GOOD

IS ALIVE AND WELL
AND LIVING IN EACH ONE OF US

Other Books By
Naura Hayden

HOW TO SATISFY A WOMAN EVERY TIME . . .
and have her beg for more!

ASTRO-LOGICAL LOVE

Isle of View (Say it out loud)

*Everything You've Always Wanted To Know
About ENERGY . . . But Were Too Weak To Ask*

*The Hip, High-Prote, Low-Cal, Easy-Does-It
Cookbook*

GOOD

IS ALIVE AND WELL
AND LIVING IN EACH ONE OF US

by

NAURA HAYDEN

Bibli O'Phile Publishing Company
NEW YORK, NEW YORK

Distributed by Penguin USA

What appears to be evil
is but the absence of Good. . . .

Front cover photo by Bob Kahn, 1993

Published by Bibli O'Phile Publishing Company
170 E. 61 St., New York, New York 10021

Printed in Canada with earth clean ink/Blaze I.P.I.

Library of Congress Catalog Card Number: 95-68421

ISBN: 0-942104-12-9

Distributed by Penguin USA

10 9 8 7 6 5 4 3 2 1

First Edition

Contents

Good is <u>absolutely</u> here and there and everywhere,
alive and well,
but very few of us are aware of it.
However,
our unawareness of it
doesn't make it not there.
Once we become aware of our own Good
inside us,
that Good will take over our lives
and lead us
to everything we want and need.
I wanted you to know this,
and <u>that's</u> why I wrote this book. . . .

Foreword

I'm a simple person and I like simple, uncomplicated things. I find that the most intricate ideas can be stated simply.

Everything in this book is stated simply. Some of the ideas may be very different from anything you've ever read or thought before and they may *seem* complicated, but on re-reading them, you will find simplicity and logic.

I want to be understood. I don't want you wondering what I'm talking about or what I mean. You may not agree with my thinking, but I want you to understand it. I have enough confidence in these ideas that I believe eventually you will agree.

Good Is Alive and Well and Living in Each One of Us is my sixth book, and it is very different from each of the previous five. There's been a lapse of thirteen years between this and the writing of my last book, but for most of those thirteen years I've been thinking about writing this.

I actually thought of the title first, except that it was a tiny bit different then. I originally thought of *God Is Alive and Well and Living in Each One of Us* for my title, but during those years I began to understand the interchangeability of God and Good, and one day several years ago I changed the title to what it is now.

I've never before been driven by anything until I thought about doing this book. Now everyone who knows me knows I have enormous energy and a lot of determination, but I've never been *driven* to do something. I've had the desires, in fact the *deep* desires, to do many things, but the ideas for this book have been super-naturally driving me all these years to write them down.

For over eleven years I've been thinking about it, collecting my ideas and writing them down on scraps of paper and saving them, or writing notes in each of my daily diaries from 1983 till now. I've collected all my new health discoveries (that of course I've tried on my self and still use every day), which have made me feel better than I've ever felt, *ever*, notating all my discoveries about hair, eyes, skin, teeth, weight, etc.

I'm a *very* curious person, and I read a lot and I ask a lot of questions. By being so inquisitive and such a perfectionist (see my chapter on "The *LOGIC* of Astrology"!), I've really learned a lot about life, about our human bodies, about our emotions, our intellects, but mostly about what will make us happy.

Happiness seems to be an absence of pain, but of course that's not only physical pain, it's also emotional, mental, and spiritual pain.

I've learned how to get rid of all those kinds of pain and how to have the real happiness that eluded me during most of my life up till fairly recently.

I *know* (not I think or I believe, but I *know*) that if you apply only *some* of the things I've learned, you will begin to experience the joy that you were meant to share in this life. I say "share" because it's there for *all* of us.

All we have to do is understand that there are certain simple things to think and do that will *guarantee* that joy will enter our lives and stay there. You don't have to beg or make any deals with a Super Person, it will come because *you* will control its coming.

And when you begin to experience this joy, you will start to understand that your attitude is changing, that you're becoming more receptive to new ideas, and that will give you even more joy.

And the wonderful thing is that the more you change, the more you *will* change. Each time you expand your mind and consciousness, you are making ready the next change and the next expansion, and you can never go back to your original thinking.

This is good.

This is also Good.

To Love, which is Good . . .
which is Love . . .
which is Good . . .
which is Love . . .
which is Good . . .
which is Love . . .

Introduction

It's very important for me to communicate my deep belief in Good. I don't mean Goody Two-shoes good, I mean the knowledge that what you're doing is right, as in right and wrong. Nobody ever has to tell you what's good, what's right—you instinctively *know* the right thing to do.

The good thing *always* makes you feel better, makes other people feel better. You can't be Good and be nervous and tense because then you're afraid, and Good makes you un-afraid.

Everyone has Good within, but not everyone expresses it. Those who seem not to have it appear to be evil, but evil is just the absence of Good.

Good is not a person. You don't have to be afraid of Good. You don't have to toady to Good. You don't have to beg, plead, and cajole Good. Good just is. And always was. And always will be.

Good is alive and well and living within each one of us just waiting to be expressed. It's a little like music. Music exists now and has always existed, but until it's expressed with our voices, or on a flute or a violin, we don't hear it, we're not aware of its existence.

And until we express Good through our thoughts and then our actions, we are not aware of it. Once we understand that, we will begin to understand the nature of Good.

It's not enough to just become aware of and try to change your spirit and your mind and express it through Good. It's just as important to become aware of and change your *body* and make it better. Isn't your body the vessel through which you express life (your temple of Good)?

I've concentrated on *my* body and have learned about so many new and revolutionary nutrients that I have tried that will also make *your* body feel better, age more slowly, get better-looking, get sick fewer times (if at all), and have more energy.

Also it's important that your emotional life improve, that you get rid of all the negative feelings of fear and anger that are the antithesis of Good, emotions that will stop your brain from functioning in a clear-thinking way.

And your mind—isn't it really important to clear up the confusion in your mind and get rid of the guilt and envy and vindictiveness, and use your incredible human computer (aka your brain) to accomplish and acquire all the things you want?

So as important as your spiritual nature is, it's no more so than your body (through which you express your self on this plane), your mind (through which you think on this plane), and your emotions (through which you feel on this plane).

If you can learn something in this book that will change your life for the better physically, mentally, and emotionally, you'll be much more receptive to possible spiritual changes.

If I can bring something to your attention that will make you *look* better, make your skin smoother and "juicier," make your hair thicker and make it grow fuller and longer, make your body less "lumpy" and more supple, those things will make you like your self a lot more and will maybe make you think, "If Naura figured this out, she might be on the right track with her spiritual ideas too!"

As you will see within this book, I have a lot of original thought that you will not have heard or read anywhere else. I am a problem-solver (probably my greatest achievement), and I will show you how I unraveled some pretty awful challenges for my self, and show you how to become a problem-solver in your own life.

We are *all* potentially problem-solvers; we just don't know how to start. I will show you the truly simple way to lead your self out of the maze of your troubles and find the good things you're looking for.

I have figured out how to keep from getting old thinking, old looking, old feeling and old acting, partly through some new discoveries that I, as a human "guinea pig" have uncovered, and partly through some original, intuitive and logical procedures.

I am mostly a logical person, so everything I write (and do) is based on logic and has to make sense, with some intuition that gives me insight into problems to be solved.

I am going to show you definite ways to control your emotions so that your brain can work the way it's supposed to, allowing you to figure out how to accomplish the things that will bring you happiness.

I will show you how I *never* allow a negative emotion in my life, and what this simple discipline can bring in the way of *material* gain, not just spiritual advancement.

The *logic* of astrology is very important to learn. Anyone who thinks that astrology can predict the future ("You are a Capricorn, you're going on a journey") is fantasizing, because if that could be done, astrologers would do charts on boxing matches, soccer games, horse races or the stock market, and they would all be multimillionaires. They can't, they don't, and they're not.

Astrology was given to us to help us learn our positives and negatives so we can understand our selves and everyone around us better. It is amazingly accurate and can truly help you, through self-awareness, change for the better.

I talk about right and wrong, personal responsibility, sex and love and why they go together, and about Good (aka God).

I have come up with a whole new concept of Good that has changed the way I think, act, and live my life. I will share this with you and I believe it will change your way of thinking also.

It is non-religious, non-threatening, and will give you a good feeling about your self and your life. It will also explain some of the so-called "mysteries" of life that I don't find mysterious at all.

When you understand what Good is all about, you will know that when you express Good, its power will bring *you* power to attain everything you really want.

In Chapter 9 I go into detail as to *how* to make all this happen. I *promise* you it will change your life forever!

I believe this book about Good is for everybody—married, single, religious, agnostic, atheist, older, middle-aged, young, black, white, Oriental, Hispanic, Indian—everybody.

Good Is Alive and Well and Living in Each One of Us was written to enlighten and help all of us make the most of our lives with the equipment we were born with.

I have read voraciously since I was a child, and I have learned much from many books. I hope my book will help you as much as I have been helped by others' books.

Right is the expression of Good.
Wrong is the absence of Good.
When we do right, wrong cannot exist.

1

Right and Wrong

Right and wrong. Black and white. There are no grays.

Too many people say that life is all grays, that there is no black and white. But I think that's what's wrong with the world. In fact, I believe that's the _only_ thing that's wrong.

If the moral fiber is there, if everyone makes a decision and chooses the right thing to do, it's pretty obvious most lawyers would be out of business, and jails would be closed. If everyone chose honesty and truth, life would be 100 percent different. But it seems most people deal in grays. Excuses have become a way of life. "Personal responsibility" is a dirty phrase.

Either an action is right or it's wrong. How can it be part right and part wrong? That's like half black and half white, which of course becomes gray.

Stephen Covey, in his best-selling book _The 7 Habits of Highly Effective People_, says, "We have conscience—a deep inner awareness of right and wrong, of the principle that governs our behavior, and a sense of the degree to which our thoughts and actions are in harmony with them."

But our whole perception of right and wrong seems to be eroding. When you read that a woman who bought some coffee at McDonald's in the early nineties is awarded an astronomical sum of money because the coffee that she spilled on her self and that burned her was too hot, you know we're really getting confused.

When Robert Chambers kills Jennifer Levin in 1988 in Central Park in the early hours of the morning, uses "rough sex" as an excuse while he chokes her to death, and gets away with it with a light sentence, the confusion deepens.

When in 1994 a mother in the Bronx, Diane Meza, illegally double-parks her car on a darkened street with her six-year-old sleeping in it while she runs inside to do an errand, and a tow-truck driver tows the car away (which he's *supposed* to do to illegally parked cars), not knowing the child is inside, and the mother sues the city for "kidnapping and unlawful imprisonment" instead of the city collecting $150 for illegal parking and arresting her for endangering the safety of her child), it becomes more than confusion, it's almost a joke.

When Lorena Bobbitt cuts off her husband's sex organ while he's sleeping and pleads wife abuse and is acquitted, you realize personal responsibility is becoming a thing of the past.

The last day of the Bobbitt trial I was doing the Geraldo TV show about the Bobbitts, and I was center stage. I was involved because my book *HOW TO SATISFY A WOMAN EVERY TIME* . . . *and have her beg for more!* had been used as evidence in the trial.

I spoke many times to several attorneys on both sides and was sent the transcript of the trial. I read the testimony of Lorena and John and spoke to John often, so I knew a lot about the case. John told me that Lorena had never had an orgasm through intercourse until he read my book and it drove her so "crazy with passion" that when he told her he wanted a divorce, her mutilation of him was a vindictive act (if I can't have it, nobody can). Lorena testified that he had beaten her and she was afraid for her life.

I was the *only* person on Geraldo's stage who believed Lorena should pay for her act of violence. On my right was a woman who had thrown acid over 69 percent of her husband's body, disfiguring him for life, and she had been acquitted because she said he had abused her.

Another woman next to her had shot her husband dead and was acquitted because she said he abused her. I tried to make the point that these women should have left their husbands, but no one seemed to agree with me. I pointed out that *I* would leave as soon as the first abuse took place, and that if I chose to stay, I would be telling my abuser that I'm choosing to stay with him even though he hurts me, and that's giving him tacit assent to continue. If I left immediately, he would know he couldn't do that anymore and get away with it and have me stay.

Midpoint in the show we broke for a commercial, and I leaned to my right and asked the woman who had shot her husband through the heart why she didn't leave him. She said she was afraid to leave, that he would have looked for her and beaten her if he'd found her. This is exactly the same thing Lorena claimed, even though she and John (before she attacked him) had been separated for almost a year and had lived many hundreds of miles apart, she in Virginia and he in upstate New York at his mother's house. He obviously had left her alone *then*; in fact he and his mother both claimed Lorena called him relentlessly all the time he was away, begging him to come back, so her "fear for her life" didn't ring true.

The break in the show lasted about twenty minutes (usually it's about two to three minutes for commercials), and I asked the producer why. She said they were waiting for the verdict on the Bobbitt case, and as soon as they got it, Geraldo would restart the show.

Finally the verdict came in, and I was stunned when Geraldo announced it. The audience wildly cheered Lorena's acquittal. I just couldn't believe it. The audience was 90 percent women, and it had turned into women vs. men. But it *wasn't* women vs. men, it was right vs. wrong. I would feel *exactly* the same if a man who had cut off one his wife's breasts had been acquitted. It had nothing to do with gender; it had everything to do with justice. And when I pointed this out, some people in the audience applauded, but the vast majority were so emotionally charged up about the woman (Lorena) triumphing over the man (John) that any intellectualizing was lost on the crowd.

This was not a personal thing about Lorena. She may be a lovely woman. This was about personal responsibility. If everyone knows up front that he or she can use an excuse for committing a crime, and that excuse will acquit the guilty party, then our society is in for a lot of trouble. I save newspaper clippings of outrageous acquittals because I'm always so stunned that I have to keep re-reading them to finally accept that they really happened.

Thomas Sowell is a brilliant black syndicated columnist who appears in many newspapers across the country. Right after the Lorena Bobbitt verdict was in and she was found not guilty by reason of temporary insanity, he wrote:

> . . . the 'insanity' defense symbolizes the degeneration
> of law which has cost the people of this country so much
> in money, violence and lives.

Then he asks us to think about the fact that psychiatrists and psychologists can treat patients ad infinitem without *ever* finding any solutions that would end the patient's problems, and these same specialists are used in cases of people they never heard of till a crime was committed. These doctors make momentous, far-reaching, and pivotal decisions that can and do drastically change all the lives involved in the cases.

He goes on to say that it's even *more* surprising that these same psychiatrists' and psychologists' testimony is never put to the test of empirical evidence. There are no records kept of what happens to the "set-free" defendants, and if any of them have committed more and worse crimes, or how many innocent people have been robbed, raped, maimed, or killed because these criminals were turned loose on society because of the testimony of these "specialists."

Mr. Sowell says that this whole criminal-insanity ploy started in 1954 when a career criminal, Monte Durham, had his conviction for burglary overturned by Chief Judge David L. Bazelon in Washington, D.C.

> For Judge Bazelon, it was not necessary to show that Durham was literally insane. It was sufficient if there was "some evidence" that he had some "defective mental condition." This . . . was now sufficient to let criminals escape responsibility whenever they could find a psychiatrist or psychologist willing to speculate in their behalf.

Sowell says that up till then the crime rate had slowly been going down; it was only after the Bazelon decision that the whole legal system began to change its philosophy, and crime and violence skyrocketed.

In 1992, during the Los Angeles riots, truck driver Reginald Denny had his head bashed in with a brick by Damian Williams in the south central area of L.A., just five blocks from where I grew up. A videotape caught the whole sickening scene of Williams cracking Denny's head and then dancing in the street to celebrate. Unbelievably, the jury acquitted him of most of the charges because he, the victimizer, was thought to have had a terrible childhood. What about the victim, poor Reginald Denny, who will *never* be the same, certainly not normal? I saw him being interviewed long after the incident and he could hardly carry on a conversation—he was slurring his words, couldn't concentrate, and appeared confused and dazed.

And what about the Menendez brothers? It's truly hard to believe that the jury could not reach a verdict about the two brothers who admitted they killed their parents. Julia Reed in Vogue writes:

Indeed, to hear Erik Menendez's lawyer, Leslie Abramson, explain it, the boys' parents killed themselves. "They set in motion a series of events that eventually killed them," she declared, speaking of the abuse they allegedly visited upon their kids. . . . By this light there is no such thing as a failure of character—just a hard life or even just a tough day.

In the Sept./Oct. 1994 premiere issue of *Marie Claire* there was a quote of Leslie Abramson in a story by Aimee Lee Ball:

> The cases that really matter are the ones where you know your client is guilty, but the prosecution has a crummy case. . . . If they don't really have a case, you have to blow it up. . . . And if the fallout is that some swine gets off—well, we don't have a perfect world.

One of the reasons we *don't* have a perfect world is that there are lawyers like Abramson and countless others including O.J. Simpson's "Dream Team" of defense attorneys who seemingly have no consciences.

Dominick Dunne was interviewed in *Quest*, a New York magazine I love and read every month, and Dunne's interviewer, Brooks Peters, asked him about the Menendez case (which he covered for *Vanity Fair*). He was disgusted by defense attorney Abramson and the lack of ethics and morality:

> How she can say things and use the TV camera and make you *believe* that those dead bodies are so *utterly revolting* that they *should* be dead.

A close friend of mine, Wilbur Stark, heard some sixty hours of tapes (I read all the transcripts) of Lyle Menendez discussing with Norma Novelli, at that time the editor and publisher of a magazine for creative people called *Mind's Eye*, *how* he murdered his parents, *how* he gave an alibi to the police and *how* he was going to change that alibi, and *how* he was going to maneuver to make Dr. Oziel, the psychiatrist who taped his original confession, lose his license. Lyle contacted Norma originally when he saw her magazine in jail and disagreed with one of her articles, and shortly after that he started calling her (she says he's a "phonaholic"), and they became friends.

Willy also showed me a copy of a three-page letter written by Lyle and sent from jail to a witness telling her in minute detail exactly what to say on the stand. The witness did exactly as she was directed in the letter by Lyle in the first trial, and this letter will be used against him in the second trial.

Willy (the father of Koo Stark) is a TV and film producer, and we met when he was producing *Brothers Brannigan* at MGM and he hired me to play a lead in the show. He went on to executive-produce *The Thing* with Kurt Russell and *The Cat People* with Nastassja Kinski, and now he wants to do a film on Lyle Menendez (from those sixty hours of tapes) showing the *inner workings* of the mind of a psychotic killer. Maybe *that* would help us to understand how an "actor" like Lyle Menendez can convince (or confuse) a jury to think he's innocent.

I have very strong feelings about right and wrong. Everyone who believes in Good does. And in my own life I've surely encountered some moral wrongs that have made me feel even *stronger* about the difference between them.

The $9 Million Inheritance

It was a lovely Saturday morning in 1986 and I was sitting in my living room going through my mail, when I came across a letter from one of my cousins, an attorney. I couldn't imagine why he would be sending me an official-looking envelope. So I quickly opened it and read with much pleasure that a relative I'd never heard of, a first cousin of my father, had died in his late nineties and left a huge fortune. It said he had been a Harvard-trained lawyer, and a businessman, yet he died intestate, so his fortune of $9 million would be divided among the relatives. The letter was sort of legalesey, but that's what I made out.

Well, what a way to start a Saturday! Wow! Nine million dollars divided among maybe twenty people is pretty exciting. During the next few weeks I got other letters from my cuz, and it was starting to get a little complicated. It seemed that Edward Clark had died in Oklahoma where he'd owned oil wells, and that Oklahoma has a law that only the *living* close relatives are entitled to share in an estate. The ones who died are *out*!

It seems there were only three living close relatives, and they were my Aunt Stella, my father's older sister whom I loved dearly, my Aunt Frances, my father's younger sister who had no children and lived near Aunt Stella and her kids, and someone from another side of Ed Clark's family. Now Aunt Stella was in her nineties and senile, and Aunt Frances was in her eighties and senile, and I didn't know much about the third person. So Aunt Stella's eight offspring (one of which was my attorney cuz) and Aunt Frances's favorite nieces and nephews who grew up around her were to soon get two-thirds of $9 million, or $6 million. And the rest of us were to get zilch.

Talk about a comedown. Well, I decided to find out about this Oklahoma law that did me, my brother, and all my other cousins out of a *lot* of money. I went to an attorney and found out that forty-eight of the states in the United States had laws that *all* descendants receive a pro-rata share of an inheritance, but that Oklahoma and Arkansas were the only two whose laws held that only the close *living* relatives were entitled to anything. And some of Ed's oil wells were in Arkansas, so we got clobbered by both states.

In other words, because my father had died, and my Uncle Mort, Uncle Don, Aunt Gladys, Uncle Hody, and Uncle Bill had died also, we, the descendants, got nothing. If Ed Clark had died in California or New York or Illinois or Florida or *any* other of the forty-eight states, his $9 million would have been shared by *all* of us.

What an unfair law. How unjust to punish all of us whose related parent had died. I have such an innate sense of fairness and justice that I was sure that if my cousins really thought about it, they'd see how unfair it was.

Before I tell you what happened, I want to tell you that I was extremely close to my Aunt Stella (she was my favorite aunt), and when my father died, Aunt Stella came to California and took me back to Dubuque, Iowa, for a month. I was a teener, and I don't know how I would have pulled through without her help.

She even arranged a big dinner at a restaurant so I could meet all my father's brothers and sisters (he had left Dubuque at a very young age), and all my uncles got potted (they *are* Irish!), and one of them during the evening's conversation yelled out "Bull ship!" and all the others shushed him so he wouldn't say it again. For many years (I'm embarrassed to say *how* many) I was mystified by what "Bull ship" meant and why they all thought it was so awful. What could be bad about a boat with bulls on it? One day *years* later, after wondering about it all that time, I realized he'd yelled "Bullshit." So much for twelve years of Catholic schools.

Anyway, I adored my Aunt Stella and got close to her younger kids who were around my age. I loved them all, and not long after my father's death they all moved to Los Angeles. I used to visit them a lot in the Valley, where they settled, and we always had a great time together. Of course, my Aunt Stella and I had a *special* closeness, but we all loved each other.

I decided to write a letter to all of the eight cousins explaining that if Aunt Stella were rational and not senile, she would have *insisted* all the family share, not just her kids and Aunt Frances's favorites. Aunt Stella was kind, loving, honest, and just.

I composed a *brilliant* letter and called upon their sense of love, justice, loyalty, and fairness for all the rest of us. Not only did I never get a reply from any of them, when I called to talk to them at different times, each one mumbled something about just running out and hung up on me.

The lawyer cuz who wrote the original letter about the inheritance finally answered my letter with copies to all the other cousins. And in it are three wonderful sentences. The first: ". . . we children would be more than willing to share equally in the portion of the estate that descends to our generation, but I must advise that we are not included in the descent and distribution that comes down to our generation. Mother has inherited her interest and she has that interest, and no percent of that has passed through to her children or to her grandchildren or to her great-grandchildren."

Was he kidding? We *all* knew that the money was inherited by my two aunts and *not* Aunt Stella's kids, but we *also* knew that the darling old women were in their eighties and nineties, both were senile, and neither could live more than a couple of years if that; and as it turned out both passed away not long after. So *after* their mother died, what happened to ". . . we children would be more than willing to share equally in the portions of the estate that descends to our generation . . ."?

Then he says, "I'm not even going to mention this to Mother or Fran for fear they would feel that someone was trying to take their inheritance from them."

It was a joke. Being in the last stages of senility, neither aunt would have been even remotely aware of what he would have been talking about had he even *tried* to discuss it.

I never would have believed that money could have changed these people. I'd heard many stories about what money does to people, but I always thought those were exceptional situations where there was animosity *before* the money came into the picture. I was truly stunned and shocked to see these eight people, with whom I had great relationships, close ranks among themselves and their new-found money.

After my original letter, my brother and many of my cousins wrote letters, which obviously fell on blind eyes. My brother's was a gem, and he answered lawyer cuz's statement that an equal sharing would turn into a "legal nightmare" by saying, "What could be simpler than equality?"

Several of my disappointed cousins consulted lawyers, and some called Oklahoma and Arkansas and were all told the same thing—the laws in those two states are different from all the others. Several attorneys in Oklahoma told me that indeed the law is unfair and will probably eventually be changed, but for now, no chance. What a law to cause a major rift in a family, and this is probably one reason why every other state made it different, the other reason being it's stupid *not* to prorate it to *all* the descendants.

The end of this beautiful tale of familial love is that none us has seen or heard from any of our nouveau riche relatives since. But I really feel sorry for them (I know you think I'm kidding, but I'm not). They appear to be afraid that someone might try to take their money away, and that's pathetic.

I believe in compensation, as does Ralph Waldo Emerson: "All infractions of love and equity in our social relations are speedily punished by fear."

It's difficult to live with guilt and fear. They knew they weren't *legally* wrong, but what about *morally* wrong? It may appear that they're happy with their money, but can someone be happy knowing that what was done was not right, and not wanting to even talk to or see the ones who were done out of what's right?

When you do the right thing, the Good thing, you're happy and relaxed and confident, and when you don't, you're not. End of the $9 million inheritance. (Sob!)

Non-persons

When someone, anyone, treats me badly, treats me with no respect, makes me feel less than a terrific person, I drop that person from my life.

Why would I ever want to be around someone who not

only doesn't love me, but doesn't even *like* me? Now we all know that you must like your self first before you can like someone else, and it is obvious that the person who treats me badly and with no respect doesn't like him or her self, and I accept that. When those people who don't like themselves discover their inner problems and hopefully change and apologize to me because now they understand what they did and why they did it, I will enter their lives again.

But until then, they do not exist in my life. Now I have a woman friend whom I love dearly. And she allows people in her family to treat her very badly. It might appear that she's a "saintly" person, but in reality what she's doing is not only bad for her, the insultee, and her own self-esteem, it's terrible for the insulter. If you allow someone to continue in negative actions, you're giving tacit assent. If you "take it" and say nothing, you're giving a message to the insulter that it's not only okay to do that, but that you'll still be there no matter what.

There is no such thing as unconditional love!

Leo Buscaglia writes in his wonderful book *Love*: "Real love always creates. It never destroys . . . One grows in love." So if the person you love is cruel and tortures you with anger and hostility, causing great pain and self-doubt, can you love that person? You might fear him or her, you might fear the loss of that love because of the loneliness it will bring, but if it doesn't allow you to grow as a person (whether you're a friend, a lover, a parent, or a child), then it's not real love. *That* is the condition of love.

Don't we know that if we do a certain thing, we'll either be praised or punished? And isn't that how we learn? When you were a little kid, if your mother had allowed you to scream at her or hit or kick her, or talk with your mouth full of food, or be vulgar in public, you'd have a pretty tough time dealing with society now.

We are taught what is right and what is wrong. We are

taught that if we're good, we're rewarded, and if we're bad, we're punished. And that's the way it's *supposed* to be.

One of the things wrong with the world we live in now is that too many people do wrong and are *not* punished.

Where do we start to reverse that, and how? I have a member of my family who doesn't exist in my life anymore. People seem amazed by this, but I find it very logical. It doesn't make any difference if a person is your brother or sister or cousin or son or daughter or mother or father. You have to let everyone know that you expect and deserve respect.

Isn't it better to have a friend who likes you, respects you, treats you well, and lets you know you are loved than a member of your family who doesn't?

Chemically, blood is thicker than water. So is mud. But to allow a family member to make you feel you're not a wonderful person is stupid. Move away from that person. Don't be around jealousy or anger or envy. There are lots of people out there who *will* appreciate you, but they won't get a chance to if you spend your time around people who don't.

A friend of mine, a very sweet man, and his wife (I don't know her) have two daughters (I don't know them), one in her early thirties and one in her late twenties. He recently told me a story that appalled me.

The older daughter had given the younger one $10,000 to hold for her "in trust" so she wouldn't spend it and wouldn't be tempted to use even a part of it. The younger one took her sister's money out of the bank and spent it all. The older one was so upset that it has made a rift in the family. She will not speak to her sister.

The appalling part is that the father is siding with the younger one and blaming the older one for ripping the family apart. He says because the older one won't talk to her sister, they never have family get-togethers anymore.

I asked the father how he could so easily excuse his younger daughter for stealing $10,000. He said that the younger one is going to pay it back. I asked if she's paid *anything* back yet, and he said no. He kept repeating that he knew the younger one would pay it back.

I asked how long ago this happened (thinking it was maybe a few weeks or even months), and when he said six years ago, I couldn't believe it. She hadn't paid a *penny* back in six years. I asked how he could totally excuse the one daughter and rationalize why what she did wasn't so bad, but I got no answer.

When he said it happened six years ago but he knew she'd pay it back, you can see how emotionally blind this man is.

And by allowing the thief to have *no* punishment, *no* loss of esteem, *no* chilling of love, you can see how the thief undoubtedly feels she did the right thing by stealing the money. She's had nothing but pleasure since. She got to spend all the money and was never punished.

And the father was actually blaming the *victim* for breaking up the family. He obviously favored the younger daughter and allowed her to get away with a terrible act, but why should the younger one feel bad? Her father still favors her, never insisted she pay it back, and went so far as to make the victim feel guilty.

Isn't this what's happening all around us? Aren't we getting fuzzy about right and wrong?

It's up to us, me and you, to reward the Good and punish the bad, to reward the right and punish the wrong. That's what Good is all about.

Right and Wrong in Przemysl, Poland

Stefania Podgorska's mother had taught her daughter two things that were the most important to her, a strong belief in Catholicism and a powerful sense of the difference between right and wrong.

Her father had died before the Second World War when Stefania was a teen, and her mother and brother had been deported from Przemysl to Germany into forced labor. So she and her eight-year-old sister, Helena, had stayed behind in a house belonging to a Jewish couple she had worked for when the Germans occupied the city. The couple had asked her to stay in the house to protect it when they were sent to one of the concentration camps, so she and her sister now lived there.

One day in 1942 when Stefania was nineteen, someone knocked on the door and when she opened it and saw Josef Burzminski, she froze—he was the twenty-seven-year-old son of the Jewish couple whose house she was living in. Several months before, the Nazi SS had marched into the ghetto where he and his family had lived, and his parents were taken as prisoners with many of the other twenty thousand Jews in the city. Thousands more were put into boxcars going to Belzec, one of the worst of the concentration camps.

A few weeks later Josef and one of his brothers were put into a boxcar crowded with many other Jews. They were told by the sadistic SS guards that they were going to Belzec to be made into soap. Josef was so terrified that he wanted to kill himself, so he took his pocketknife, cut the barbed wire in a little window in the boxcar, and squeezed through it, thinking he would be killed when he fell to the ground. He lost consciousness and was badly injured.

He came to and painstakingly found his way to the house and begged Stefania to hide him till he recovered. Though there were German signs all over the city warning that anyone who hid Jews would be killed, her mother's words telling her about right and wrong rang in her ears, and she agreed to hide him. Within weeks twelve other hidden Jews, friends of Josef, arrived.

Soon after, all the remaining Jews left in the ghetto were shipped off to the death camps.

There were numerous chillingly close calls as they were almost discovered by the Nazis, but her belief in right gave her great strength, which overcame the terror, not only for her self and her little sister, but for her thirteen new Jewish friends.

She hid them for over two frightening and traumatic years, and several months after the Germans finally left and the war was over, Josef asked Stefania to marry him. They now live in Boston, where they raised a son and a daughter, and today when I spoke to them, I found out that yesterday, November 25, 1994, was their fiftieth wedding anniversary.

Lawyers & Justice

From childhood on, I was mystified by the fact that lawyers take cases where people are very obviously guilty, and those lawyers will not only defend each person, he or she will try through any means to get the guilty person adjudged not guilty, and then set free.

I could never understand how a lawyer would use any and all possible means, obviously allowing the perpetrator to lie outrageously, to get the client out of jail and free to be back in society.

I always wondered if the attorney ever thought that his mother or his wife could have been the victim of the rapist, if he ever considered the possibility that his child could have been the victim of the child abuser/murderer (or might be the *next* victim of the set-free murderer if and when he attacks again).

This had truly bothered me and mystified me a lot all those years until I married an attorney. I kept asking him over and over how can an attorney in good conscience do this. He gave me many answers and not one satisfied me, until one day in the car when I *again* asked him and he again tried to explain, except this time he was a little cross (and exasperated), when he blurted out "a lawyer is a mouthpiece because the defendant doesn't know how to handle himself in a courtroom—he doesn't know the rules and he wouldn't have a clue as to how to defend himself, so I become his mouthpiece."

All of a sudden I finally understood. A "mouthpiece." The lawyer *becomes* the accused and speaks *as* the accused and *for* the accused.

The only problem with that (and it's some problem) is that when a guilty person is lying (which he or she *always* is because if he or she weren't, there wouldn't be a trial, the accused would just tell the truth and be punished), the lawyer is accepting the lie and defending it.

Not only is the accused lying, the attorney (his mouthpiece) is lying too.

Truth doesn't enter into it at all. All the lying doesn't seem to bother anyone, certainly not the accused, but also not his attorney.

To quote Dominick Dunne, again in his interview in *Quest* about the first Menendez trial:

> I am riveted by how people buy the lies that these lawyers tell. There is no other word—lies!

He goes on:

> I just believe in the importance of *truth*. I know that sounds corny, but truth is something that just almost doesn't exist anymore. There ain't no morality. No ethics. Truth is a joke. People swear to tell the truth so help me God and then they sit on the witness stand and lie, lie, *lie!*

A terrific man I work with, Steve West, was on jury duty several years ago, and when the case was settled, the judge walked into the jury room and told all the jurors a very interesting piece of information. Judge Francis Pecora noted that *everyone* who is part of a case in a courtroom has to take an oath to uphold the truth—except the lawyers. All judges, jurors, plaintiffs, defendants, etc., swear to tell the truth. The *only* people working in a courtroom who are *not* required to take an oath to tell the truth are the lawyers in the case.

Lawyers take an oath when they are sworn in:

I _____, do solemnly swear that I will support the Constitution of the United States, the Constitution of the State of _____, and that I will faithfully discharge the duties of the office of Attorney and Counsellor at Law to the best of my ability.

But not a word about telling the truth.

Doesn't this make a travesty of the judicial system when not telling the truth (and playing tricks with lies), is part of that system? And how can there be *justice*—I mean real and true fairness—when it also really depends on who has the better lawyer?

If one person is telling the truth and the opposite side is lying, then the judge and/or jury has to guess/perceive/intuit/feel who the liar is. And if the mouthpiece of the truth-teller is weak and not too smart and not a very good lawyer, and the mouthpiece of the liar is strong, very smart, and a terrific lawyer, obviously no one will end up believing the truth-teller, and the liar will not only be believed, he or she will be set free.

In the April, 1995 issue, *Newsweek* had a great article written by John H. Langbein about the O.J. Simpson case being an example of the deeply and seriously flawed American criminal-justice system.

He tells us that in many advanced European countries— Holland, Sweden, Germany, Switzerland and others—they have a "thorough, impartial, judge-supervised investigation of the *facts* in the pretrial process." These judges are not out "to convict (or to defeat conviction) but only to find the truth." We in America give our lawyers license "to engage in truth-defeating distortion and trickery at trial."

Langbein says that at the end of the eighteenth century, jury trials were very quick procedures, often taking minutes, not months, and lawyers were seldom present. Over the past two hundred years, criminal lawyers have slowly and insidiously transformed criminal trials to the money-eating monsters and media circuses they are today.

He goes on that lawyers charge enormous fees and are not only immensely wealthy, they're powerful enough to have an "entrenched vested interest for the perpetuation of our failed system. One of the blessings of serious European-style reform in the United States would be to cut the lawyers down to size. They won't go quietly."

And as bad as lawyers are, what about judges? At least with a jury you have six or twelve people trying to come to a decision. Some of them might be very emotional with preconceived ideas, others might be not-too-bright and slow to understand the intricacies of a case, but out of six or twelve there's a good probability that *some* of them (or at least one) will be bright and fair and honest.

But with a judge, you're only dealing with one person. And what if he or she is emotional with preconceived ideas? What if he or she is bigoted? Or dishonest? You can see how fair the decision would be with *that* kind of person.

In France they have the Napoleonic Code, and it seems to me a million times more fair than what we have. There are *three* judges who sit on all the cases, and it's pretty obvious why three judges are a lot more fair than one—all three wouldn't have the same prejudices, and also with three it would be highly unlikely that there would be dishonesty.

They do have juries there, but only in some cases, and even then the jury only *advises* the judges, not the reverse as we have here, the judge advising the jury.

Doesn't that sound a lot better and fairer than what we have?

I've read a lot about unfair judges, and just the other day a case came up.

Andrea Peyser, a writer for the *New York Post*, did a great story about a Supreme Court judge, Justice Franklin Weissberg, who threw out a damning 911 tape as evidence in a terrible murder case similar to the Robert Chambers case. A thirty-five-year-old man, Gerald "Jed" Ardito, choked his twenty-four-year-old girlfriend, Marie Daniele, to death in a hotel room in Manhattan. He admits it but says his girlfriend died of rough consensual sex. And the 911 tape, recorded five months earlier, has the girl screaming out that he was trying to choke her to death. The judge declared it "ambiguous" because he says the now-dead woman did not believe her boyfriend was going to murder her. He also ruled it was a "prior bad act" unconnected to her death. Peyser said, *"The tape could prove that her death was not accidental, that he had tried to murder her before."* There were also three witnesses the night she called 911—one, a neighbor who stopped the guy from dragging the girl, who was trying to escape, back into his apartment. The neighbor threatened the guy with a baseball bat, and he let her go. And two witnesses who had seen her neck discoloration from the attempted strangulation had differed as to the location and severity of the marks, so the judge deemed this information as unimportant. Also, a policeman and another neighbor each reported that the girl said he was trying to kill her, but the judge said they were unreliable witnesses.

After withholding all this evidence, Judge Weissberg gave the verdict, and the victim's family screamed out curses as Ardito was sentenced to eight and one-third to twenty-five years for manslaughter. Had he been convicted of murder, he would have faced twenty-five years to life.

Robert Chambers strangled Jennifer Levin. Joseph Porto strangled Kathleen Holland. Gerald Ardito strangled Marie Daniele.

All three got away with murder.

Cathy Burke wrote in the *New York Post*:

The men who perpetrated jurisprudence's cruelest joke—the rough sex defense—stood trial for killing their lovers, but never had to take responsibility for their deaths. The Chambers, Porto and Ardito cases point to a troubling trend of sanctifying excuse-making. If the criminal-justice system sees no need to hold murderers accountable, why should we expect it of educators, of politicians, of our children, of ourselves?

For killing these three women, Chambers got 5 to 15 years, Ardito got 8-1/3 to 25 years, and Porto got *out* after 2-1/2 years. Cathy Burke says:

Judges compounded the stupidity by handing out sentences that combined, don't add up to one of the murdered women's lives.

There was a letter to the editor in the *New York Post* the other day about a judge in a child-custody case, where John Heard, the actor, *lost even partial custody of his son*, and this judge severely limited his parental role. "Supreme Court Justice Phyllis Gangel-Jacobs, who ruled in the case, is also a prime example of a judge whose anti-father reputation is exceeded only by her rampant arbitrariness . . . Further, in forcing Heard to pick up his ex-wife's legal bill to the tune of $370,000, it sends a clear signal to fathers that they should not even think of contesting custody, lest they risk suffering dire financial consequences."

A housing court judge was jailed in 1994 on charges of pocketing bribes to fix cases. Judge Arthur Scott, Jr., was arraigned for taking money from landlords and tenants, and in each of the stings he ruled in favor of the undercover bribe-payer. In one of the stings he approached a "pretend landlord" during a recess and said he would evict a tenant if paid by the "landlord." That very same day a lawyer was arrested and charged with bribing Judge Scott in an earlier landlord-tenant case.

The *New York Post* does great exposés. Recently they had a weeklong series by columnist Jack Newfield and reporter William Neuman: *NEW YORK'S 10 WORST JUDGES The men and women who bring shame to the city's court system*. I'm only going to mention four: Bernard Bloom, Surrogate Judge of Brooklyn who "lied under oath to protect a corrupt employee," Robert Sackett, Manhattan Criminal Court Judge who "let an accused armed robber with six prior felony convictions go, and the suspect then allegedly killed the witness against him," Brooklyn Supreme Court Judge Edward Pincus who "gave a convicted wife-killer no jail time," and Martin H. Hershey, Manhattan Criminal Court Judge who is "characterized as erratic and irrational, and routinely gives crooks light sentences."

There are, of course, many great and honest judges (the *New York Post* named thirteen), but these unjust, corrupt, and dishonest judges I list are enough to make you lose faith in justice, and/or realize we need drastic changes in *all* our legal systems. Plus, of course, the federal court judge on the following case . . .

Injustice Is Blind

I think the worst thing I ever went through was a lawsuit. Up until this lawsuit I thought justice always prevails—I honestly thought so—but I found out that it doesn't always work that way.

And any of you who think that you have to be black, or Hispanic, and/or poor, to have injustice heaped upon you are living in a fantasy. Believe me, injustice *is* blind.

I am a white, tall, reddish-blonde female who went through a horrendous experience, which, had you been there, you would have found hard to believe (as several attorneys who were there told me).

It started in 1978, when I had a royalty agreement with a California-based company that made my Dynamite Energy Shake for me. Now the formula was totally mine, and this company didn't spend any money at all on advertising. They sent me to different cities where I had a PR person book me on TV and radio shows. As most of you probably already know, I don't make any money on the sale of the Dynamite Shake since I started it in 1978. I give all profits to a foundation that

I named after my late father, The John Ellsworth Hayden Foundation, which gives free Dynamite Energy Shake to mental-health institutes, prisons, old-age homes, and youth centers.

The man who ran the company was arrogant beyond belief (my least favorite trait), and he acted as if he thought he could get away with his arrogance as long as his company made money. I was getting a 5 percent royalty, and all of *my* money (not the company's) went into the foundation.

Some problems started almost immediately when they put my photo on drinking glasses without my OK. Then, in 1981, a very serious problem arose when customers started complaining about bad product. It was my name and face on the can, so I was very upset and concerned and demanded that this problem be stopped. The more I complained, the more everyone denied that there was a problem. At a certain time I was sent a case of shake for my own use, and every one of the twelve cans was bad.

Well, by the time 1982 came around, I was in a constant state of anxiety, making phone calls day and night and writing letters and seeing my attorney, who would tell me what to say in my next letter. I begged my attorney to start a lawsuit, but he kept putting me off. I later found out there was a conflict of interest because he handled the NNFA, a big health-food organization of which the company I was suing was a member, so I changed attorneys.

Finally, I could stand it no more and I told the people in charge of the company I wanted out of my deal with them. At first they said no, but after a few more months of my refusing to publicize the product, they said they would allow me to *buy* back my contract. Now remember, it was my formula and all of my promotion selling it. They made the product for me and sold it to the stores. Period.

They said they wanted $500,000 from me to give me my freedom so I could then make the Dynamite Energy Shake myself. I told them I didn't have $500,000, and had no way of getting it. They said they would give me a year to start making the first of five payments, and they would sell me all the inventory in their warehouses and give me three months to start paying for it. I was so emotionally distressed with what I had been through that I was extremely anxious to end our relationship as soon as possible.

Even though I knew it was a terrible deal for me buying back my own formula, I said I would do it.

But they had to guarantee me that the warehouse inventory was not bad at all—not one can. The chairman of the board gave me a verbal guarantee in front of my self and two other witnesses.

I signed the deal and started my own business, Haydenergy. I hired a man to run the day-to-day business as I was traveling the country with my fifth book, *HOW TO SATISFY A WOMAN EVERY TIME . . . and have her beg for more!* which first came out in 1982.

Within months trouble started and stores were calling our 800 number to say the shake wasn't right. They had sold me their whole warehouse full of bad product.

Well, I started a lawsuit against them, and the case was assigned to a certain judge. I knew I would win, because I knew when I told my story to a jury, they would believe me. I had many really good witnesses to testify for me.

The bottom line is I changed my second attorney because he kept telling me to settle, and I had to keep telling him, my own lawyer, that I was in the right and would *win* with a jury.

I then got my third attorney, and one night shortly after I retained him, he called me and told me that the very next morning I was going to trial. I asked him how we could go to trial so quickly—didn't it take time to pick a jury? He said there was no jury. I said of *course* there's a jury, why would I go to trial without a jury, and he said I'd better be in court tomorrow morning at 9:00. I was in a state of shock. How could I *not* have a jury?

I since learned that my second attorney had signed a paper

(a waiver of jury) giving up my Constitutional right to a jury. I cannot tell you how upset I was not to have a jury, which I'd been counting on since the case began. I *knew* the jury would see how wronged I was.

During the trial I had twelve witnesses from all over the country, and I had to pay not only their travel expenses, but their hotel and food in New York. One woman had an adorable child, and I had to pay for both her and her husband with the child to come here for several days, including the weekend, to get them to make the trip.

Then the judge took that Monday off to play golf, and my witness had to leave and go back to Los Angeles without testifying. The judge could have told us about Monday and I could have had my witness fly in for Tuesday and I could have saved the whole weekend expense, but he didn't. Plus, of course, I lost her as a witness.

The other side had *one* witness, the president of the company, who said that I and all my twelve witnesses were not telling the truth, that he was the only one who should be believed. He said the product had all gone bad after we made the deal.

The last day of the trial I had my most important witness left, a biochemist. We had saved him for last. The other eleven witnesses were store owners, consumers, warehouse owners, etc., but this man (to whom I had to pay a lot of money every hour he sat in the courtroom) was going to *prove* that the other side was wrong, that the product was bad long before we made the deal. He had done many laboratory tests and had all his documentation with him.

On this last day at 4:00 P.M. the judge arose, hit his gavel on the bench, and said, "This case is closed!" and started to walk out of the courtroom. I was beside myself and ran over to my attorney and said that our biochemist hadn't testified yet, so my attorney quickly stood up and said to the judge, "Your Honor, you haven't heard the testimony of our last and most important witness, a biochemist." The judge arrived at the door of the courtroom, turned around, and yelled, "I said this case is closed!" Then he opened the door and walked out, slamming it behind him.

It was all downhill from there. A few months later the decision came in: I lost, and the other side got a judgment for $950,000 against me. That's the $500,000 I had agreed to pay to buy my own product back, $200,000 worth of *admitted* bad shake in the warehouse that I had to pay for, and $250,000 interest since I started the case.

I was going to appeal it because of the incredible injustice and because I was told that Judge Robert Sweet is the most overturned-on-appeal judge in the Federal Court of the Southern District of New York, but when told what it would cost, I didn't have enough money to even begin.

I was in total shock. They put a lien against my house, and if my husband's attorney had not earlier put the house in my husband's name too, I would have lost it. The lawyer on the other side tried everything he could to harass me. He sent his attorney-assistant often to stand in front of my house staring at it, as if they were going to get it. It took a lot not to let him reach me, and I had to practice my detachment every day (see Chapter 2), but I never responded to his ploys to disturb me.

This attorney would not allow me to try to settle the case. He kept telling me and my attorney that the other company (which had been bought and sold four times since the case began) was now not interested in settling for *any* amount, they only wanted their $950,000 (which could as well have been $100 million, for all I had).

So I used my thinking and contacted my darling friend Sam Reiser (Paul Reiser's late dad), who had been one of my twelve witnesses (he took a day off from his busy office, spent a whole day in court with his wife Helen, and was my strongest witness) and a good friend for many years. He owned a chain of health-food distributors across the United States, and was one of the nicest, kindest, most decent, principled human beings I've ever known.

At this point he went behind the attorney's back, contacted the company for me, told them I wanted to settle (which they knew nothing about), and we started negotiations with their in-house attorney (so el creepo was now totally out of a job and did *that* give me great joy!), and my husband flew to California and met with the very nice new attorney from the company.

Over a period of months we came to a settlement of $75,000, which I borrowed from a very dear friend; I paid off the company and had the lien lifted.

The nightmare was over.

It cost me over $200,000 in legal fees and took five years from beginning to end.

I'm not going to go into what happened to everyone on the other side, but as Ralph Waldo Emerson said, "The fallacy lay in the immense concession that the bad are successful, that justice is not done now."

When I think about what *could* have happened to me, it could have been so much worse. And I learned a great lesson about justice and lawsuits.

So even though I spent a lot of money on the case and I suffered greatly in aggravation and pain dealing with the attorneys on both sides, the defendants on the other side, and of course the judge, I'm much better off now than I was then.

I'm a much wiser person now than I was before, and I learned a lot about right and wrong that I wouldn't have learned without going through this.

Even though it was the worst experience in my life and I felt paralyzed by ignorance of legal procedures making me totally dependent on my lawyers, I look at it as something I really *needed* to go through. And that's how we have to look at every terrible injustice that we experience and have no control over.

And even those terrible situations that we actually *cause* to happen and then later regret—these are also learning situations that we should *not* regret. We did each one for a reason (at the time we did it there was a reason), and no matter what the results, if we use them and learn from them, then we will have grown mentally and emotionally and even possibly spiritually. And we will begin our learning about Good.

Everything is a growth experience, and if we have patience, don't get emotional, and keep our clear-thinking abilities fine-tuned (Chapter 2), right and Good will *always* win out.

Right and Wrong for Kids

If kids see adults lying and cheating ("The woman at the checkout counter gave me twenty dollars too much by mistake, but that store is overpriced anyway, so I kept it," "When I cheat my customers, it's bigger profits for me," "If I lie just a little to the IRS, they'll never find out,") how can these kids *not* grow up like their parents?

Kids must be *taught* the difference between right and wrong, and they must also *observe* their role models doing right and eschewing wrong. For children and teeners to learn ethical behavior and moral values (not whacking playmates, nor stealing candy, nor lying to teachers), they must observe the *advantages* of doing right—how listening to our consciences makes us happier by de-stressing our lives and making us feel Good about our selves.

Kids will also start to feel better about themselves when they start listening to their consciences instead of their peers. But they have to learn this from us.

Moral Values

In 1987 Norman Podhoretz wrote a column, "Perspective," in *The New York Post*. This particular column's caption was "When Horror No Longer Horrifies," about the sixteen-year-old girl who paid a classmate to kill her father, who had been sexually abusing her. He states, "Even incest is viewed as an 'illness' rather than as a moral evil."

He tells of an English literary critic in the 1940's who had

written patronizingly about the great Victorian novelist George
Eliot because Eliot admired chastity and self-restraint and
disapproved of self-indulgence and loose living.

Another English critic replied to the first one that, at the
risk of exposing himself to ridicule in literary circles, he shared
George Eliot's viewpoints. Then he added that feeling "above"
those moral values leads to triviality and boredom, and from
boredom comes evil.

Mr. Podhoretz states that in America (in 1987) sophisti-
cated and enlightened classes *still* feel above these values, and
it all leads to the same triviality and boredom, and "what could
be more trivial and more boring than a life in which no act, not
even incest, matters enough to inspire horror and revulsion?"

And then he says that "out of this denial of evil comes more
evil. As the unspeakable becomes a casual subject of babble
and chatter, restraints and fears are shed that would otherwise
have deterred."

He continues, "What once would have seemed inconceiv-
able now becomes possible. What once would have seemed
too weighty a burden for the spirit to bear now becomes fairly
easy to live with."

The difference between right and wrong is easy to discern.
The moment the thought of an action crosses your mind, your
conscience beeps either a warning or an OK. Many of us are
so used to not paying attention, we aren't even aware of the
beep. But it's there. And when the beep goes unheeded, and
we don't listen to our inner voice and our awareness of right
and wrong, confusion takes over.

We may *think* we're focused while we're not doing the
right thing, but true life-focus comes *only* with doing the right
thing. When we follow what we know to be a basic and
fundamental truth, we know and we feel the power of that
truth, that principle. And when we're around people who
ridicule us for following not them but the truth, we know
and we feel that right will *always* triumph as it has since
time began.

John Fitzgerald Kennedy

The late president JFK loved a particular quote of Dante that he repeated often, and it electrified my intellect:

> The hottest places in hell are reserved for those who, in a time of great moral crisis, retain their neutrality.

There *is* a right and wrong, and deep within each of us we know which is which. We must act on this instinct or die emotionally and spiritually. Mentally, we can kid our selves, but way down inside we know we can't retain our neutrality; we know we must decide that right is where we belong, and we must speak out for it and take a side. It takes courage at the beginning, but eventually we find there's *only* right, and there's really no decision and no courage needed.

The Power of our Good
combined with our thinking-without-emotion
will lead us to
<u>every thing we want.</u>

2

Emotions vs. Intellect

Something has become very clear to me recently. I had a glimmer of it before, but never realized the real truth of it until recently.

The *only* thing that gets us in trouble is our emotions, our feelings. And then, of course, it is only when those emotions are the negative ones—fear, hostility, anger, hate, jealousy, vindictiveness, etc.

Many people think that love gets us in trouble, but what we sometimes think of as love—a love-obsession, or overpossessiveness—is really fear, as are any of the other negative loves masquerading as the real thing.

Many people also think that it's thoughts and actions alone that cause problems, but without fear as the root, there would be no anger, hate, fighting, or any of the other negative thoughts and actions.

I remember so clearly about twenty years ago when I was married to a very emotional man who was very negative. Our relationship started out OK, but then as intimacy started crawling in, he became tense and afraid and built a cement wall around himself.

One day he started screaming at me about something, and he picked up my typewriter and threw it at me. I was so shocked at his outrageous actions of screaming and violence that something clicked in my head. No anger, no fear, just a coolness of attitude and a relaxation in my body as I felt a power of control over my self and over my feelings for my husband. He could no longer make me respond to any negative act he might do. From that moment on I detached my self from him emotionally and stayed calm no matter what he said or did.

It was the very beginning of my experiencing detachment. Up till then I would react to things more or less emotionally. I would *respond* to things emotionally. Basically, I always was a pretty calm person except when something angered me, and then I'd go crazy. I remember as a child twice being punished for having tried to injure two playmates. I was about four the first time, when I threw a heavy metal toy gun at a kid's head, and five and a half the second time, when I picked up a brick and threw it at another kid's head. How lucky I was that neither was seriously wounded, but I've never forgotten either incident. I don't remember what caused me to be so violent or what my feelings were at the time my obvious anger took over my body, but I've never forgotten the punishment and my remorse afterward.

However, since then I've always worked at staying calm. But this newfound detachment gave me a sense of peace and power. No matter *what* my husband did, no matter how loud he screamed or how nasty he got, I was calm and clear-thinking. *Nothing* he did or said could rattle me.

And it made my humor come out in small ways. Like the time he told me he could *only* drink freshly squeezed orange juice and that he could *always* tell if it was canned or frozen or in cartons. So every week I bought a large carton of Tropicana and hid it in the back of the fridge behind some health bottles of mine I knew he'd never move. Then I bought one fresh orange every week, and I'd float one orange seed on the top of the store-bought juice and get my kicks when he'd gulp it down (after removing the lone seed), smack his lips, and tell me how much he loved fresh-squeezed juice.

This went on for four years, till I couldn't take my constant detached relationship with him anymore and I left. The purpose of a love relationship is to grow individually and together, and you can only do that with a freedom of feelings and a blending of emotions. If you have to be detached constantly, on guard against a terrible temper, you're with the wrong person.

Carl Jung says in *Modern Man in Search of a Soul,* "Nothing is more unbearable than a tepid harmony in personal relations brought about by withholding emotion." I don't know if Carl ever had to detach himself from a love, but he certainly understood the anguish in that situation.

Now even with the detachment that I learned from being with my husband, and believe me that was the very beginning of any detachment I *ever* felt, I still didn't make the mental jump that I recently made.

But whatever detachment I learned then *did* help me enormously in every area of my life. I was able to keep cool when all others were going nuts, but I never really realized how the intellect, the thinking process, is in charge of life, and if it isn't, how that life is doomed to failure.

Recently, I've been going through a lot of *extra* stress in my life, and I think that has forced me to be even more intellectual and less emotional in my response to my problems. I've been more observant of people around me than I've ever been before.

I've observed three people very closely in the last few weeks and watched what their emotions have done to their lives.

One is an attorney with whom I've been very close as a friend. This man has always been a disaster with his emotional tantrums and screaming about almost everything that bothers him. He's got a really brilliant mind, but his feelings are so strong that he is almost never in control of himself, and I've watched him destroy most things in his life.

Another is a Spanish friend who is extremely talented but more than extremely emotional. She screws up most things she does because she appears unable to think clearly about anything because of her strong, uncontrolled feelings. She is a chain smoker (a sure sign of emotionalism), and even though I got her to quit for two months, her emotions overtook her desire for mental and physical health, and she resumed smoking.

The third friend, another male, is so emotional that everything he does is based on his feelings. When I point out that he's not thinking clearly and he's screwing up his life, he at the time seems able to understand what I'm saying, but then he reverts right back to his emotions.

All three have failed in most areas. Not one of them has any money, or prestige, or power. And all three of them are dishonest in varying degrees.

I believe these past few weeks I saw them clearly for the first time. And I saw how a lack of control on the emotions creates a vacuum in the intellect department. When you feel strongly in a negative way, you jam your body-computer (your brain), and you cannot think clearly.

British philosopher Bertrand Russell said, "The degree of one's emotion varies inversely with one's knowledge of the facts—the less you know, the hotter you get." When intellect is not being used, our feelings run rampant.

If something—*anything*—is stopping us from thinking clearly, *we must get rid of it!*

A fellow I work with and love dearly, Harold Rand, used to come into my office often, and he'd always say, "I don't understand how you can be so calm when you have so many tremendous problems and pressures," and I'd answer, "I'm calm only because I'm not responding emotionally to any of them. I recognize *all* of them intellectually, and I'm working on each one with my thinking-without-emotion, and trust me, Harold, I'll find an answer to each one."

And I did. I couldn't make the $4,000 a month rent for our offices I'd been paying for two years for a floor and a half in a small office building, so I talked the very nice owners into sealing up the stairway leading to the half-floor below and cutting the rent to $2,600 a month. Now I had less room and fewer desks, so I had to cut the staff from nine to six. I couldn't afford Harold anymore (he was very expensive and worth every penny), so I stopped using his PR services (I'd already let several people go earlier to cut the payroll when our income fell).

Harold would come around several times a week as he was looking for PR accounts, and he *always* said, "Naura, you're my role model, and you've taught me not to panic, not to get emotional, so I'm staying cool, and I know I'll get something."

Several weeks later Harold got a great account, and he says if he'd panicked, he couldn't have gotten it, but instead he went through his Rolodex and non-emotionally called anyone and everyone who might know of something. And that's why he was successful.

It really does work. Just remember, the intellect sees a problem, recognizes that it *is* a problem, and starts working on it immediately if you *keep* it intellectual and don't respond to it emotionally (which tightens and tenses you up), and I guarantee you, *you will find the answer*.

The intellect is that part of us that learns and reasons and thinks profoundly, and, when unhampered by negative emotions, allows us to *understand* how only Good and Goodness will lead us to real happiness.

The positive emotions of love and joy, which are subjective feelings rather than a conscious mental effort of the intellect, allow us to *feel* Good and Goodness within.

That's what's so good about Good. Good works through both the intellect and the positive emotions—*not* the negative ones—to lead us to whatever we want.

How To Use Emotional Detachment

The power within us can never be used until we learn *how* to detach our selves *emotionally*. The moment fear or anger enters our bodies, we must let go of our physical tension (fear and anger *always* cause physical tension), and that will *automatically* release the fear and anger emotionally.

By working what appears to be backwards, by relaxing the body muscles first (and you can actually do this physiologically by taking dolomite—coming ahead—which is calcium and magnesium, and which *really* un-tenses you), instead of trying to *will* the emotions to subside (almost impossible when you're tense), we are able to physically relax and distance our selves, detach our selves from our problem, and then solve it by using our intellect.

Without the emotional detachment that I have taught my self, I would undoubtedly have tensed up and panicked with some of the larger problems in my life. But with my constant awareness of any tension in my body and my deliberately and immediately relaxing it by drinking lots of water every day (coming in Chapter 4), which helps enormously to keep me calm, the relaxing and detaching has become a good habit that is sort of second nature now.

Just remember, *relax* and *detach*. It really works!

Life Preservers

A few years ago I had a relationship with a man who loved the horses. He really loved all gambling, but he particularly loved the track. So every Saturday in the summer for the first year, we would go to Monmouth Racetrack in New Jersey and spend Saturday night after the races in Jersey, where he played cards with all his track buddies. It wasn't too exciting to me to watch a bunch of guys play high-stakes poker, but hey, when you're in love, you sometimes put up with a lot of boring moments.

Anyway, one weekend he decided that instead of spending

it with his gambling pals, we'd spend it with another buddy, a very successful contractor from Jersey, and his wife, a young and beautiful novelist. I loved both of them, and after the races and dinner, we went to their gorgeous home in Rumson to spend the night.

In those days I was under tremendous stress because of this relationship, and I used to take a lot of dolomite pills, which are calcium and magnesium in a natural balance of two parts calcium and one part magnesium, and both really do calm your nervous system. Every night before bed I'd swallow ten pills (that was before I started chewing them), and I'd always leave ten more on my nighttable to take if and when I awakened in the middle of the night and couldn't get back to sleep (dolomite *really* works to relax you *naturally*, and ten pills is roughly equivalent to the calcium in a quart of milk, so you can see how tense I must have been). This particular night I took off my racing button, which is a piece of metal about two inches long by one inch wide with two round ends, and when you fold it over your lapel the authorities and doormen recognize you when you go in and out of the clubhouse.

I unbent the thing and laid it on the dresser. I undressed, and before going to bed, I laid out my dolomites in two piles of ten each, and a container of plain yogurt (this was long before I found out I have a milk allergy and gave up all milk products).

Well, this particular night I must have picked up the unfolded metal ID (again, it was about 2" × 1" and very sharp) and swallowed it with the pills.

The moment I did it, I realized what I had done. I stood there in the darkness of the bedroom and knew I would have to stay calm. I could feel this huge metal thing (believe me, it *felt* huge) in my throat, and as long as I stayed calm, it would be okay. If I panicked, I knew I would either choke to death or bleed to death from the sharp metal edges of this thing.

I calmly walked over to my sleeping husband and woke him up. It was about 3:00 A.M. He asked what was wrong, and I turned on the lamp and pointed to my neck. When I didn't speak, he realized I couldn't speak, and he asked if I had a sore throat. I shook my head no. He asked if I had swallowed something, and I shook my head yes. He got me a pencil and pad and I wrote down what had happened. He told me to get dressed, which I did quickly, and he threw on his clothes and drove me to the emergency room at the closest hospital.

The emergency room put me on a gurney, and I lay there for about five hours waiting for someone to do something. I later found out everyone there had misunderstood my husband and thought some vitamins had lodged in my throat and they were waiting for them to dissolve.

Finally, they got the story straight, and they took me into the operating room and put me to sleep. In the middle of the operation to remove this thing, I woke up. I couldn't breathe, and I was petrified *because* I couldn't breathe, and I know this may seem strange, but I had an orgasm on the operating table. I passed out again, and when I woke up I was in a hospital room and the doctor was standing next to the bed. My throat was *really* sore, and the doctor told me not to talk. So he did the talking.

He told me how lucky it was I didn't let the nurses force bread into my mouth (they had thought the bread would force the "vitamins" down my throat). I certainly would have choked to death with the bread caught on the metal pin. He said it was "miraculous" I never panicked in all the six or so hours I had this thing in my throat.

It was *not* miraculous. It's just that my power of thinking was stronger than my emotions. Fear is an emotion. And fear kills. Any time you allow panic to take over your life, you're a goner.

If you're in a fire or on a sinking boat, your only hope is to use your brain to save you. I *never* check into a hotel room without looking for the fire exit. I count how many doorways I'd have to pass to get there just in case it's dark and/or smoky.

I never get on a boat of *any* size without checking where the life preservers are, just in case.

Now all this came with training—my *self*-training. I wasn't born like this and I didn't grow up with these ideas. I realized that some day I might be in a life-threatening situation, and if I knew what to do, I wouldn't panic.

The Blue Angel

A few years ago, I used to go once in a while to The Blue Angel, a nightclub on East Fifty-fourth street in New York. One day I read in the paper about a big fire there the night before where many men and women were killed, most of them huddled in the ladies' room. What had happened was that when the lights went out, everyone felt against the wall and walked in the direction of the front door. What they hadn't realized was that the wall was curved and led to the ladies' room, where they were all trapped.

I was so mentally traumatized by this story that I couldn't forget it for weeks. The vision of all these people in the pitch blackness of the club being trapped was so scary to me because I knew the ladies' room, I knew the whole layout of the place, and I kept envisioning my self trying to get out and becoming trapped.

From that day on I have carried a small flashlight in my purse. If the lights ever go out wherever I am, I'll be able to light the way for me and everyone else.

It's thought over emotions. And thought *always* wins out!

My Mother

I had a terrible relationship with my mother. So many people have, that this is not really a big deal, and to tell you the truth, if she hadn't battered me emotionally (and sometimes physically), I wouldn't be the person I am today. I wouldn't have the understanding of mental illness that is so clear to me if she hadn't been manic-depressive.

She wasn't the classic four- or six-month manic then four- or six-month depressive, she was more ten minutes manic then six hours depressive or two hours manic then three hours depressive.

Her mother had died when she was four, and her aunt (who had lost a baby boy) raised my mother, and was not only very inattentive to her, she was also very uncaring (my mother lived on doughnuts and cakes for breakfast, lunch, and dinner for many years, suffering twelve broken bones by the time she was sixteen because of a lack of calcium and other nutrients), and her aunt was cruel, constantly telling my mother she wished she were a boy and not a girl (which must have given my mother a *lot* of self-esteem as she was growing up).

So my mother was the victim of abuse herself, and of course I now understand why she was so cruel, but to a child or a teener or a young adult who is emotionally needy of the female parent, it's traumatic to have to live with it and through it.

Going back to my early childhood, I had a deep emotional need for my mother and a tremendous love I felt for her, but because she was sometimes so mean to me and so insensitive to my feelings, when I hit puberty, I put up a protective barrier, and I couldn't call her anything but Mother. She wanted me to call her Mama, which I did till the barrier, but after that I tried not to call her anything—and if forced I would say Mother.

Now the worst part of a bad relationship with a parent (or with *anyone*) is that he or she is never *always* mean or *always* insensitive. Once in a while my mother would be nice and kind and loving, and that made it much more difficult. I knew she *could* be nice, but it didn't happen often, and even when it did, I knew it wouldn't last for long.

Had she not been a manic-depressive (caused no doubt by all the chemical imbalances stemming from the worst possible sugar-diet a child could eat), she probably would have been a very successful woman. But her illness made her emotionally unstable. She cried a *lot*. And it was very embarrassing to me to have her come to my high school, because she always ended up crying in front of people. Had she not been so emotional, she possibly could have accomplished something. But she was almost always either angry-screaming or depressed-sobbing. She never used her intellect. She probably didn't even know she had a thinking machine. She was extremely sentimental and kvelled when anyone gave her a slobbery birthday card or *any* card that was full of runaway emotion.

But thinking was not on her agenda. And that's why she lived a miserable existence and was unhappy every day of her life. I honestly don't remember her being happy for more than a few hours at a time. She couldn't express Good because her negative emotions stopped all thinking.

She was also a heavy smoker all her life (starting as a teenager), and smoking goes with emotionalism, either overt or covert. You may see a seemingly cool person puffing away, but within is a raging turmoil of unresolved negative emotions—fear, anger, etc.

I used to be a smoker and I know emotionalism first-hand, and my stopping smoking (which was one of the hardest things I've ever done) was the beginning of getting control of my self.

The smoking made my mother even more tense and uncontrollable (imbalancing her body chemistry even beyond her childhood and adult sugar-diet), and when I stopped smoking, I tried to get her to stop, but her addiction was strong and her desire to stop was nonexistent.

A few years ago I was thinking about her and concentrating on her good qualities and thinking about some really kind and nice things she had done for me. It was near Mothers' Day, and I decided to compose a beautiful letter to my mother and tell her how much I loved her and send it as a telegram.

Well, I wrote it out and I put in any and all really nice things I remembered her doing for me from childhood on, any sweet things she did for me, the times when she scrimped and saved to buy me something I really wanted, the times when she gave me the love I so needed. It was *very* emotional, but I knew it would mean more to her than any gift I could buy (and of course I knew how sentimental she always was), so I called Western Union and started to dictate it to the operator. Well, I got so emotional I had to hang up. The memories were so touching to me that I couldn't stop the tears. It took me a while to compose my self, and then I tried again. I still couldn't get through the first sentence, and again I hung up. Finally, I figured out how to do it. I called for the third time, and I told the operator that my boss wanted me to send this telegram for her, and I very slowly and deliberately enunciated every word and was very businesslike in my delivery.

Off it went to California and my mother's house to be hand-delivered the Saturday before Mothers' Day. I was sure my mother would be thrilled beyond belief and would be ecstatic when she first read it. She had always been incredibly sentimental, and I had just put in some of the really loving and touching things she had done for me while I was growing up, so she *had* to be thrilled with it.

I waited all day Saturday and no phone call. Well, I thought, she probably didn't get it till late in the day, and with the three-hour time difference I'll hear from her tomorrow. On Sunday there was no call by mid-afternoon. I was positive Western Union must not have delivered the telegram; something must have gone wrong. I called Western Union, and the operator said yes, my mother had signed for it on Saturday, early Saturday. I didn't know what to make of this. It was a truly beautiful and loving letter.

I decided to call her on Mothers' Day after I had found out she had indeed received the telegram and hadn't called me. I was so mystified and curious, and when I called her and wished her a happy Mothers' Day, I asked her if she had gotten my telegram and she said yes. Period. So I asked if she liked it, and she said she didn't understand why I sent it.

You can't imagine how I felt. What a jerk! What an *emotional* jerk! I must have fantasized that she would be ecstatic. But how could she *not* have loved all that sentiment? I had never seen her not melt at mush. To this day I don't know why she wasn't thrilled, and I will never find out. She died soon after.

My brother believes that because she was so overly sentimental, that kept her from feeling and reacting to *real* sentiment, *real* feeling.

If she hadn't been an emotional basketcase, we probably could have had a loving relationship. She was basically bright and might even have been very bright had she been able to think clearly. She *never* read anything. She was so full of fear and anger and self-pity that she watched TV, went to bed at 7:00 P.M., got up at 4:00 A.M., and drank tea all day long as she sat with a pencil and pad and mucho cigarettes figuring out her finances.

Stephen Covey wrote a wonderful bit about his mother: "She writes us love letters. I was reading one the other day on a plane with tears streaming down my cheeks. I could call her up tonight and I know she'd say, 'Stephen, I want you to know how much I love you and how wonderful I think you are.' She's constantly reaffirming." The reason I put this in about his mother is to show the difference between his mother and mine, his constantly reaffirming and mine not, but the end result is the most important part. He had an advantage of constant love and reaffirmation of his self-image that must have helped him enormously, and I didn't, but it forced me to find strength in other areas. And if it had been reversed and he had had my mother and I his, we still would have wound up the same because *he* would have found his strength in other areas.

You work with what you have, and if you're fortunate to have advantages of loving, supportive parents, you're ahead of the game. But it's *your* game, *you're* the one who's playing it, not your mom or your dad, and self-pity is one of the most insidious of all the negative emotions. It'll suck you down so fast you probably won't even know what happened. And feeling sorry for your self immediately stops *all* thinking as you wallow in negatives, so you'll *never* figure out how to move ahead.

If you have *any* difficult relationship, relax and detach. And then when you start thinking-without-emotion, you'll realize that it's *your* life and *you* are in control, and ideas will start flowing. If you respond to negatives and *don't* relax and detach, you're empowering the other person and un-powering your self.

When you relax and detach, you really *do* take the reins, whether it's with your spouse, your mother, your dad, your kids, your boss, a salesperson, anyone. The important thing is *not* to respond to *any* negative emotion, your own or someone else's. No matter the waiter is short-tempered and rude, detach your self, don't answer him back, but do quietly report him to the manager *after* you've finished your meal. When you're detached, it gives you such a feeling of power that *no one* can rattle you or make you respond in anger.

Two things make me sad about my mother. The first is that when I was a little girl she came home one day and told me that her doctor told her to take yeast—that it would make her nervousness and tensions go away and would make her feel a lot better. So she went out and bought some cubes of Fleischmann's baker's yeast that you use to make bread. She put two of them in two glasses of tomato juice and mashed them all up with a fork and gave me one. You just can't imagine how foul it tasted, but we both drank it. She said the doctor said it's not only great for your nerves, it's also great for your skin, so of course little ten-year-old me wanted great skin. We both took it every day for about a month, but she didn't feel better and my skin hadn't started glowing, so we stopped.

Many years later, after I got into nutrition, I started reading about brewer's yeast and how great it is for you because of all the B vites, and then there was a warning about how you should *never* take baker's yeast by mistake, that it does just the *opposite* of brewer's yeast, it *robs* your body of the B vites. When I read this, a terrible sadness came over me, because if the doctor had only specified *brewer's* yeast, my mother could have felt so much better. The B vites *do* get rid of depression and anxiety (as I found out for my self) and *would* have helped her feel so much better. Her doctor sure meant well, but he probably didn't even know the difference, that there were two different kinds of yeast. So near and yet so far. . . .

The other part that really makes me sad about my mother is that she was born fifty years too early, that were she a young, newly married woman today with manic-depressive symptoms, she could have been helped with all the new body chemistry-balancing drugs today. But back then she screamed and ranted and raved and hit, and after my father died (my anchor in a sea of twenty-foot waves, storms, and undertows), she sank so low and became so desperate for relief that she went to a psychiatrist who put her through electric shock treatment. For those who don't know, they strap electrodes on your temples and wrists and pass electric current through your body.

That helped her outbursts somewhat, but her long-term memory was dimmed, and it's such a barbaric treatment, second only (to me) to a lobotomy, that I would hope that few people would think of doing it today.

The Good NEW Days

Speaking of barbaric treatments, anyone who talks about "the Good Old Days" has forgotten all the problems we used to have, *like* lobotomies (detaching part of a brain, for you innocents), which Joe and Rose Kennedy allowed their daughter Rosemary to go through because they sincerely believed it would help her, as did Tennessee Williams's family, who allowed his sister to be lobotomized.

Also "the Good Old Days" had washing machines with wringers (and no driers, so you *had* to hang the wash outside on "clotheslines"), horrible messy carbon paper instead of copy machines, safety razors that put nicks all over your face or legs instead of Trac II, dentistry without Novocain (aaachh!), etc.

When I did *Naura's Good News* on WMCA radio for over two years in New York in the early to mid eighties, I had a feature called "The Good *New* Days" (and I did it again in 1994 when I was a guest-host on KFMB-AM in San Diego). *Every* person who called in (they had to be over thirty to be eligible!) said the old days were better, with less crime, less noise, fewer social problems, less crowding, etc., but when you think about the *incredible* new technology going on all around us, the new days are better in so many ways. We have to *use* all this new technology to stem crime, and this *can* be done. We've got to start *controlling* our rampant negative emotions and start *using* our intellects to further our well-being—and then we'll have a world of today that will *dwarf* the "Good Old Days."

Truth Pill

If there were such a thing as a "truth pill" that was 100 percent infallible, and it became a legal tool that was known and accepted worldwide, and any people involved in crimes or disputes or lawsuits knew ahead of time that they would eventually have to take it, and of course whoever was lying (and someone in a crime or dispute or lawsuit is lying) would be punished accordingly, do you think it would change our world/society?

Do you think society would get behind it to make it legal?

Do you think that our legislators *would* legalize it?

I feel strongly about all three questions because truth is such an important part of Good. Truth is intellect, not emotion. Truth is fact, not fantasy.

If truth continues on its downhill spiral, the world can only get sicker. The reason almost all people lie is, first, because they are afraid of the consequences of telling the truth (telling the truth sometimes takes courage), and second, and most important, because they get away with it. And like everything else, the more successful you are, the more you continue with your successful formula.

But it can't continue. Courtroom dramas are sucking money out of state and federal governments the same as lawyers are sucking it out of hapless victims (not *all* lawyers are conscienceless, just *most* of them). A few do have integrity and morals, a few do know the difference between right and wrong; I just wish there were more.

Someone in the not-distant future *will* come up with some new technology that will obviate lying, so prepare for a brave new world where truth will reign because no one will be able to get away with lying.

In my *Isle of View (Say it out loud)* book I have a section about "creative lying" relevant to sensitivity to others' feelings and also to doing Good (like Stefania saving Jews in Nazi Germany), but that is a totally different situation from lying to further your self, not others, or to do selfish things that will actually hurt others.

Abortion

If you look at abortion intellectually and not emotionally, you'll see what it really is.

Two people have sex, and neither the man nor the woman is using protection to stop the sperm from reaching the egg.

The woman becomes pregnant and doesn't want the child, or she does want it but is afraid she can't handle it because of her age, or lack of funds, or some other reason, so she gets rid of the unborn baby. Abortion has become an alternative birth control method.

No matter what anyone says, it *is* a human baby and it *is* being killed. Those who support legal abortion *call* it "aborting a fetus"—but a fetus is an unborn baby, so it's *still* aborting a baby.

Negative emotions play the biggest part of abortion. First the woman is afraid the guy will be turned off if she stops to put in a diaphragm or if she insists he use a condom. Or she's afraid she'll ruin the romantic mood with dialogue. Or she wants to pretend it "just happened" without any thinking or preparation ahead of time (which relieves her of any possible guilt).

Then of course there's the fear of having the baby, being a parent while still in school, having her youth sabotaged and becoming an instant adult, or for a woman not a teener, the fear of not being able to care for a child alone, or if married, the fear of not having enough money for all the other kids.

Intellectually, the answer is simple:

When the sperm doesn't reach the egg, there is no baby.

All women must be taught about and, if they can't afford it, supplied with protection.

Either all women of childbearing age who have intercourse wear a diaphragm *all* day *every* day (because "you never know when it might happen"), or these same women take birth-control pills and chemically regulate the eggs in their bodies.

And of course single Catholic women who don't believe in birth control can be celibate (which is what they're taught to be), and the Catholic marrieds can use the "rhythm" method based on the woman's ovarian cycle.

Certainly a diaphragm is inexpensive once a woman's gynecologist measures her for the right fit and gives her a prescription for it. And once it's inside a woman, she never feels it (that's one reason why a right fit is so important; the other is only a right fit will keep the sperm out).

The pill costs more, it alters your hormones, and you do run the risk of forgetting to take one on a particular day, but it *does* work.

Then you have the subcutaneous implant that is easier than the pill because you don't have to do anything for months and sometimes over a year. But it also alters your hormonal balance.

Every body is different and has a different body chemistry, and it's important to find out which is best for you so you will only become pregnant when and if you want to.

Intellect vs. Emotion

The important thing is to see that when the negative emotions run amok, nothing good can happen. And when the intellect is in charge, *only* Good can happen. That's what's so good about Good. Good works through intellect and the positive emotions—*not* the negative ones—to lead us to whatever we want.

We know what the negatives are—fear, anger, self-pity, etc.—but let's look at the positive emotions—love, caring, nurturing, compassion, awe (and all these really are love-based), and any feeling that is strong and deep within us without any physical tension.

Physical tension is negative feeling.

Absence of tension is positive feeling.

Who can experience the feeling of awe while looking at an incredibly beautiful part of nature, a vivid sunset, a majestic stallion, waves pounding the shore, and not be overwhelmed by nature's greatness? And who can hear of a terrible sadness and not be overcome with feelings of compassion? I dare anyone to read Eugene Field's beautiful poem "Little Boy Blue" and not be deeply moved.

Little Boy Blue

The little toy dog is covered with dust,
But sturdy and stanch he stands;
And the little toy soldier is red with rust,
And his musket molds in his hands.

Time was when the little toy dog was new
    And the soldier was passing fair,
And that was the time when our Little Boy Blue
    Kissed them and put them there.

"Now, don't you go till I come," he said,
    "And don't you make any noise!"
So toddling off to his trundle-bed
    He dreamed of the pretty toys.
And as he was dreaming, an angel song
    Awakened our Little Boy Blue,—
Oh, the years are many, the years are long,
    But the little toy friends are true.

Ay, faithful to Little Boy Blue they stand,
    Each in the same old place,
Awaiting the touch of a little hand,
    The smile of a little face.
And they wonder, as waiting these long years through,
    In the dust of that little chair,
What has become of our Little Boy Blue
    Since he kissed them and put them there.

My father read it to me when I was seven years old, and I cried and never forgot that moment or the poem. Every time I read it, I dissolve. It's a beautiful poem about sadness, and it stirs up beautiful emotions of love and loss. There's nothing there of fear or anger or envy, just the overwhelming sadness about the loss of a beloved and innocent child.

All beauty is overwhelming to our emotions, and when we respond, *that* is beautiful. Be it awe or love or compassion, they are all positive emotions and are Good. They make us feel as one with the universe.

We are open when we feel the positive emotions, just as we are closed when we feel anger or fear.

So the more relaxed and open we keep our selves, the more able and ready we are to express the beautiful and loving feelings that are so much a part of us, and the less likely we are to revert back to our uptight and tense feelings of fear and anger.

Good is always positive and always makes us feel relaxed and open.

When you control your negative emotions and allow your intellect to take charge, the answer to *every* problem will come to you. In my own life, once I stilled my fears and allowed my intellect to lead me, I found the answers to all my problems.

And I'm not talking about only mental or emotional or spiritual problems (and of course these are all *very* important), but I'm *also* talking about paying the rent, buying a car, finding a life-mate, getting a raise, starting a new business, adopting a child, or getting *any* and all the things you really want.

The power of our Good combined with our thinking-without-emotion will lead us to *every thing we want*.

Good does not <u>give</u> us anything—
<u>We</u> have to figure out with our own brains
how to get what we want,
and once we figure it out,
our Good Power will lead us to it.

3

Problem-Solving

I am a problem-solver, and I really do believe it's my greatest achievement. Everyone is a *potential* problem-solver, but not everyone knows it. I know it.

Any problem enters my life, I *immediately* think, "How can I solve it?" I *never* think it's not solvable. I *never* think, "Why did this happen to me?" I know it's there for a reason, for my growth. I don't care how overwhelming it appears, I know there is an answer just waiting for me to find it.

So many people who come upon a problem, any problem, big or small, think they are doomed to live with it. How sad that they don't know that every so-called problem has an answer just waiting to be discovered.

THERE ARE NO PROBLEMS, THERE ARE ONLY CHALLENGES.

Let's say you flunk a class at college and you're despondent about it. You can either stay depressed and live with it, or find a way of taking the test again (after cramming), or taking the course again at night or on weekends or by correspondence. Or maybe there's another answer. Trust that the power of your ability to think-clearly-without-emotion will lead you to find the right answer once you give the problem some focused thought.

Or here's a challenge if you just broke up with your mate and you're lonely. How do you meet someone besides going to a bar or a club?

Well, I came up with a great idea when I was doing *Naura's Good News* on WMCA radio and people were calling me and asking how to meet new friends. Everyone loved it, both males and females.

You are going to give a unique, ingenious, inexpensive, and the most *fun* party ever given.

First, if you're a woman, you make a list of all your single girlfriends, anywhere from five to ten of them. They have to be unattached (if you're a guy, you do the same thing with your single, unattached pals).

Now each woman has to ask anywhere from two to four men friends who are unattached. They can't be someone you still are in love with, or a drug addict, or a sleaze, the men have to be normal, fairly well-adjusted people (don't pass off some nut job on a poor unsuspecting girlfriend of yours who'll be at the party).

Now each of your girlfriends will bring a food dish or wine or soft drinks/juice. For instance, you supply the potato salad, someone else brings a quiche and a mixed bean salad, someone brings a box of super coconut-brownie cookies, someone else two bottles of wine, one red and one white, etc. So the food costs little per person. Each woman who invited the two to four men must introduce her guests to all the other women at the party so everyone meets everyone else. And you must have a guest book that everyone signs with name and phone number.

I had two such parties and they were great. I had five girlfriends who each asked three male friends, so there were six women and eighteen men, and it was fun! Everybody made lots of new friends and several made new romances. And a male friend of mine gave the same kind of party, and he had seven guy-friends who each asked four women, so he had eight guys and thirty-two women (he's got a *big* apartment!).

The fun is its lopsided male/female ratio, and you meet lots of opposite and same-sex friends. Having the guest book is important when a girlfriend calls and asks who was that tall, lanky guy, or one of the men calls and asks for the redhead's name and phone number, and you've got 'em all right there.

Another good way (not as good as my party idea because nobody knows anybody ahead of time) is the personals ad. But it can be exciting, particularly when *you* run the ad! One girlfriend of mine ran an ad and got over one hundred replies. She culled it down to six she thought were the most interesting and made lunch dates with all of them. Of the six she liked two and went out at night with them.

One she went to Las Vegas with, and when he stayed in the casino all night, she told him the next morning she wanted to go home, and he had his limo drive her right back to L.A. and she never saw him again. The other, a darling guy she's still with several years later, gave her a diamond engagement ring, and they are very happy together and are really compatible. Sometimes it works!

I've heard of lots of successful "meets," and even if you just make some new platonic friends, that's great. Through them you might meet some un-platonic friends.

Another friend, a male, answered several female personals ads and met a psychologist and a teacher and is not too compatible with either of his two new acquaintances. So he's going to run his *own* ad and is looking forward to the results. The bottom line is keep trying and don't give up. There are a lot of individuals out there looking for a new friend (and romance), and why shouldn't it be you?

Now back to business. Maybe your business failed because of something out of your control—a recession or depression. Try to figure out how you can start up again, where you can borrow some money, or maybe look for a partner who would bankroll and take half the profits. Or figure out another business that might do better in the financial climate of the times, a business that you would like to get into and that you feel you could do well with because of your knowledge or instincts or love of that particular field.

A dear friend of mine, a truly great talk-show host, was really challenged when he was suddenly let go from a major radio station in the Midwest when the station was sold. He and his wife decided to sell their house and move with their two kids to Florida. He wasn't able to get a job right away, and his wife, a former dancer, tried to think of something she could do to help bring in some bucks, so she opened a dance studio for kids. It was something she'd thought about but never had the guts to do till Fate stepped in and she *had* to do it to help support the family. It was slow at first, but she now has over two hundred students and her business is *booming*. And my friend, the talk-jock, after looking for the right station for many months, finally found it, and is again doing his thing on the airwaves.

Or maybe your business fails because of some failing of *yours*—lack of organization, sloppy bookkeeping, your lack of supervision of your employees, failure to collect monies due you from clients—whatever it was, it was your fault. So stop and think about it. Maybe you didn't belong in that kind of business. Maybe you're a more creative kind of person who needs to create and let others handle the business aspects of running a business.

Or maybe you really loved your business and just were too naive and inexperienced to know you needed help. *Everybody* needs help. Nobody can do it all. We all need a good accountant, bookkeeper, secretary, assistant, receptionist, typist, file clerk, etc. So maybe you could restart your business, but this time start it more slowly and make sure you get your books started right by an accountant and make sure the accountant or bookkeeper gives you a report every week. This time do it right. Profit by your mistakes.

Several years ago it looked like curtains for me financially. I was so close to losing everything I'd worked so hard to attain that I could not only touch it, I could smell, taste, and feel it.

One of my businesses had a major problem. We had to recall all of my record albums because something (we didn't know what) had ruined them, and we had to get all of them back from thousands of stores all over the country.

We plummeted from almost a million dollars (and climbing fast) in 1989 down to $30,000 in 1990. Plus we had to pay for the recall, which is expensive. To get stores to take products from their shelves and pack them and send them back, and this could be books, records, *anything*, you have to pay all the shipping, plus promise them to replace them with new good products.

It was a nightmare, and all the money owed us from distributors went right into paying for the recall. This first happened in January 1990, and by February I didn't have the money for my mortgage, my suppliers, or my payroll.

I started getting cash from my credit cards (you can see how desperate I was at 22 percent interest!) and I made my payroll that way, but when you've got eight people working for you, it's some payroll. I also paid my suppliers from the cards, but there wasn't enough for my two mortgages, the first and the second, so eventually I fell behind four months on my first and eight months on my second.

Things were closing in on me, but I never got emotionally panicked. I was constantly trying to figure out what I could do to instantly bring in a large income.

I was getting just a little apprehensive about my first mortgage. It was huge, $1,150,000, and the monthly payment was $12,000. I was four months behind, so I owed the bank $48,000.

One day I received in the mail foreclosure papers, and even *then* I didn't panic. I just *knew* I would get out of this. I didn't know *how*, but my mind was *constantly* thinking about possible solutions. That same day in the summer of '90 a lightbulb went on in my head . . . *HOW TO SATISFY A WOMAN EVERY TIME* . . . and have her beg for more!

My book had come out in 1982 and had been a huge bestseller in hardcover. It sold over 200,000 copies and was ten weeks on *The New York Times* and *Time* best-seller lists (plus many other lists all over the country) in 1983. After I stopped promoting it, an amazing thing happened. It kept selling by itself, by word-of-mouth, and each year it sold anywhere from 10,000 copies up. So from 1984 to 1990 it was steadily being reordered by bookstores around the country.

But in the back of my mind, way back, I'd every once in a while think about how important the book was for married couples, and how my sexual technique had saved countless marriages. I'd received thousands of letters over the years from husbands and wives telling me the book should be given to couples by churches and marriage-license bureaus.

So here I was, the foreclosure papers in my hand, I didn't even have *one* month's mortgage payment, and I'm thinking positively about re-promoting my book. This was midsummer and I was excited about the idea. Then reality set in—where was I going to get the money to *print* the book? I only had a few thousand in the warehouse, and to do TV and radio shows, I'd need at least 25,000 copies, which would cost me maybe $40,000.

I thought of a man I knew very well and decided to call him, which I did. I made an appointment within the week and felt good about that.

Then I called E. P. Dutton, my book distributor, and talked to Frank Heidelberger, my contact there, and told him of my idea to re-promote the book. He was wildly enthusiastic and really made me feel good about that.

Now I turned my attention to the foreclosure papers. I called my mortgage broker, a wonderful Irishman named Gleason, and asked his opinion of what to do. I knew that when the bank went so far as to send these papers, it meant that even if I got the $48,000 for the four past payments, they wouldn't take it. Foreclosure means you gotta cough up the whole $1,150,000. Jack said he would call the bank, but he wasn't too optimistic about it.

I *still* didn't panic. I *still* felt something was going to work out. And worst-case scenario I'd go live in Europe, maybe on the Riviera. This was always my "escape fantasy." If it's meant to be that I lose everything, then it's for a good reason and for my growth. Maybe I'm *supposed* to live in Europe (the thought of Switzerland always intrigued me because it's so clean and pristine and uncluttered and beautiful). And I mean Europe with hardly any money because I obviously had a *lot* of problems and very little bread.

When you don't panic and get emotionally overwrought, you give your brain a chance to function, and mine was cooking on all four burners. The next day when the mail came in, I found a letter from the mortgage bank, and it was from a woman in the mortgage department. As it turned out, she had made a mistake in sending it, because it said that if I paid the four payments totaling $48,000, it would bring me up-to-date. It was obviously sent in error because it nullified the foreclosure temporarily, and the poor woman was undoubtedly in hot water for mistakenly sending it.

Well, at least I knew I didn't have to come up with the million right away. Now I tried to think of someone I could borrow $50,000 from. I racked my brain and nothing came out. For days I thought of little else but where I could come up with $50,000.

Later that week I went to Chicago on business, and while in my hotel room I got a call from my brother telling me our mother had died. She had been in a hospital for a long time suffering from emphysema brought on by fifty years of heavy smoking. She also had Parkinson's, which was awful enough without the emphysema. So it was a blessing that she passed away.

My brother told me she had left me $50,000.

He was the executor of her estate, and he told me there was a lot of paperwork but that I would probably get it in a few weeks. When I told him I really needed it now, he said he'd try somehow to advance the money to me; I don't think he was legally supposed to, but being the angel he is, he did.

Well, that was the turning point. I paid the first mortgage and made it current, I told the second-mortgage woman that I would start paying her next month. She kept threatening to sue me, but I convinced her I really would make double monthly payments till I got caught up.

I flew out to Los Angeles for the funeral, and when I got back, I went to my meeting with my friend to borrow the money (or part of it) so I could print the books.

Let me tell you a little bit about my friend. I had known him for fifteen years and considered him a *good* friend. We had lunch often and really liked each other's company. He always called me when I appeared on a radio or TV show in New York and told me he was my biggest fan. He was married (I'd never met his wife), but we had a totally platonic relationship. And an important fact is that he had just sold a *giant* business and had split $56 million with his partner. Fifty-six million dollars! That's $28 million into *his* bank account.

There wasn't even a question in my mind that he would lend me the $40,000. He knew I had a great credit record (meaning I had over thirty credit cards and I always paid my debts), and he liked and admired my determination (or so he had always said).

I offered to pay him back out of first profits and give him 10 percent of all future earnings on my book.

Well, he said he'd have to think about how to do it, and would I call him the next day? I said sure, and when I called, he asked me to call again the next day. He had me going for over a week, and one time he'd asked that I call at exactly 11:00 A.M., and I was in a TV studio in Tulsa waiting to do an interview and what I had to go through to get to an outside phone was incredibly difficult, but I did it.

The end of the story is that after stringing me along for eight days and leading me to believe he would do it, he finally said to me that he wouldn't do it. I was so stunned, I literally couldn't believe it. I was in shock for about twenty seconds, and then I asked him why, and he actually said to me that he had lent money to his two sisters and they hadn't paid him back. I told him that I wasn't these two women and that he knew that I always pay my debts, but he said sorry, no can do.

Needless to say, I haven't seen or spoken to him since, but it was sad to me to lose a friend of fifteen years. However, as soon as I realized (almost instantly) that he obviously *wasn't* my friend (a friend is someone who cares and will help if possible, and Goodness knows it was *possible* for him to help), my sadness disappeared and reality set in.

I had lost valuable time wasted on this cluck, so I right away called another friend. This one I didn't know as well, and he certainly didn't have as much money as the first one (who does?), but I knew he did invest in certain things. On the phone he asked what the meeting would be about and I told him I needed some money, $40,000, to print my books, and that I would pay him back first and give him 10 percent of all future earnings from it. He said sure on the phone, he would do it. I breathed a little easier with his commitment.

He came over to the house to make the deal and asked to see my press kit on the book, so I showed him all the previous newspaper clippings from when the book was first out, and my brand-new press kit that my PR woman had put together.

He sat browsing through all the sensational stories about the book, *The New York Times* and *Time* magazine's best-seller lists for the ten weeks in 1983, and he came to one quarter-page review of the book in *The Orlando Sentinel*. The review was spectacular. It ran a headline:

A CLEAR-EYED VIEW OF HUMAN INTIMACY
by Samuel Roen

It has been said, "When a wise woman tells you something, you should listen." Naura Hayden is a wise woman who tells you something in her new book, *HOW TO SATISFY A WOMAN EVERY TIME*.

With this book of revelations, Hayden takes her place as an authority, joining an elite group of doctors (medicine and philosophy) who have for the past several decades drawn open the curtains of intimacy.

Although Hayden does not enjoy the prestige of a doctorate, her personal experiences entitle her to a degree in the practical. She presents the feminine view and that has more validity than theoretical premises and conclusions advanced by males, even those with doctor's degrees.

Although small in size, the book carries a giant message. Hayden is a strong advocate of propriety and marriage: "Now we come to my favorite subject, marriage. I don't believe in living together—"playing house"—and I truly believe in the commitment of marriage. I think it's the greatest relationship that two people can ever have. A partnership with someone who loves you. What could be better?"

It's no wonder that the book has caused a stir around the country.

Well, my friend asked me if the reviewer worked for the paper, and I said he must or why would the story be in the paper? He said no, it looks like he's a free-lance writer whom the paper hired to do the review. I asked how he could tell, and what difference would *that* make if it were true? And he said that it wasn't as good as if he were an employee of the paper. I couldn't believe his negative so-called logic, but asked him about all the *other* terrific reviews I showed him written in newspapers and magazines around the United States, and he said no, he just didn't think he could lend me $40,000.

I asked why had he made a commitment and told me yes on the phone, and he said after giving it some thought, he didn't think he should do it. Every time I see this guy now at the Friars Club, he tells me and everybody else what a dodo he was and how tremendous his 10 percent would have been, and I'm happy he turned it down 'cause I made 10 percent more.

Okay, now what do I do? My PR person had already started booking me around the country to appear on TV and radio, and I had hardly any books.

Well, I called my "book-maker," a wonderful man named David Zable, who takes care of all my book production, and ordered 25,000 books. I knew how people would respond to the book because they had before, so I told Dave that I had no money, but that in three months I would be able to pay him (book distributors hold all monies from sales for ninety days in case of returns). He trusted me to pay him, and he printed the books (why didn't I think of him in the first place?).

The rest is history. The book has sold over 2 million hardcover and is *still* going strong.

But had I panicked and not stayed calm, had I let my fears take over, I would have been done for. I never even *acknowledged* any fears. I relaxed and I detached.

When you stay calm, fear can't grab hold of anything. It takes tension to be afraid. And if you really *work* at staying calm, if you really won't *allow* your self to become physically tense, you can keep your brain working and allow Good to lead you to figure out what to do.

The bottom line is discipline, relaxing and detaching, and *knowing* that your brain (with Good's help) *will* come up with a solution.

Trust me. It *always* does.

Personal Responsibility

It's always amazing to me how few people want to take responsibility for what they do. They only know to stay passive and react to everything around them. This is what they were taught.

And this is one of the hardest attitudes to change, but it's probably the most important. Because until you can see that no one or no thing can affect you unless you *let* it, unless you *respond* to it, you will never get to the detachment stage where you *can* use your thinking-without-emotion ability.

So if you *are* a responsible person, you are able to choose whether you *will* respond or not, and you are able to choose *how* you will respond.

So many people, for whatever reason, will *not* say, "Yes, I did it and I made a mistake," or, "That was one of the dumbest things I *ever* did." When you use an excuse, "Well, Bob wanted to do it so I went along with him," or "She was such a bitch that I had to scream at her," or "It wasn't my fault, I was told to do it," you are giving power to the other person. When you empower people or things, you lose your *own* power.

People accept you at your own evaluation.

If someone senses that you have no "center," no inner strength, that person senses that your self-esteem is low, and unfortunately, it's been proven in prison tests, that a person in power (a prison guard) will often take advantage of a subordinate (an inmate). It's happened in concentration camps and sometimes, sadly, in preschool classrooms. If an unprincipled person feels he or she *can take advantage and get away with it*, he or she will.

It takes a response to further the negative action, but you can train your self to *turn off* the emotions and say to your self, "I refuse to respond, and *that* will drive him [or her] crazy." If someone knows how to trigger you off and does it all the time and you constantly respond, what joy that gives your tormentor because that person is the actor and you are *re-*acting. Can you imagine what will happen if you all of a sudden don't respond to the trigger-word? You all of a sudden will change roles—you will become the actor and the former actor will become the *re*-actor.

Remember there is a quick moment (maybe even a split second) between the word or action and your response. Just pause a second. Relax and detach. The more you do it, the easier it becomes. Relax and detach. Make it a habit. Relax and detach.

That's taking personal responsibility for your self and for your life.

Liking Your Self

An absolutely *foolproof* way to like your self is to make a commitment to your self and then follow through. It sounds too simple, and it is simple, but it works. Money-back guarantee!

First you start with something really basic. You're overweight and you want to firm up your body, so you promise your self that you're going to walk the three flights up to your apartment for a week after work instead of taking the elevator. And every day at 5:45 you schlep up the stairs feeling good about your resolve (and the wonderful part about exercise is even small muscle-flexers done every day really start to strengthen the muscles much better than doing a half hour of strenuous flexing once a week). Your legs are starting to feel stronger, so at the end of the week you decide to do it for a month and see how you feel.

Or you've been seriously trying to cut out junk foods from your diet, so you promise your self you won't buy the Cheez-Whirls (that you love) every day for a week at your coffee break, you'll buy an apple instead. And you keep it up for the week. By the end of the week you're so proud of your self you decide to change your morning glazed jelly doughnut to a bran muffin.

The important thing is to make your first promise an easy one and be sure to set a time limit, like one week. Once you've proven to your self that you *can* depend on your self to keep your word, you'll be amazed at how much your self-esteem will grow.

But if you make it *too* difficult ("I'm going to give up cigs forever," "I'm going to go to the health club every day for an hour") and you *don't* follow through, you will more than dislike your self, your anger and disgust will make you *despise* your self ("You see, I can't rely on my self," "I knew how weak-willed I always was and I still am").

And the added benefits are the side effects:

• "I'm going to listen to my French audiotapes for fifteen minutes for five days."	• You'll slowly begin to learn French.
• "Every time my husband criticizes me, I will stop my self from defending my self, I will take a deep breath, relax my body, and just say, "You know, you're right." I'll do this for three days.	• You'll begin to learn detachment.
• "I'll get a rebounder (trampoline), and every day for a week I'll jump on it for five minutes in the morning.	• You'll start to strengthen all your internal organs and muscles, making you feel better.
• "I'm going to sign up for that computer class at the Y, and for the next eight weeks I'll go every Tuesday night for three hours."	• You'll finally learn the computer.

There are so many (thousands of) fun and constructive things you can make small promises about and *keep* that will enrich your life and be the beginning of your liking your self.

I have done this *many* times, and it really has helped me in my climb toward self-esteem, and I've learned many interesting things besides.

And of course another foolproof way to truly like your self is to realize the Good within and then to express it. How can you *not* like a Good self? . . . . (coming in Chapter 9).

Aptitude Tests

So many of us drift about in our lives not knowing what we may be talented at and what we could be making a living doing that would not only pay our bills but give us fun, pleasure, and gratification.

What a pity grammar schools don't have aptitude tests so little kids could have an idea where they might be headed. Those lucky few who know exactly what they want to do from age five *are* lucky, because they never veer till they become a doctor or a concert pianist or a mechanic or a hairstylist.

What a waste of a life for someone temperamentally suited to be a physical therapist to become a sales clerk, or someone perfect as a salesperson to wind up a gardener and work alone. What a waste of talent for a potential pastry chef to become a masseur. Or someone who should be a nurse to end up a legal stenographer.

Each job has people perfectly suited to it, and each person has an innate talent for one particular thing that he or she would be better at than anybody else.

The best way to find out is to take an aptitude test. It costs, but not a terrible amount, and if you weighed it against the cost of a new suit, and also weighed all the benefits of finding out what you're best fitted for, it can do a lot more for you than ten new suits.

These aptitude tests can be taken at any number of places in your city, and you can find them in your Yellow Pages under Career Counseling Centers. Some are less expensive than others, but when you think about finding something you're fitted for as opposed to trying out lots of different types of jobs till you find one you like—or *never* finding one you like, just getting stuck doing something you're not only not suited for but something you dislike intensely, you'll see the tests are worth every penny.

If you count the hours till the end of the day, if you're bored out of your skull doing whatever it is you're doing, you *should* test your self to see where you really belong in the career field.

Remember, the harder you work, the luckier you get!

But you won't *want* to work hard if you hate your job, and you will want to work hard if you love it.

What a thrill to get up each morning and know you're going to spend a day doing something that excites you, be it meeting lots of new people as a receptionist in a literary agent's office or assisting a vet in an animal hospital.

Maybe you'll decide *you* want to be an agent or a vet after that experience, or maybe you'll continue what you're doing because you enjoy it so much.

Maybe you'll find you excel at fashion or as a mechanical engineer, maybe you'll wind up a school social worker helping kids adapt to school life. Or you could find a talent as a photojournalist, so you get a job as an assistant to a photographer so you can learn the ropes.

The thing that you can *always* be successful at is anything that is a *service* that people really need. A fellow I know likes cats and learned how to bathe and groom them, and actually goes right to the cat's house to do it. He charges a lot, but it's such a great service that he's booked solid weeks in advance.

If you're fortunate enough to be doing what you love every day, you are blessed, but if you're not happy with your work, run, don't walk, to the nearest "career counseling center" in your area.

Or if you want to try something much less expensive to begin with, and maybe it'll tell you all you need to know, there's a wonderful book out called *Discover What You're Best At* by Barry and Linda Gale that lets you test your self to discover your real abilities so you can find the right job. Try the library or any bookstore.

There's another aptitude book called *Do What You Are* by Paul D. Tieger and Barbara Barron-Tieger which tests you to discover and understand your own personality type, to help you find the work that will make you happiest, and to learn how to best use your work-related talents. This particular book I saw in a catalog called *Wireless*, 1–800–669–9999, but you can either buy this book or check it out at the library.

And while you're at it, see if there are any *other* aptitude-testing books that sound good to you. The bottom line is you have talent (we *all* have talent) and if you don't find it, you'll waste your life in a job that makes you unhappy, but if you *do* find your talent (and it *is* there, I promise you), you will be more productive and more fulfilled and that will make you happier than you've ever been. Try it. All you have to lose is your boring job.

Grammar School and High School Lawyers

Since I've gotten into nutrition, I've always felt that kids should learn about vites and mins and protein while in school, so even if Mom and Dad don't know that sugar's bad for you and why, the kids can teach them. In fact, when I went to Washington, D.C., several years ago and gave testimony for the Congressional Hearings on Nutrition, I suggested that:

> There is also a lot of confusion in children's minds. They are inundated with TV ads telling them that sugar-coated cereals are good for them and they'll get all the vitamins and nutrition from these kinds of junk foods, but these ads aren't just misleading, they're downright lies.

> We need courses in *every* school in America to teach all kids about what vitamins are and why we need them and which foods build strong healthy bodies to play soccer and little league and fuel their brains so they can think more clearly—and which foods are junk and how they cause bad grades, mental disorders, weakened muscles and disease.

> Finally, people and kids are slowly beginning to be taught and are slowly learning about how to get healthier, and it is a

forward move. But there's another need we should look at, and it's *almost* as important.

The incredible ignorance that most of us have about legal matters is astounding and really feeds into the choke-hold that attorneys have on us. Most of us are going to have some kind of legal problems (and some of us in business a *lot*), and unfortunately this will happen yearly if not more often, *particularly* if one is in business.

And I for one am fed up with my own ignorance and my need to depend solely on my attorneys' knowledge and abilities. I felt the same way about doctors, so I read up on nutrition so I'd know more about *health* than they do; they certainly know much more about sickness than I do because they went years to medical school and studied sickness and how to cure it with drugs (which is what I *don't* want). They are not taught how to keep you from getting sick.

It's much simpler to learn about nutrition than it is about law because there are so many books out for laypeople explaining it in simple, uncomplicated terms. But these kinds of books (to my knowledge) don't exist for law.

So how great it would be to have simple courses starting out with seven-year-olds, explaining courtrooms and judges and the simpler aspects of legalities. And each year the course could get a *little* bit more detailed, until high school, when the kids could really get into it.

And I'll tell you something for sure—the moms and dads would love to learn from the kids what they're being taught every day in school about different kinds of legal problems and how the lawyer solves them.

Had I had this knowledge taught me as a kid, I would have saved many *hundreds* of thousands of dollars in my lifetime, and tons of aggravation of having been taken advantage of by too many attorneys.

Certainly grammar is important—knowing when to say "who" and when to say "whom" marks you as a literate person. And knowing how to spell Afghanistan and where it is on a map is important. And basic math is important. But before all that comes nutrition (if you're not healthy, what difference does it make *where* Afghanistan is?), and then law, in my opinion. Geometry, algebra, etc.—I had no need for them then or now.

But how much vitamin C is good for me is *urgent* for me to know, as is knowledge of the best sources of calcium, magnesium, and potassium.

And knowing the basic intricacies of law would make an *immense* difference in my life and would change the attitude of lawyers the same as the popular knowledge of nutrition has done for doctors.

Doctors are no longer able to arrogantly do whatever they will; now they are asked to explain and are then told the patient is going to get a second opinion. Now of course some doctors and lawyers have never been arrogant; unfortunately many of them are.

How wonderful it would be if all of us knew a *lot* about legal procedures (after ten years of courses) and those lawyers would have to get rid of *their* arrogance and their *incredible* fees.

My dream come true!

(See page 284 at the back of the book for the American Pro Se Association.)

Small Problem Solving

When I travelled to Australia the first time with my second book, *Everything You've Always Wanted To Know About EN-ERGY . . . But Were Too Weak To Ask* in 1978, I went with one under-the-seat suitcase, a tote bag, and my purse. I was there for a month, so I didn't have many clothes with me (I still travel light, everything is color-coordinated, and I *never* have to wait for the baggage, I run right out and get a cab).

The first week was Sidney, which was great, then the second week I went to Adelaide, and it was really *cold*. One night in my hotel room I was freezing, and when I called the desk for more blankets, they said that so many guests had already called that they now didn't have any left. So my brain clicked, and I filled the bathtub up with hot water and left the faucet on with a small amount of hot water dribbling into the tub all night. The steam soon warmed the whole two rooms.

"Dear Abby" last week had a letter from a reader answering a previous letter (which I hadn't seen). Evidently, the first letter had been from a left-handed person telling about putting stamps on a stack of letters from a roll of stamps, and complained that the stamps always ended up upside down on the envelope. So the second reader suggested putting the envelopes upside down (or bottoms up) before putting the stamps on, and the stamps would end up the right way on the envelopes.

The late, great Ethel Merman used to travel a lot and always drank tea every afternoon wherever she was. The teacup always had a brown tea stain on the inside, and every day she'd ruin the hotel towels by wiping out the brown stain. Then she got a great idea that ended the problem forever. She bought herself a brown teacup!

Many years ago when I wanted to look bustier, I figured out that if I put some folded tissues on the bottom and sides of my half-bra, it lifted up my bust and I looked much larger with great cleavage. I'm sure many women figured out the same thing, and just recently there's been a big advertising boom on a "wonder bra" that does exactly that. We were just way ahead of our time by figuring it out for our selves.

I used to have "dry eye," particularly in the morning but usually all day long. I went to an ophthalmologist who told me it's a pretty common problem, usually caused by stress, and all I'd have to do is use eyedrops of a saline solution very similar to my own tears and that would take care of that!

Well, I tried the drops for a day, and then I thought, "How ridiculous—let me get my *own* eyes to make tears." So I yawned and sure 'n' begorra some tears came into my eyes, not a lot, but at least some. Then I stuck my finger down my throat, and you wouldn't *believe* the amount of tears I got. So between the yawning and the gagging, the problem went away, first by my not having to use the phony tears ever again, and secondly the problem went away permanently.

I found out later that tension in your throat can be a cause of "dry eye," and when I gagged, it released the throat tension. So many doctors just go after the symptom and relieve that temporarily and leave the problem to stay with you forever.

What makes life fun is coming up with unusual answers to little problems. We all have thinking machines, and using them creatively solving these little problems is the first step to using them creatively to solve our bigger problems which, when we get to that point, we'll begin to see as challenges and not as giant problems anymore.

And that's Good in action!

When we express Good through our bodies,
they become healthier and more energetic
because Good is a healing factor.

4

Health and Energy

If I had my choice to be breathtakingly beautiful and have my face and my body drive the world wild for the rest of my life even as I got older, *or* to be incredibly healthy without any tension, anxiety, or depression, and feel full of energy every day for the rest of my life, the health would win out, hands down.

I've been through anxiety attacks and serious depressions when I didn't want to go on living (just think of rock star Kurt Cobain's unbelievably sad suicide in his early twenties to what could have been a beautiful life), and I wouldn't wish that on anyone.

Good health is the greatest blessing we can have, and if we've misused it by abusing our bodies (either consciously or unconsciously), it's now up to each one of us to become receptive so our Good can lead us to all the new health discoveries.

Basically, the answer to getting *anything* we want is to quiet our negative emotions through using our intellect, our clear-thinking ability. To act and not to react.

And this will get us great health and energy too.

When we are tense and uptight physically, it's very difficult *not* to react negatively to a situation.

Tranquilizing drugs have been very popular for many years to reduce tense and nervous reactions to just about anything that could happen to us.

The tranquilizer chemically alters a body so that it will *not* respond in a tense way. But tranquilizers have side effects, as do most drugs.

The most important thing to remember is that *no* outside stimulus has the power to disturb us. It is only our *response* to something that can disturb us. A tranquilizer doesn't change our environment. Whatever problem was there is still there.

When we feel anger or fear, it's because we're tense. When we are perfectly relaxed, we cannot feel negative emotions.

In one of my earlier books, *Isle of View (Say it out loud)*, I tell about sodium pentathol and why it works as "truth serum." Sodium pentathol is a chemical, and when it is injected into the body, it so totally relaxes every muscle in the body that it is impossible for a person to feel anxious or afraid or insecure or angry. And with those feelings absent, a person will tell the truth. The relaxation will be so total that no negative emotion will exist. When there is no fear, truth will come out.

It is impossible to feel *any* negative emotion when the body is perfectly relaxed.

The same thing happens in everyday life. If you're full of tension, you're also full of fear. So you should first make sure your body is in good shape and not deficient in any of the B vites or calcium or magnesium. And once your body cells are filled with these vites and mins, you'll notice how much less tense you are in every situation.

I always thought fear came first, that I got tense because I was afraid, but it's the opposite. First you're tense, *then* you're fearful. *Most* people think they're fearful first, but it's not so.

I also used to think that everything that was wrong with humans was mental and/or emotional, certainly not physical. I thought that violence, anger, and depression could be fixed on a therapist's couch. I was in my late teens and was constantly beset with terrible depressions and awful anxieties. They started in my earlier teens and had gotten progressively worse.

I thought I was going crazy. I thought I was emotionally unstable. I thought I was doomed to live a life filled with fear (anxiety brings you the most horrific fears you can imagine) or, with my terrible suicidal tendencies, I was doomed *not* to live at all. Once, at nineteen, while visiting my mother, I went to the medicine cabinet and took out a bottle of some of my mother's pills and was going to down them all when something stopped me—I didn't know what—but *something* (now I know it was my "inner voice") made me put the pills back in the bottle and put the bottle back in the medicine cabinet.

So at the age of nineteen I went to my first shrink. He gave me uppers to bring me out of the depressions, and then I found I couldn't fall asleep at night. So I told him the problem, and he gave me sleeping pills to help me fall asleep.

I was constantly drugged, morning and night. Then I developed worse anxiety attacks, and he gave me tranquilizers to calm me down. Now I had three separate drugs in my body—plus of course all the coffee (at least ten cups a day) and the cigarettes (a pack a day) that I was putting into my poor receptive body that trusted me to know what I was doing and to take care of it.

Looking back on my self during those years, I wonder how I survived all those toxins. And then I had a physical collapse when very young the last day of shooting *Bonanza* at Paramount Studios in Hollywood. My boyfriend/fiancé/husband was that wonderful actor George Kennedy, and I was a dance hall girl, Big Red, and Hoss (the late, beloved, dear friend Dan Blocker) got George and me finally to the preacher.

Had I not had a physical collapse on the *Bonanza* set the end of the last day of shooting after which I was rushed to Cedars-Sinai Hospital where I stayed for a week, I would have *continued* to believe that everything was mental and/ or emotional.

I (with the shrink's help) tried to find out *why* I had suicidal tendencies, *why* I was so full of anxiety, *why* I had awful anxiety attacks that scared me to dealth. I remember walking down Hollywood Boulevard one day and praying I wouldn't scream out or do something equally crazy, and rushing home and having a beer, which calmed me down.

It was in the hospital that the breakthrough came. A girlfriend, Rachel Perry (of those great Rachel Perry cosmetics), gave me one of Adelle Davis's books, *Let's Eat Right To Keep Fit*, and I, for the first time, started learning about vitamins and minerals. Nowadays there's information all around us, but then there was not nearly as much.

I had read Gaylord Hauser (he was very good) and several other nutrition people, but they seemed a little fringe-area to me. But Adelle Davis was much more down-to-earth and logical, and I liked that. Then I read her *Let's Get Well* book, which goes more into detail about nutrition. Both books are terrific. I read about the B vites and all the minerals and how deficiencies could cause chemical imbalances that could cause depressions or anxiety attacks. Wow! How come el shrinko never told me this?

When I got out and went home, I bought all the ingredients to make my first Dynamite Energy Shake. At that time I made it with brewer's yeast (which tastes awful), but when I started packaging it and selling it in health stores (listed in the back of the book), I took out the yeast and put in really nutritious ingredients that taste delicious.

I took it every day and started feeling much better and was able to cut out all table sugar, the pack of cigs a day, the ten to twelve cups of coffee a day, the booze, and all the other drugs. All the B vites in the shake gave me an "up" that made all the drugs (yes, coffee, cigs, and booze *are* hard drugs) unnecessary for my sense of well-being. No more uppers, no more downers, no more tranquilizers. I now didn't need them. My body started to get healthier and less tense and more relaxed, and all my *natural* energy started flowing through me.

To me it was a miracle. From that day of the first Dynamite

to now I haven't had one depression, not one anxiety attack, and no tension. I sleep well, and everyone knows about my energy.

So now I've completely reversed my beliefs on everything being mental and/or emotional. I now *know* that if your body is chemically imbalanced, you will *automatically* be tense, depressed, and full of anxiety. And the reverse is that if you balance out your body chemistry, you can not be (not will not be, but *can not be*) tense, depressed, or anxious.

When I hit my forties, I still felt terrific, but as I got into my forties, I started feeling a little less terrific.

I'd been reading for years that adults should not drink milk. But because I had a *passion* for milk and milk products, I thought these articles were written by nuts. Now I started re-thinking. I'd had a bad postnasal drip all my life. When I woke up in the morning, my head was so stuffed up I had to breathe through my mouth.

So I finally decided to cut out all milk. I didn't need it for the calcium, because four tablespoons of my Dynamite Shake gave me the calcium equivalent of a quart of milk, but giving up milk was tough because I not only drank three or four glasses of skim milk a day, I also ate yogurt (which I loved) every day and I loved cheese of *any* kind.

But I did it. I didn't touch a drop of milk or milk products for three weeks, and my head started to clear up, the postnasal drip started to go away.

Now all my life I'd thought I had a sinus problem, which I felt I must have inherited from my father. *All my life* I had a really stuffy head, so I was very excited about my body-discovery that was going on.

My postnasal drip cleared up about 60 percent since I gave up milk, but when I went on a lot of talk shows, which I did for two years traveling with *HOW TO SATISFY A WOMAN EVERY TIME* . . ., I started clearing my throat a lot. It drove people crazy, particularly me. So one day when I was back in New York for a few days between trips, I went to see Dr.

Wilbur Gould, the most famous throat specialist in New York (and probably the world).

Unfortunately, Dr. Gould passed away recently, and the world lost a wonderful man and a great doctor. Most opera stars and pop singers went to him, and he worked his magic. He found a slight sinus infection and cleared that up, and I cleared my throat less, but it was still a problem. He suggested I meet with a man in his office, William Reilly, a DMA, or Doctorate of Musical Arts. Bill had me speak, then sing, and he asked me if I drank water every day.

I told him that in my whole life I don't think I drank ten glasses of water total until about three years ago. I mean *literally* I never drank water. I *hated* water. In fact, I probably drank *fewer* than ten glasses during my lifetime. I found water boring. Why drink some boring liquid when you could have diet cola drinks, decaf coffee, juices, Postum, other carbonated diet sodas, etc.?

I told him I used to drink Postum a lot after I gave up coffee. I always put milk and sugar substitute in it, and I *loved* it. It really tasted good. I probably drank at least ten cups a day. Maybe more.

Then one day about three years ago I started musing about all the sugar substitute I was using, not only in the Postum, but in everything else I wanted sweet (which was everything). All of a sudden I got this inner vision of huge amounts of these chemicals (sugar substitutes *are* chemicals) going into my stomach, and something in my brain clicked. At that moment I decided to stop using any sugar subs and also to stop all other liquids I was imbibing (the stuff would have tasted awful to me without all the sweet) and to drink nothing but water.

There was no thought process. I just got the vision of all the chemicals going into my body, and the decision came.

No arguments with my self ensued, no thoughts about "Why not juices?," no thoughts whatsoever. Just a decision.

So I told Bill that from that day three years ago to this I drank nothing but water, but very little of it. After stopping all the Postum, etc., I cut down my liquid intake and probably drank maybe three or four glasses of water a day, tops. He said I should drink eight glasses a day, and I asked him why. I'd always heard you're supposed to drink eight glasses a day, but nobody ever said why. So I thought there obviously wasn't a good reason or someone would have stated it.

Bill said water's very important to the body to dilute the mucus that's there. Finally, someone gave me a reason, and what a reason. If anybody needed to dilute mucus, it was throat-clearing me. As of that day I started drinking eight glasses every day and *voilà!* Another miracle happened—most of the remaining mucus went away. I would say that from the 60 percent that it went down to from the 100 percent mucus I had when I drank milk, it now went down to 25 percent. I told Bill that he was the first person who ever explained *why* water is so important. I don't want to do *anything* unless I know why. And I hardly ever do.

And I have some more incredible things to say about water, but that's later.

Deffing

Some people thought I was doing an act when I wouldn't use graphic sexual terms on TV or radio when I was telling audiences about my *HOW TO SATISFY A WOMAN <u>EVERY TIME</u>* . . . marriage manual. I explained that it was not difficult to write "penis" in my book, but I would not say it on the air. In fact, I wouldn't say it off the air. I believe most people don't want to hear graphic terms spoken, and that's why we have euphemisms. I think most people are embarrassed by graphic terms.

Well, now in this book, I'm going to get graphic about other bodily functions, and I feel the same about this as I did about sexual terms. I think most people would be embarrassed or grossed-out to hear me talk about personal body functions. I know I am.

So right now I'm going to explain the words I will use. I find the words "bowel," "shit, " and "crap" embarrassing, and "defecation" is too long, so from now on instead I will use the word "def" for "defecation."

Matt Groening, one of the great contemporary cartoonists, who does the *Life in Hell* cartoons, did a *Teachers' Guide to Words That Make Kids Snicker*, and one of the cartoons is a buck-toothed kid sitting at a desk snarfing and giggling and snurfling as the teacher says, "It's extremely hot in the bowels of the earth."

It's only fairly recently that I became aware of how important it is to get rid of the wastes from our bodies. I always thought that only what you put *into* your body was important, but the last few years I've learned how important it is to empty our bodies *every day* of all the residue and waste left over inside us from all the food we eat several to many times a day. These residues become toxic, and the longer they stay in our bodies, the more toxic they become.

This toxic matter lies in our colons, and the older we get, starting in our thirties, the more important it is we get it out. When we're very young, in our teens or early twenties, our bodies are so resilient, almost anything goes. When I was a kid, I ate anything and everything. Unfortunately, I ate a lot of junk, later drank a lot of alcohol, used a lot of drugs from uppers and downers to grass (and of course booze is a drug too), smoked a lot of cigarettes, and overall really abused my body.

Most people's intestines are in awful shape because of years of eating chocolate-covered jelly doughnuts and candy bars and sugary carbonated drinks and coffee and fatty meats (all things I used to love and gorge on).

I've seen photos of the cross sections of people's colons that are so narrowed by sludge attached to the colon walls that it's incredible. When I realized that my colon was probably as bad if not worse than the photos I saw, I did some study and came up with a substance that would pull the sludge away from the colon walls and eliminate it from my body.

It was a special product (listed in the back of the book) I read about in a health newsletter and it consisted of psyllium seeds, which I mixed with water and drank, followed by a large spoonful of a thick liquid made from some kind of lava (bentonite, which is a kind of clay-like lava) that would act as a magnet and go through my colon and pull the hardened waste clinging to the sides and clean out all the years of debris—chocolate cream pie when I was eight, banana splits when I was fifteen, etc.

I took it four times a day, and I was stunned when I saw what came out. Up till this time I would not and could not look at waste—the thought of looking at it would make me throw up. But now I was so fascinated by my new information about the colon (about which I knew *nothing* until then) that I couldn't *not* watch to see what would come out.

It was amazing and non-gross. Black "floaters" that measured anywhere from half an inch to one inch were there every day. They looked like little pieces of rubber tire or burned-black polyurethane "popcorn" used for packing, and they floated in the water. *Every* time I deffed, some came out, and that's for over a year. I learned that they were the hardened "carbon" lining of my colon that had been packed solid and stuck to the sides of my colon for my lifetime, probably since I was a very little kid.

I'd never seen anything like this before, and they continued for over a year and then slowly finally stopped. As soon as they stopped, I knew my intestines were rid of this awful solid lining that had kept my body from absorbing many of the good things I was taking every day, like vitamins and minerals and protein, and kept my colon from functioning the way it's supposed to.

I believe everyone has this awful rubber-tire lining in his or her colon and this is the main reason for overweight.

Fat or Healthy
Healthy or Fat

You cannot be healthy and be fat. You cannot be fat and be healthy.

The colon is the part of your body that the stomach puts the partially digested food into, and it moves the waste materials down so it can be excreted. When the toxic-waste material is *not* excreted several times a day, the body is in shock. The body *wants* the waste *out*, and when it doesn't move out, the body does everything it can to get it to move out. The thinking part of the body (the brain) tells you to eat more foods to stimulate the colon to get it to get rid of the waste.

So you eat any kind of food and/or sugar, and the message goes to the colon, but the colon is clogged and nothing moves. Food is a stimulant, so you instinctively eat *more* food, but nothing can happen to move your colon more than a teeny bit 'cause the poor thing has a solid rubber-tire lining plus waste from up to eight past meals that keep much of the colon from experiencing peristalsis, the rhythmic waves of involuntary contractions that would move the waste out.

The compulsion to eat that *all* overweight people have is because of this. Once you get the toxins out of your body and stay away from any foods you may have allergies to (later in this chapter), you'll find your compulsion to eat has left, and obviously it'll be a *lot* easier to keep your weight down when you're healthier. But you *must* get rid of the toxins.

I'd like to mention glycerine bullets, aka suppositories, which I was told about by a doctor when I was in my teens. He said it was the best and safest thing to use if you had a problem deffing. He said in fact they could be used every day if necessary, so I did. They cause the lower part of the colon to go into peristalsis (which it's *supposed* to do after you eat), so it's a natural reaction. I recently asked another doctor, an internist, if he felt they were safe to use, and he also gave me an unqualified yes.

Because we eat so many of the wrong foods (wrong because we have food sensitivities or allergies that we are probably not aware of) over a period of years, that's another cause for the colon to slow down its peristaltic action, and the waste residue from the foods we eat backs up in the intestines.

Of course, this doesn't happen overnight—it takes years to happen, but it absolutely does happen.

And what does this waste do? It seeps out toxins into the body. It *poisons* the body. You won't know you're slowly being poisoned, you'll just feel tired, and depressed, and tense, and anxious.

As important as what you put into your body is what you get out of it. *The waste must come out several times a day.*

Now mind you, you're never *aware* of any of this—you don't get violently ill or break out in a rash—you just feel not-so-good to possibly awful.

Now physiologically, again, when you put new food into your stomach, it stimulates the body to go into action and eliminate the waste in the colon. But when the colon is packed with waste from up to eight past meals, it's unable to move.

But the reflex of the body doesn't know that—it just knows that if you eat, you'll move your colon. No wonder so many people keep eating and stuffing themselves and they're not really hungry. And unfortunately not too much comes out.

Some authorities believe that over 90 percent of civilization's diseases are caused by improper functioning of the colon. *All* animals, *all* babies, and *all* natives (people who live and eat "naturally") def shortly after eating *each meal*, but how many of us do this?

I used to crave sweets and overeat other foods all the time. I was literally a food addict. And now I know why. I was so clogged up and my poor body was doing everything in its power to get rid of the junk, so I kept instinctively eating more and more food and of course more and more sweets. And all it did was clog me up more.

And speaking of clogging, everyone is an individual and

has individual needs. Any kind of bran clogs me up. It may be good for many people, but it doesn't work for me. It does just the opposite to me. But fresh fruit is the greatest fiber for me and for most people. After I have my Dynamite Energy Shake for breakfast, I always have a fresh apple, and midmorning I have another piece of fruit. Between lunch and dinner I again have a piece of fresh fruit like a banana or grapes or a persimmon or another apple (I *love* apples!).

I used to suffer constantly with a never-ending desire to eat. I was always trying not to eat so I could lose weight, which made my food compulsion *unbearable*.

Finally, several years ago I received a mental message. I loved wheat items—anything made from wheat, particularly bread. I tried not to eat very much wheat because I'd always felt it would make me fat. In fact, I hardly ever ate bread. But in an Italian restaurant that I frequented they had the most incredible hot, crusty rolls, and they were irresistible to me. But to lessen the weight gain, I pulled all the soft insides out of the roll, put a little butter on the inside of the hot crust, and was in heaven.

I started to notice that when I did that, I couldn't def for a whole day the day after. I mean not at all. It didn't hit me at first, but after the third time, I noticed a pattern. So I stopped the wheat cold turkey, and that problem went away. Believe me, it's not easy giving up something you love (hot rolls), but I can't stand to feel not good, to feel not energetic, to think with a clogged brain, and to feel down or tense.

This made me even more aware of the food/body connection.

Food Sensitivities and Food Allergies

I found out (for my self) about my food sensitivities and allergies. I found I can't eat wheat or it does something to disrupt my intestines. I can't drink any milk or milk products or it makes me so mucus-y that my head is all stuffed up, and it also clogs my intestines. Then I noticed that rice clogged my intestines, so I gave that up. I was really beginning to cut down on my menu.

But amazingly to me, when I stopped eating those things that I loved and craved, I started to lose weight. Now I'm at the point that I don't *want* to lose weight anymore (see Chapter 6), so every day I take several tablespoons of olive oil or flaxseed or any other vegetable oil in the kitchen to keep my weight up.

The key word is "crave." When you crave something, that's a sign that there's a food allergy. Certainly, I was a sugar nut my whole life, and when I cut it out years ago, my craving left. The same with wheat and milk and rice. But if I take a bit of one of them (particularly milk), the craving returns.

It's very similar to alcoholism, which is a craving and an addiction. If you can stay away from booze, you're fine, but take one sip and you're a goner. It's tough for me to take a bite of a chocolate mousse cake because I'd like to eat the whole cake, not just a bite or a piece. So I keep it from my lips. Easy it's not, but it's a *lot* easier than feeling awful and draggy and tense or depressed.

Since I found out for my self what my allergies were, I went to a great New York allergist, Dr. Richard Firshein (who wrote *Reversing Asthma* about how to control this disease naturally), and I took some tests and found that those three things that I knew instinctively I was allergic to (wheat, milk, and rice) I really *was* allergic to, plus lettuce, vanilla (vanilla!?!), artichoke, coffee, sugar, and egg white.

I didn't know I had an allergy to egg whites, but I totally stopped eating them about two years ago and since then have eaten only the egg yolk. Everybody says I'm the only person in the *world* who eats scrambled egg yolks (or fried egg yolks—and I leave the whites on the plate).

The reason I do this is I got a mental flash two years ago that egg white is mucus (it looks and feels exactly like it, and I believe it *is* mucus), and it surrounds the yolk in the shell *only* to protect it and the baby chick. The baby chick embryo does not eat it, it lives on the yolk, and I believe no one should eat this mucus-protection. I also believe that those who do are putting a stress on their bodies because of the allergic reaction to what their bodies perceive as a foreign substance, mucus.

The egg *yolk* is a complete protein that the baby chick embryo lives and thrives on till it hatches, and it's loaded with incredible nutrients including arachidonic acid and an omega-6-type fatty acid, plus lecithin (which I learned about in Linda Clark's great book *Stay Young Longer*), and which is incredibly important to every cell in your body because it:

1. Acts as a brain food and helps rebuild brain cells (one study showed that the brain of an insane person had only half as much lecithin in it as a normal brain).
2. Acts as a tranquilizer and helps nervous exhaustion.
3. Softens aging skin and keeps the skin in good shape while you're reducing.
4. Helps acne, eczema, and psoriasis.
5. Increases the gamma globulin in the blood, which fights infection.
6. Produces more alertness in older people.
7. Lowers blood pressure in some people.
8. Reduces cholesterol and helps dissolve plaques already in the arteries.
9. Redistributes weight, shifting it from unwanted parts to parts where it's needed.
10. Aids glandular exhaustion and nervous and mental disorders.
11. Is a sexual aid and restores sexual powers (seminal fluid contains a large amount of lecithin).
12. Helps in the assimilation of vitamins A and E.
13. Prevents and cures fatty liver.
14. Lowers the requirement of insulin in diabetics with the additional help of vitamin E.
15. Lengthens the lives of animals and produces healthier coats and more alertness.

The word "lecithin" comes from the Greek word *lekithos*, which means egg yolk, and before we learned how to extract lecithin from soybeans, our only source was egg yolks, which were expensive (compared to soybeans).

A few years ago when Regis Philbin was doing a local Los Angeles TV show, I appeared on it to talk about egg yolks, which most doctors were warning everyone against eating. Regis and I are good friends, and he wanted me to enlighten his audience on how good eggs are, so I researched it and found that the yolk has more lecithin in it than cholesterol, and of course lecithin gets rid of cholesterol. Egg yolks are *very* healthy.

Liquid lecithin is a main ingredient in Pam, the spray we use in frying pans so nothing will stick to them, and lecithin in our bodies does more or less the same thing and is *very* important to take.

Getting back to allergies, the difficult part to perceive is that you don't break out in a rash or get sick (unless you have a *serious* life-threatening allergy) or get any *obvious* physical sign of allergy—you just don't feel as great as you should. Maybe you're not deffing several times a day (which you will when you're eating right), or you're depressed or anxious. So just know that if you want to feel terrific every day, you have to use your *intellect* to figure out why you're not.

Remember, the normal way you're *supposed* to feel is healthy. You're *supposed* to be full of energy; you're *not* supposed to have to take caffeine, or chocolate, or any of the stimulants to feel good, or alcohol to relax. Your body should feel good on its own. And if you're putting in the right foods, drinking lots of water, and moving your body either walking or doing some exercise, you *will* feel terrific.

Traveling Virus

When I was in my early thirties, I woke up one morning and couldn't get out of bed. I couldn't move. I had an excruciating pain in my back that was so painful that I could not sit up.

I started to think about what I could have done to cause this pain. Had I twisted my back? Had I lifted something heavy yesterday? What could I possibly have done to make this unbearable pain? I couldn't think of a thing.

After a few moments of wondering what I would do, I painfully rolled out of bed onto the floor with a thump. I couldn't sit or stand up, so I rolled to the kitchen and knocked my bottle of vitamin C to the floor with a yardstick leaning against the wall, and took 2,000 mg. (two pills) with no water. It took a minute to get enough saliva, but I got them down.

The pain started to slowly subside, so I took two more, and ten minutes later I was able to stand up, and a half hour later all the pain was gone. It was an amazing experience. I thought I had forgotten about it, but years later when I started to get lower back pains, which were very painful, my mind jumped back to my past experience.

I started to think a great deal about it (that's the awful thing about pain—all you can think about is your pain and how to get rid of it), and I realized that it was a virus years ago and was now a virus. That's why the vitamin C got rid of it years before.

Now it wasn't easy to think of it as a virus—all anyone reads about is arthritis. So on certain days I had the lower back pain and could hardly bend over, and then hours later or the next day the pain would leave my back, and all of a sudden I would get a sore throat or a stomach ache and my back would feel fine. That's when I realized it's a "traveling virus." It could start in my back, then go to my tummy, then to my head, then my throat, then forty-eight or sixty hours later come back to my back.

I now believe most aches that people have are caused by this traveling virus. And it takes up residence in a person's weakest parts. My stomach, my eyes, my throat, and my lower back are my four weakest parts, and they're the parts the virus goes to on a continuing basis. But instead of staying in one of them and making me really sick and unable to function, the vitamin C keeps it in check, and it keeps moving through my body.

I believe this traveling virus is responsible for the colds, headaches, sore throats, aching muscles, etc., that most everyone gets.

The virus is dormant until you get tired or overworked or get less sleep than you should or eat delicious unhealthy things that clog up your system, or get older, whereby your immune system starts to wear down.

I think lots of people have this "traveling virus" and don't realize it's not a physiological problem with their back that's bothering them, it's this ubiquitous traveling virus that temporarily inflames back joints then moves to the tummy then gives a sore throat, then back again.

You need a *lot* of vitamin C, beta-carotene, and all the other antioxidants to fight this and all other viruses, cold germs, and all the rest of the disease-causing germs floating around.

I'm taking lots of new kinds of supplements (Chapter 5), and some of them seem almost miraculous in their problem-solving abilities in my body. The ACF 223 alone (and you will read about it in the next chapter) makes me feel terrific as it's repairing my body cells and doing its antioxidant work during the day and as I sleep at night.

When you read about all these new and amazing health discoveries that I now use every day, I believe that they will do for you what they're doing for me—changing my life much for the better.

Vitamin C

One important thing I must let you know is that I took vitamin C in large amounts (15,000 mg) every day since I got into nutrition about twenty-five years ago (when hardly *anyone* believed in megavites). So it's my belief that the vitamin C strengthened my immune system and kept me from having incapacitating back problems or stomach problems or throat problems that would have put me in bed. In fact, in twenty-five years I have *never* had to go to bed because of sickness, not even one day, and I absolutely believe it's because of my taking large amounts of vitamin C every single day.

Whenever I do start to get a sore throat or the beginning of a cold or virus, I zap it immediately with 2,000 mg of vitamin C, then 1,000 mg every quarter hour, taken with sips of plain tea. I've taken 50,000 mg and sometimes more in a day with lots of liquid when I've needed it to get rid of some virus or bug in my system.

Remember, everyone's different and has a different chemical balance or imbalance and different vitamin and mineral requirements. You have to find what keeps *you* well.

The little bit of tea I drink stimulates the vitamin C synergistically (I *never* drink tea unless I start to get sick). But it's very important that with the large amounts of vitamin C you *must* drink lots and lots of liquids (water or juices, water preferably), to flush out the toxins.

How the vitamin C works is that it "eats up" the virus or germ and then the vitamin C is destroyed by the virus in the process, and that's why you need massive doses. If even just a few germs are left because you stopped too soon or didn't take enough vitamin C, they will multiply rapidly and the cold or virus will get worse again. And you do need the large amounts of liquids to be sure to clean out all the "eaten up" viruses (viri?) and germs.

I used to bruise very easily—in fact my arms and my legs had lots of little bruises all over—and that's why I started the heavy-duty vitamin C to begin with. When the collagen is weak (see Chapters 5 and 6) and you touch or bump your body, the weakened collagen just under the skin spreads apart and lets the blood come through, and that's what a bruise is. So I started with 2,000 mg, and when I got up to 15,000 mg the bruises stopped.

But remember, everyone is individual and needs different

amounts. You may need only 3,000 mg a day (the very mini-mum according to Linus Pauling), or you may need more. If you catch colds easily, you obviously need a lot of vitamin C. Experiment. As long as you drink a *lot* of liquid (particularly water), it can only do your body good.

At the back of this book I recommend a great book written by Irwin Stone, the biochemist friend of Linus Pauling who got Pauling started on vitamin C, and in Stone's book, *The Healing Factor: Vitamin C Against Disease*, he explains that vitamin C isn't a vitamin at all, and that every animal on earth except man, the monkey family, a fruit-eating bat in India, and the guinea pig manufacture ascorbic acid (what we know as vitamin C) in its liver. Through some mutation millions of years ago we lost this ability, and if we don't get some vitamin C from food or a supplement, we will die within weeks.

The USRDA (U.S. Recommended Daily Allowance) or MDR (Minimum Daily Requirement) is 60 mg a day, which is a joke, because that's the amount that will keep you from getting scurvy, the last disease of a vitamin C deficiency before you *die!*

But when you realize that animals not under stress manu-facture the human equivalent of around 3,000 mg a day in their liver, and under stress anywhere from 10,000 mg a day and up (and who of us isn't under some kind of stress?), you can see how ridiculous 60 mg a day is.

Many of the signs thought normal for old age have been proved by science to be merely disease symptoms, and if you look at pictures of children of eight or ten with scurvy, you'll see they have wrinkled skin, have lost their teeth, and look like very old midgets.

Irwin Stone recommends a child of one receive 1,000 mg (one gram) of vitamin C a day, a child of six, 6,000 mg, a child of ten, 10,000 mg, and then stay on 10,000 mg a day for the rest of your life.

I took his and Linus Pauling's advice since I read both their books, and I'm really glad I did.

Water

"Even a stopped clock is right twice a day."

That's one of my favorite quotes because we're all prone once in a while to pass someone off as not too smart, or a nut, or as just too inconsequential to affect us. But the amazing thing is that sometimes these people from whom we think we could never learn anything are those from whom we learn the most.

I am constantly searching for truth and answers, and I subscribe to many health newsletters. Some are terrific and some I've cancelled because they have nothing new in them.

There is a newsletter out called *The Last Chance Health Report*, written and published by Sam Biser. Now lots of people would say that Biser is a bit of an eccentric, a young eccentric. I have been reading his newsletter since 1976 when it was called *The Health View Newsletter*.

He's gone out of business several times and I've lost my prepaid subscriptions each time, but I still hang in there and subscribe to whatever he's doing because his newsletter is always full of offbeat info that is great. He *is* eccentric and he sometimes writes shock-type headlines just to grab your attention. But grab he does, and he goes after interviews with doctors who have alternative treatments to drugs that most regular M.D.'s would ridicule.

I've really learned a lot from his newsletters, including the psyllium and lava (bentonite) bit, and as strange as some of his stories about himself are, his interviews are *great*. He comes across as a very nice, kind man who sincerely wants to help people.

One of the most important things I've *ever* learned about health is also the simplest, and I learned it in 1994 from *The Last Chance Health Report*. Sam Biser interviewed an Iranian medical doctor, Dr. F. Batmanghelidj, who received his medical degree from St. Mary's Hospital Medical School of London University.

In 1979 after the shah was deposed, Dr. Batmanghelidj was taken to Evin prison (built for 600 people and packed with over 8,000) in Iran by the revolutionaries, and was to be executed. His "crime" was that he had been part of the establishment and he owned many assets that the revolutionaries wanted to take over. He was in court nine times in seventeen days, and he had to defend thirty-two indictments. If he had been proven guilty of any one of those, he would have been shot. But he wasn't, he was put in prison.

A few months later, in 1980, a man was carried into Dr. Batmanghelidj's cell in excruciating pain. He had a peptic ulcer, and the authorities wouldn't take him to a hospital. He needed medication for his terrible pain, and the only thing available in the cell was water, and Dr. Batmanghelidj felt water might help relieve the pain (when he was a medical student, he drank water whenever he had heartburn and it helped). He gave the man two glasses, and within eight minutes the pain was gone. The doctor kept giving him two glasses every three hours, and he kept getting better.

Another inmate with an ulcer (the stress of never knowing if the guards were going to come and take you away to be shot must have been overwhelming) was lying on the floor in great pain. He had taken an anti-ulcer drug and a bottle of antacid in a ten-hour period, and they had done no good. Dr. Batmanghelidj gave him three glasses of water within twenty minutes, and the pain went away. The most potent medicine for ulcers, cimetidine, had done nothing in ten hours, and three glasses of water stopped the pain in twenty minutes.

Dr. Batmanghelidj now started studying cases of ulcer patients, and in every case he found that chronic dehydration was the real problem. The stomach produces acid that cannot be allowed into the intestines, so the pancreas neutralizes the acid, but when there's not enough water for the pancreas to do this, a spasm blocks the acid and keeps it from going to the intestine, and that's what causes the pain.

Dr. Batmanghelidj also says unequivocally that water will

alleviate asthma symptoms, and sometimes cure it. When the body is low on water, it does everything it can to conserve it, and one of the biggest water losses comes from your lungs when you breathe out (you can see it on a cold day when you breathe out the warm air as steam). To conserve the water loss, the body constricts the lung tissue. Natural body histamines save and regulate water, block the loss of water through evaporation, and can trigger bronchial inflammation and spasms. The greatest antihistamine is water because it's anti-inflamatory.

He says the chest pain of angina is temporarily relieved by nitroglycerine, but water will *cure* it: The body histamines regulate prostaglandins and some of these are constrictive, and if these get into the circulation, they can cause vasoconstriction in the heart, which is how a sudden heart attack comes on. When you hydrate your body with water, the prostaglandins won't get to your heart.

Dr. Batmanghelidj says that high blood pressure is caused by water deficiency. When the body has to force water into tissues because they're dehydrated, it has to raise the pressure, and this is hypertension, which is *caused* by water deficiency. The *worst* thing a person can do is take a diuretic and force water *out* of the body (which is already desperately in *need* of water). Salt is not the problem. The body needs salt to keep more water in the tissues. The doctor believes diuretics are extremely dangerous.

He says thirst is *not* a good barometer of your need for water because over a period of time the body loses its alertness to dehydration. Many times a person will think he's hungry and go eat, and in reality his body is screaming out for water. There are many signs of dehydration, some of them being stomach pain, anxiety attacks, depression, high blood pressure, and tiredness.

Dehydration is one of the main producers of free radicals in the body, and water is the greatest free-radical remover. Water is a primary antioxidant, and to stay trimmer and younger-looking, you'll get rid of a lot of those free radicals by drinking a *lot* of water. (I explain free radicals in Chapter 5.)

Since I read Dr. Batmanghelidj's great book *Your Body's Many Cries for Water*, I've upped my daily water from eight glasses to from twelve to sixteen glasses a day (I drink bottled spring water and tap water—any kind of clean water is fine). I really try to get sixteen because I believe I need it. I feel better than I've ever felt, and my energy level is even higher than it used to be. And remember, I drink *nothing* but water (except the apple juice I make my Dynamite Energy Shake in). I also use a little salt on my food to make sure the water doesn't *all* come out. My body really needs it, particularly when I'm drinking a lot of water.

During the day if I feel even a little bit "off," I take another glass of water, and within minutes whatever was bothering me is gone. I visit the bathroom *often* (at least once an hour), but all that water has to come out, and as big a drag as it is to keep going there, I'd gladly go even more often if I can keep feeling this great.

In another book that I read, *Sinus Survival*, Dr. Robert S. Ivker says, "Regular water drinking might be the simplest, least expensive self-help measure for the maintenance of good health. Every bodily function occurs through the medium of water . . . many Americans are chronically dehydrated . . . In general, we need to drink more water than our thirst calls for."

Jackie Elie West has been working for me for several years, and she's terrific, high strung, a hard worker, and a *very* fast talker. She started out caring for my Aunt Millie, who lived with me until she died, and Jackie did a great job. She's very nurturing and *very* patient. Aunt Millie was basically a sweet woman, but Alzheimer's got her, and she became mean between her sweet times. Jackie never lost her temper with Aunt Millie. I could never have taken the verbal abuse, but Jackie's own understanding and empathy were so beautiful that all the nasties rolled right off her.

Jackie is from Trinidad and is a beautiful black woman, tall, well built, and physically *very* strong. But she's always been nervous and has scars on her wrist as a result of her terrible depressions. I of course started her on the Dynamite Energy Shake (the price was right), and she loved it. It calmed her down, and a lot of her tension abated.

But one day about six months ago she called me from her home at about 8:45 A.M. and said she'd be late because she felt so anxious and tense and just really awful that she was going to see her doctor, and her girlfriend was on her way over to take her because she didn't think she could make it alone.

I asked her to tell me exactly how she felt, and she said she was having an anxiety attack and thought she was going to die. Her heart was pounding and she was having trouble breathing.

I told her to put the phone down and go get a big glass, fill it up with water, and come back to the phone.

She came back, and I told her to slowly drink the water down, which she did. Then I told her to put the phone down again and get another big glass of water and come back. She did and she drank the second glass.

I had her do this three more times. When she had finished the fifth glass (this all took about ten minutes), I asked how she felt, and she said it was a "miracle" because she felt good. All the anxiety, all the heart-pounding, all the troubled breathing was over. She said she was going to call the doctor and cancel the emergency visit and would be in to work within the hour (she lives in Brooklyn).

When she came in, she told me that whenever this had happened in the past, her doctor gave her tranquilizers and she *never* felt really right. But since the water, she felt great.

Every day since then I ask her how many glasses she's had so far, and she says "three" or "seven" or whatever, depending on what time I ask her. She says she'll stay on ten to twelve glasses a day for the rest of her life.

It's so amazing to me that something as simple as water,

which is everywhere and which is *free*, is the bottom line to so many problems.

Virginia Graham (she was the star of *Girl Talk* for years on TV, and I was her guest *six* times!), an absolutely fabulous and beautiful woman and a good friend, looks at least twenty-five years younger than her age, and she drinks eight glasses of water every day. She says her doctor told her about it when she was a young adult, and she's been drinking it ever since. How lucky for her she had such a knowledgeable doctor.

Another good friend, Sheila MacRae, I met when she was appearing with her late husband, Gordon, at The Coconut Grove in Los Angeles and I was dating their agent, Marvin Moss. I remember telling Marvin that Gordon had a great voice, but Sheila had all the comedy talent—her impressions of Zsa Zsa and Carol Channing had the audience screaming.

Sheila and I have been friends since we met, and she is truly gorgeous. She looks incredibly young for her age—her skin, her hair, her eyes, are all sparkling, her posture is fabulous, and she drinks at least eight glasses of water, minimum, every day. She credits her English-born mother, who was *really* into health and nutrition, with giving her *all* her healthy habits.

I want you to experiment, to become a "water guinea pig." Even if you feel okay, take a big glass and know you're keeping your body hydrated, which will keep you younger longer and give you a lot more energy (water is a *great* energizer).

And if you have asthma or an ulcer, or heart problems, or *any* malady, try the water. If you feel fearful about something, drink a glass of water.

If you're anxious or depressed, drink five *big* glasses within ten or fifteen minutes. I *guarantee* you you'll feel better and the anxiety or depression will start to leave.

But you *must* make this a *daily* habit. You'll be *amazed* at how good it will make you feel.

And feeling good is what Good is all about.

Keep your eyes and your mind open
and trust that your Good
will lead you to everything
that will heal you . . .

5

Wonder Supplements

I *am* a health nut and I'm proud of it! But hey, isn't that a lot better than the opposite? I mean, I don't think anyone *wants* to be a sickness nut, but it sure looks suspicious when so many people do so many things that obviously don't make them healthy.

I admit I'll do almost anything to make my body better, stronger, and healthier. And I have since I was a teener, in fact even younger. I can remember when I was nine asking my mother to steam lima beans because I read they were healthy. But as a kid I was ignorant because my mother knew nothing of nutrition and there was little information and very few books about it then. But after my physical collapse on *Bonanza* I really *became* interested in health and vites. I started to then, and of course now, try anything and everything that sounds logical at least once to make my Temple of Good better. I *try* things. And if I have any kind of a negative reaction, I stop.

I remember years ago I heard about an herb tea, Red Zinger, and I tried it. It made me tense (I was probably allergic to something in it), so I never made a second cup. But I've taken dozens of other things that have made me feel terrific *naturally*—no stimulants, just good healthy products.

I liken my self to a human guinea pig. If you don't try it, you'll never know. And that's how I learned about so many incredible new chemical and natural formulations that have made me feel better than I've *ever* felt.

I have such trust that my Good will lead me to things in my life that I need when I need them, and that's exactly how it happens.

Many of these new nutrients I'd never even heard of five years ago, and some have been around a while but are just getting the word-of-mouth publicity that it takes to become popular. And all of the ones I write about I personally take every day.

At the end of the book I list the sources of all the products I write about and use.

GH3

I'll start with GH3 because it's the first health-substance, other than a vitamin, that I started taking a few years ago and have been taking ever since. Now I'd heard about GH3 maybe five years before that, but I thought it was only for very old people. I remember going to dinner with my husband at a lovely East Side restaurant and having the owner come sit with us because they were friends. He was in his sixties (at that time that was very old to me), and was telling us about this wonderful new pill called GH3 that took away his depressions and made him feel so much better.

Then I read a little about it in a magazine that stated that the formulator of GH3, Dr. Ana Aslan of Romania, a cardiologist who later became a gerontologist, was a national heroine in her country because of her work with this powerful substance.

Then in 1974 a dear friend, Herbert Bailey, who's one of the most knowledgeable and respected nutrition researchers and writers in the world (he's written eight major books in the health sciences), told me he had a meeting and interview scheduled at the New York Hilton with Dr. Aslan and would I like to accompany him? Would I?!

What a wonderful and enlightening interview it was. Dr. Aslan was a charmer and an obviously brilliant, yet down-to-earth woman with a mission. She was seventy-eight years old when I met her, and she looked many years younger, had the energy level of a much younger person, and had a cute little figure.

Even though she didn't actually discover GH3, she was the first person to discover its use as an anti-depressant and an anti-aging substance.

At first I entered into the conversation with Dr. Aslan, Herb, and Andrei Raiescu, who was chief of the Romanian Tourist Bureau. Dr. Aslan said she'd been taking GH3 for twenty-three years, and that's the reason she felt so good. I told her that Herb was going to try to start a move to get her the Nobel Prize, and she said she wasn't looking for prizes, all she wanted was for the world to have the benefits of GH3 so every body could feel good too.

Then I only listened as she and Herb discussed how and why GH3 works. I was fascinated. In all bodies, human and animal, there exists in the brain monoamine oxidase (MAO), which is an enzyme, and when a person is around the age of forty-five (sometimes as young as the mid-thirties), MAO begins to build up and increase in the brain, displacing other vital substances. One of these substances is norepinephrine (noradrenaline), a hormone essential to our vitality and sense of well-being. It was found that real aging begins around the time that the MAO starts its buildup, and at that same time age-related depression begins.

It has been well known for some time that the suppression of MAO with drugs could cure depression and lessen the symptoms of aging, but it was found that all the drugs tried were *irreversible* inhibitors of MAO, and since MAO is necessary to maintain the homeostasis of the body (it regulates blood pressure, protects the liver, etc.), anything that *permanently* destroys MAO is dangerous.

Dr. Aslan found that GH3 *temporarily* inhibits MAO, and

allows it to return when needed. GH3 also increases the level of serotonin (an important and essential brain amine), and allows it to coexist with noradrenaline in the brain.

The bottom line is that an MAO increase and a noradrenaline and serotonin decrease equals aging and depression. Premature increase and decrease equal premature aging—the person gets "old before his or her time." And aging is almost always accompanied by symptoms of depression.

I was so excited to be hearing all this from the woman who started it all that I asked her if a person under forty could take it, and she said yes, that if you start in your thirties, it will act as a preventive, so I started taking one pill a day for twenty-four days and then for twenty-four days I didn't take it, as the directions specified.

Then in the late eighties, Herb suggested I try the injections, so I did. I had learned to give my self vitamin B12 injections in the butt after a West Coast book tour trip where I couldn't find a doctor in Portland, Oregon, who gave them, so when I returned to New York, instead of going back to the doctor who had been giving me a weekly shot, I got my gynecologist to prescribe Cyanocobalamin (vitamin B12) and needles, and the cost went from twenty-five dollars a shot once a week to twelve cents a shot every other day. Anyway, I gave my self the GH3 shots in my behind three times a week for a month, then off a month, then started over.

Herb had written a book about GH3, *GH3: Will It Keep You Young Longer?* and is planning an updated version because he maintains that GH3, with certain other nutrients and antioxidants, is the only really safe and effective antidepressant and "rejuvenator" for millions who desperately need it.

Sylvester Stallone was interviewed in *Longevity Magazine* and said he injects himself with GH3 in his butt three days a week for three weeks twice a year. Sly says he uses this for anti-aging—he's looking to stay as young as he can as long as he can.

Personally, I don't like injectables. With the vitamin B12 it's a necessity because the stomach acids and enzymes destroy B12 taken by mouth so you sort of have to take B12 by needle, although fairly recently a "sniffer" and a "sublingual" B12 came on the market.

But several years ago I went back to the GH3 pills and I take one every day as soon as I wake up, except now I take it every day without a month off. Dr. Aslan said, and it's on the box, that you're supposed to take two a day, and maybe later I'll feel the need for two, but for now one really works great for me. Within ten to fifteen minutes (the time it takes to dissolve in my tummy) I feel very different. And better.

I get the GH3 pills from Europe (almost all the European countries have them, so whenever I'm there I get them, usually in Germany or Switzerland), but you can also get them in any city in Nevada, the only state in the U.S. that now sells them, so plan on going to Las Vegas or Reno and stocking up. Most people in the health field believe that in the very near future, GH3 will be sold all over the United States.

I plan on staying on GH3 for the rest of my life.

SOD—Superoxide Dismutase

I met Dr. Richard Brennan on a TV show in Seattle, and we became instant friends. He was a charmer and really knew preventive medicine. Richard was the founder of the International Academy of Preventive Medicine in Houston, which is, I believe, the largest group of medical (and other) doctors in the world who practice preventive medicine.

I was on the show with my Dynamite Energy Shake and Richard was plugging one of his books, and when he heard and saw me retort to the male host who was bugging me about people not needing vitamins or minerals beyond their food diets, he was ecstatic. The host was very unknowledgeable (ignorant?) about nutrition, and he was almost angry that I appeared to know a lot about nutrition and I wasn't shy talking about it. I said you need lots of vites and mins, and I explained why. He seemed so angry that I silently wrote off ever doing *that* show again.

It was my last city on a two-week tour, and the next Monday in New York I got a call from the producer asking me to come back that very week. She said the at-home audience responded overwhelmingly in my favor and they were all angry with Mr. Host, so she beseeched me to return, which I did.

Back to my good buddy, Richard. He was so thrilled to see I could hold my own against nutrition attackers that he asked me to be the keynote speaker at the next annual meeting of the International Academy of Preventive Medicine, which was taking place in a month in Dallas. They expected 500 doctors from around the world to attend, big names like the brilliant Hans Kugler, Ph.D.; Professor/Dr. Linus Pauling, Ph.D., whose research and books started me taking megadoses of vitamin C; Professor Roger Williams, Ph.D.; my good friend Richard Passwater, Ph.D.; Dr. Hans Selye, M.D.; Dr. Wilfrid Shute, M.D.; Dr. Fred Klenner, M.D.; and many more world-famous and highly respected medical doctors, professors, and researchers.

Of course I accepted. It was a great honor not only to attend, but to speak in front of these very astute and renowned doctors who weren't (and aren't) afraid to buck the tide and talk against the medical profession's overuse of prescription drugs, overuse of operating rooms, scare-tactics to keep people from taking larger amounts of vitamins than the ridiculously low government RDAs, etc.

But the biggest thrill awaited my arrival back in New York when I received a beautiful parchment document with my name inscribed on it making me an honorary fellow of the International Academy of Preventive Medicine.

Richard and I became closer friends in time, and I learned a lot from him. Sadly, he passed away several years ago, but he was way up in years (I never knew how many), and he certainly lived a full life dedicated to helping sick and hopeless patients.

One of the most important things I learned from him was about SOD (Superoxide Dismutase), a protein—an enzyme found in all body cells—whose function is to fight the aging effects of superoxides (the medical term for free radicals) in the body—and the body is constantly creating these awful by-products.

These free radicals are oxygen molecules that lack one molecule, making them unstable, which starts their degenerative work.

Dismutation (deactivation) is what the SOD does by transferring the free radical into stable oxygen and hydrogen peroxide. This prevents irreparable cell attack and damage, which causes rapid aging and deterioration.

I've been taking three SOD pills every morning as soon as I get up (at least an hour before food) for over ten years. They're enteric coated, which keeps them from dissolving in the stomach and allows them to enter the small intestine, which is where most things are absorbed into the bloodstream, and where the SOD begins its good and powerful work.

Zell Oxy

Every single morning just before I take my Dynamite Energy Shake, I take a small, .64 oz. glass vial of a German supplement, Zell Oxy with Royal Jelly. It's super-delicious pre-mixed with apple, lemon, and grapefruit juices and wheat-germ oil.

The Zell Oxy (oxygen) is made by a cold fermentation process using a special yeast strain, and it takes five days for the growth-culturing process, at which point the yeast production is permanently stopped, and you get the whole yeast, which has never been heated or dried. Because the whole yeast cells have been softened by enzymes and are oxygenated, they are quickly and easily digested and travel to all the cells in the body.

What it does for the body is increase energy, improve oxygen use, establish healthy intestinal flora, and support the body's immune and nervous systems.

One vial contains the nucleic acids RNA and DNA and over 100 billion whole yeast cells, and enzymes I never heard of before, plus eighteen amino acids including arginine and lysine, which the Italian National Research Centers on Aging in Ancona, Italy, state can reactivate the neuroendocrine network and stimulate the thymic hormones, which are very important in reversing the aging process.

CoQ10

CoQ10 (Coenzyme Q10) is a non-vitamin nutrient with vitamin-like qualities, and it's also known as ubiquinone because it's a naturally occurring chemical in every cell in the body.

CoQ10 is manufactured in the body and found in some foods, particularly polyunsaturated oils. It's an essential substance in cell respiration, electron transfer, and the control of oxidation reaction. It works in the transport of electrons from the inside to the outside of cell membranes, is necessary for energy production, and is an antioxidant acting as a free-radical scavenger and protecting cell membranes from their damaging actions.

CoQ10 has helped heart ailments, increased muscle strength, improved gum tissue, helped with the synthesis and secretion of insulin, and in animals restored some of the age-induced decline of the immune system.

I heard about it through my friend Herb Bailey and started taking it about four years ago. I take three small capsules of 10 mg each after every meal, so I get 90 mg a day.

Dr. Robert Willix, who has one of the best health newsletters around, *Healthy Longevity*, which I subscribe to and get every month, and who wrote *Healthy at 100* and co-authored *Natural Health Secrets From Around the World*, takes 120 mg of CoQ10 every day. He's a brilliant preventive medicine

M.D. and is on the forefront of info about all the incredible antioxidants available to us.

Ginkgo Biloba

Everyone has heard of wonder drugs that come from plants, but Ginkgo biloba is a tree, and the very powerful extract is made from its leaves.

The Ginkgo tree is the longest-surviving living species of tree on earth, growing during the dinosaur era 250 million years ago, and it survived the ice age in Asia. As far back as 4800 years ago (2800 B.C.) the Chinese treated memory loss and poor circulation with this herbal mixture.

Ginkgo biloba is made up of flavanoid glycosides (a part of the bioflavanoid family), which benefit circulation, keep the capillaries from becoming brittle, aid the healing process, and have an anti-inflammatory action.

It's also made up of ginkgolides, which work synergistically with the flavanoids to reduce inflammation, and prevent the clumping of blood cells, which can lead to clots, which could cause a stroke or heart attack.

In 1985 in Germany Drs. Weitbrecht and Jansen studied forty patients sixty to eighty years old, who all suffered from some form of dementia. All those who took the Ginkgo improved remarkably in mental capacity, mental alertness, and mood.

Then in the same year another German study was done with sixty patients, fifty-seven to seventy-seven years old, and they all showed some mental deterioration. The researchers stated that the Ginkgo biloba extract had a positive effect on the deterioration of mental performance and that this was reflected in the patients' behavior.

I've been taking it for over two years, and I can see a difference in my memory (which was awful when I was twenty and it's *still* awful, but getting better). It seems that because Ginkgo helps the circulation it can be a brain stimulant, and being an antioxidant, it neutralizes free radicals before they can do their damage.

I take nine drops of the almost tasteless liquid Ginkgo biloba in a glass of water three times a day. It's recommended to take 30 mg of Ginkgo from one to three times a day.

I don't know if the Ginkgo is responsible for making my hands and feet warmer than they've been since childhood, but when I started the Ginkgo is when I noticed the difference.

ACF 223

Another non-vitamin nutrient I take every day is ACF 223, and it was actually patented in the U.S. Patent and Trademark Office on September 22, 1987.

It's an antioxidant formula that prevents oxygen toxicity caused by free radicals, and the benefits show up *internally* as it slows the onset of atherosclerosis, stroke, and cancer, while *externally* it slows the hardening and wrinkling of the skin. The same free radicals that cause hardening of the arteries cause hardening and wrinkling of the skin.

Both the skin and arteries have a gelatine-like substance called collagen, and another supportive substance called elastin. The collagen is directly under the skin, and it's what gives your skin its plump, juicy look. It's the major protein of the white fibers of the cartilage and connective tissue, and without it you would look cadaverous, as many bulimics or anorexics do, and also as people get older, the collagen starts disappearing, and the skin has nothing to plump it up, so you have just skin pulled over (or hanging over) bone.

Elastin is an elastic-like protein of all the parts of the body that have to stretch or expand and then go back to their original shapes, such as happens with your skin and blood vessels.

Both elastin's and collagen's fibers are bound together by chemical-imide bonds, and when these oxidize they become amide bonds, which are less elastic and flexible and tougher and harder than the imide bonds.

ACF 223 is a *super* antioxidant with a combo of NDGA (Nordihydroguairetic Acid), vitamin E, BHT (Butylated Hydroxytoluene), MEA (Mercaptoethylamine), and Catalase in this patented formula. And it's important to know that these antioxidants stimulate synergistic reactions among themselves, so the combined effects are much greater than if you just used vitamins or any of the others separately.

I've been taking it twice a day for over a year now, and I plan on taking it forever (if I live that long!).

Glutathione

My friend Herb Bailey told me about Glutathione six years ago, and I've been taking it ever since. It's a natural substance found in the body, and as you get older and the body starts to shut down, you can delay signs of aging with this powerful antioxidant. It links three of the amino acids together—glutamic acid, L cysteine and glycine, and 80 percent is absorbed into the bloodstream within three hours.

Glutathione works by itself but works better when combined with the other antioxidants like vitamin C, vitamin E, selenium, beta-carotene, etc. Herb says, "It prevents glaucoma and macular degeneration in the eye (the cause of most blindness), and my own ophthalmologist noticed the favorable results obtained with a combination of vitamin E and glutathione, and in fact it stabilized my incipient glaucoma. It's also a detoxicant and a possible reverser of malignant cells to healthy cells."

There was a news release mid-1994 that said glutathione is being found by researchers to be an important ingredient in the fountain of youth. You can imagine how good I feel to have been taking it (and so many other good things) all these years.

I take it every morning with my SOD (KAL makes a combo of the two) as soon as I get up.

More Food Allergies

I had been taking a heavy-duty estrogen kind of pill for many months in late 1994 while preparing for my second in-vitro fertilization (the first was in 1991, and I lost the embryo transplants both times), and one particular month I noticed that soon after taking it I had heart palpitations, trouble breathing, and anxiety. I felt I had to continue, so I did, but I was very bothered by my pounding heart for several hours every day after I took it. One day while at the hospital talking to the doctor who was in charge of the in-vitro, I told him of my problem.

He said it sounded like I had an allergic reaction to something in the pill and he wrote out a prescription for skin patches (why didn't I tell him about it sooner?), so with the estrogen bypassing the stomach, I had no allergic reaction.

We started discussing food allergies and I told him that as a kid I could eat anything, but now I was becoming allergic to many foods, which affected my deffing (certain foods I noticed did something to my intestines and I didn't def for a whole day), and I had to severely restrict my diet.

He then told me a story about himself that was really shocking to me and made me realize for the first time how serious food allergies can be and are.

He had gone to a medical meeting one evening and they had hors d'oeuvres during a break, and he took one. He put it in his mouth and immediately sensed it was crabmeat, so he spit it out (he knew he was allergic to seafood). He didn't swallow even a tiny bit of it—he just had it in his mouth for a short moment and immediately took it out.

He stayed for the rest of the meeting, then went home and went to bed. He awakened several hours later not feeling well, so he got up to go to the bathroom. On his way back to the bedroom he passed out, and fortunately his wife heard the thud as his big body hit the floor. He's about 6'1", weighs about 200, and is under forty years old.

His wife called 911, and an ambulance came and took him to the hospital. He had little pulse, and they thought they were going to lose him. He was in the hospital over a week, and for several days it was touch-and-go if he would live. He finally recovered, but what a shocking story. Remember, he didn't swallow any of the crabmeat, it just *touched* his lips, tongue, and cheeks, and it almost killed him.

Since then I've heard of kids allergic to peanut butter and how some have died from its swelling the throat and not allowing them to breathe.

A friend went to Florida on business several months ago, and being a vegetarian, ordered some plain pasta with sauce. When it came, he ate it all and noticed nothing out of the ordinary. About an hour and a half later, while he was still in the dining room, his lips swelled so hugely that he asked the waiter what was in it and found out the pasta sauce had seafood in it, and then he called the hotel doctor, who sent him to the emergency room of the local hospital. They gave him an antibiotic immediately to reduce the enormous swelling, and then for an hour he sat as an epinephrine drip went into his body. Slowly, the lips went down, and ever since then he's carried Adarex, an antihistamine, so in an emergency (for him or anybody else) he can save a life.

A photographer friend of mine had a terrible rash all over his body and went to so many doctors to find out what the allergy was that he lost count. The rash got progressively worse, and he felt awful inside and out. This went on for two years until one astute doctor found out what it was—he was allergic to his toilet seat! His wife used it with no problem, so you can see how individual and how *strange* allergies can be.

Vitamins & Minerals

I started heavy-duty vites in the mid-sixties right after I had my physical collapse on the *Bonanza* set. I was in Cedars-Sinai for several weeks, and when I got out I not only invented my Dynamite Energy Shake, I started taking megadoses of certain vites.

I started small doses and worked up to mega and began to

feel terrific. So I kept it up; and for all these many years I've been taking 2,400 units daily of vitamin E, 15,000 mg a day minimum of vitamin C, (and as I said, if I start to sneeze or get a sore throat, I go up to 30,000 or even 50,000 mg a day, and sometimes more, *always* accompanied by a *lot* of liquid, which flushes my system of the dead germs and viruses the vitamin C has decimated), 50,000 units a day of vitamin A and beta-carotene, 7,000 units a day of vitamin D (50,000 units a week), and one to two and sometimes three servings of Dyna-mite Energy Shake a day, giving me great big amounts of all the B vites and lots of minerals too, including calcium, magnesium, potassium, and all the others needed for great health.

And all those years I was reading and listening to all the scare tactics of so many doctors warning that anything over the RDA (recommended daily allowance) was dangerous, and some even implied it could lead to death.

The ludicrous part of this is that every day people die either of prescription drug overdose, or mixing drugs with other substances, sometimes liquor, other drugs, or even certain foods. You never hear the furor over prescription drugs that you hear about vites. The profit on prescribed drugs runs into billions, and vites don't even need to be prescribed.

Instinctively, I knew I was on the right track. How could I feel so great and be wrong? So even though many doctors warned me I was overdosing, I never wavered. Even one of the heads of the AMA debated with me on a Chicago TV show about my 50,000-unit-a-day vitamin A intake, and when he said it was really dangerous, I asked him a question (and I was pretty sure he didn't know the answer). I asked him if he recommends beef liver as a healthy meat to eat and loaded with B vitamins, and if so, how much. He said yes, six or eight ounces, and I said might he recommend it every day for super-health and he said yes. Then I asked if he knew how much vitamin A was in seven ounces of liver and he said he didn't know, and he blanched when I told him 106,000 units! So how could 50,000 units a day be toxic?

Another one-hour TV show I did with a doctor was in Washington, D.C., where I debated Dr. Neil Solomon, who later told me he had thought I knew little and was a phony and he was going to unmask me on the air. He started out being very belligerent and hostile to me, but by halfway through the show (when he saw I knew what I was talking about) he changed and started to become friendly.

At the end of the show he asked me to call him Neil, and told me he wanted me on the advisory board for a TV health show he was doing in Baltimore. At that time he was head of the Board of Health of Maryland and had written several best-selling books; *The Truth About Weight Control*, his most widely read book, has been read by millions of people (he coined the phrase *The Yo-Yo Diet*.)

We since have become very good friends and have done several TV shows together, and he's gone deeper into preventive medicine and vites and mins. He's very open-minded (which he proved on the first show we did together), a truth-seeking doctor, and a wonderful person. The point I'm trying to make is my instinct told me to keep taking the megadoses, and now, many years later, we're finding out that the antioxidants are *extremely* important for fighting free radicals and keeping the heart and all the other muscles and cells in good shape. Had I listened to all the fear-mongers, I would have stopped. Thank Good I didn't.

Thank Good for some of the knowledgeable doctors who know the *real* answers:

Dr. Robert D. Willix, Jr., states ". . . no one has ever reported *any* toxic effects from taking large dosages of vitamin E."

Dr. Harold Rosenberg: ". . . there is no possibility whatever of any danger due to an excess of dolomite" . . . etc., etc., etc. . .

I subscribe to another great health newsletter (one of the best), *Health & Healing*, by Dr. Julian Whitaker, M.D., and he is constantly and amazingly telling us things like:

FDA-approved drugs kill 140,000 people a year! That's seven times more than die from heroin, crack and all other illegal drugs put together!

Each year 2,000,000 patients pick up hospital infections that they didn't have before they were admitted. Of those, about 60,000 die from the infections.

In a major study, Boston University researchers found that 36% of hospital illnesses are caused by doctors' blunders!

He also tells us:

A six-year Harvard study of 21,000 doctors showed that those who took regular Beta Carotene supplements had *half* as many strokes, heart attacks and other heart problems as those who did not!

A UCLA study of 11,348 adults showed that death rates are 45% *lower* in men with high levels of Vitamin C in their diets!

In another Harvard study, nurses who took Vitamin E had 36% less risk of heart attack than those who didn't.

Dr. Whitaker is into preventive medicine—too bad every doctor isn't, but not surprising when you stop and realize that doctors go years to medical schools and are lucky if they get a two-week course in nutrition, so you understand *why* they don't know how to prevent disease. They're trained to treat you with drugs *once you're already sick*, they're *not* trained to keep you well, to keep you from *getting* sick.

But just as I took charge of my own health many years ago and am now bursting with energy, you too can learn from health books and health newsletters.

In two of my previous books, *Everything You've Always Wanted To Know About ENERGY, But Were Too Weak To Ask* and *Isle of View (Say it out loud)*, I go into depth in layman's terms about all the vitamins and minerals, what they are and how they work, how much you should take and where you find them, so I decided not to go into detail again. All the information is in either of those two books.

The only two vitamins you should not take too much of are vitamins A and D, and certainly the amounts I take are very safe and *far* under the maximum. All the B vites and vitamin C are water soluble, and if you ever did get a surplus, it would be flushed right out of your system. And your nervous system would sure be in good shape with all those Bs!

The following is an overview of what I take.

I formulated the Dynamite Vites for my self, and I take them every morning with my Dynamite Energy Shake, but I couldn't make the tablets as potent in vitamins A and E as I wanted for my self because, for instance, if a person has a problem like high blood pressure (I don't), he or she should not take more than 400 units of vitamin E a day (which is the amount in the Dynamite Vites), and I want 2,400 units a day, so I take 2,000 units *extra* of vitamin E and 12,000 mgs *extra* vitamin C (everyone needs a different amount of vitamin C, and *my* requirements are very high).

As I said before (and this is very important), it's up to each one of us to find the right amount of vitamin C, and the barometer is stronger collagen and *no more colds*. I haven't had a bruise, or *even one cold* in over twenty-five years. I *start* to get 'em, then zap 'em with huge amounts of vitamin C and *lots* of liquid (and I've taken as much as 50,000 mgs and sometimes more in one day).

Vites & Mins	I take 4 tablespoons Dynamite Shake	I take 12 Tablets Dynamite Vites	
Vit. A & Beta-carotene	—	30,000 I.U.	
Thiamine (Vit. B-1)	25 mg	150 mg	
Riboflavin (Vit. B-2)	25 mg	150 mg	
Niacin (Vit. B-3)	125 mg	250 mg	
Niacinamide (Vit. B-3)	125 mg	250 mg	
Calcium	1,000 mg	2,000 mg	
Iron	25 mg	36 mg	
Vitamin B-6	25 mg	150 mg	
Folic Acid	400 mcg	800 mcg	
Vit. B-12	100 mcg	200 mcg	
Iodine	210 mcg	300 mcg	
Magnesium	560 mg	800 mg	
Zinc	50 mg	30 mg	
Copper	2 mg	4 mg	
Biotin	300 mcg	600 mcg	
Pantothenic Acid	100 mg	300 mg	
PABA	100 mg	300 mg	
Choline	1,000 mg	1,000 mg	
Inositol	1,000 mg	1,000 mg	
Potassium	1,000 mg	198 mg	
Papain	100 mg	200 mg	
Selenium	100 mcg	200 mcg	
Ribonucleic Acid	100 mg	200 mg	
Betaine	100 mg	200 mg	
Molybdenum	100 mcg	—	
Chromium	100 mcg	200 mcg	
Vanadium	100 mcg	—	
Manganese	3 mg	10 mg	
Vitamin C	—	3,000 mg	(I take 12,000 mg extra)
Vitamin D	—	3,000 I.U.	
Vitamin E	—	400 I.U.	(I take 2,000 units extra)
Phosphorus	—	200 mg	
Citrus Bioflavanoids	—	100 mg	
Glutamic Acid	—	200 mg	

Calcium

One of the reasons why the Dynamite Shake is so important for older people is the calcium. Younger people all need it too, but older people *urgently* need it so they won't have brittle and porous bones that break easily as they mature.

And actually the bones are the *last* parts of the body that lose calcium. When you're not getting enough calcium in your diet, which then leads to a calcium deficiency, the nervous system and the skin and other nonvital body parts are the *first* places that lose precious calcium.

So when your bones start to become brittle and porous, you must realize your body has already lost calcium, and that's why you're tense, nervous, and not sleeping well. Four (4) tablespoons of the Dynamite Energy Shake in any liquid (juice or water) gives the *calcium equivalent of a quart of milk!* If you can tolerate milk and use it, that's even more calcium.

Dolomint

I've always been a big fan and user of dolomite, a natural combination of calcium and magnesium in the best proportion of two to one. I'm repeating this because I feel it's *really* important for you to know about this healthy and natural relaxant. Whenever stress creeps up on me because of time (a deadline for something) or money (a late bill), I either suck or chew (usually chew) three or four dolomite pills, and if that's not enough, I take three or four more. In a matter of minutes I start to feel tension draining out and relaxation setting in.

I like 'em so much, in fact, that I've formulated something delicious called "Dolomints," which are dolomites with fructose and mint flavor. I am packaging them two ways: in large and small bottles, and in a roll like "Lifesavers" so you can carry them in your purse or pocket and know that you're doing something good (and healthy) for your self to relieve stress.

Raw Garlic

I eat at least two big cloves of raw garlic every day, one usually chopped up and put on a baked potato or yam with olive oil, sometimes for lunch or sometimes for dinner, and one in my carrot juice (coming soon).

I think my body so needs it and uses it so completely that nobody ever notices the "garlic fragrance" on me. But even if they did, I'd still take it. I *love* the smell.

Garlic is the best natural anti-infection, anti-bacterial, anti-fungal, and bacteriostatic food known to man.

It's non-toxic and it's effective against bronchial congestion, circulatory problems, and heart disease.

Its anti-clotting agents can prevent heart attacks and strokes.

When it enters the bloodstream, the allicin in it acts with the same pharmacological power of any and all the antibiotics, including penicillin, except there are no side effects.

If your system is toxic, raw garlic is the best detoxifier (by chelation), and eating garlic inhibits the formation of nitrites and nitrosamines in the stomach, which can cause cancer.

One of the most exciting effects of raw garlic to me is that it not only does all the cleansing work, it also is one of the best stimulants of the immune system in all of nature.

Carrot Juice

I try to make carrot juice (which is fabulous, full of beta-carotene—that's where I get my extra vitamin A—and *very* cleansing) every day, and I put the other garlic clove in the juicer. Deee-licious! (Do you think I'm doing enough to be healthy???!)

The Sweetest

I have a tremendous sweet tooth, which I don't feed anymore with junk since I've given up all sugar (except fructose in fruit), and I've discovered the all-time sweetest and healthy combo that I really love. I've always loved stewed prunes (even as a child) because they're so *sweet*, but just once try putting a box of pitted prunes and a box of yellow raisins in a big pan, cover them with water, bring to a boil, put a lid on as they simmer for about ten minutes, and then turn off the heat and let them sit with the lid on for an hour or overnight. The combination of the prunes and the yellow raisins is *incredible*. I never heard of anyone stewing raisins, but I think you'll really love it.

Silica Gel

I've had weak and splitting fingernails since I was a kid and I've tried *everything* from gelatine to calcium to silica cell salts to you-name-it, and nothing has ever worked. I discovered Silica Gel in a health store, and it's a thick liquid made up of purified water and microscopic particles of silica that are so finely dispersed that a gel is formed, making it easier to digest.

Silica gives structure to all animals and plants and is essential to the human body, is found in the blood, lungs, and intestines, and gives strength and support to all connective tissue, tendons and ligaments, skin, hair, and nails.

I take one tablespoon in the morning when I get up and one more when I go to bed. My nails aren't great yet, but they are better.

Bee Pollen

When President Reagan was in office and was giving interviews about bee pollen, I kept thinking, "Bee pollen? If he keeps raving about it, there must be *something* to it," so I found out about a place in Phoenix, Arizona, that has what people say to be the best bee pollen in the world. It's called CC Pollen Company, and the product is called High Desert Honeybee PollenS. I ordered some (they ship it frozen, and when you get it you must refrigerate or freeze it to keep it fresh).

Bees fly from one flower to another gathering the pollen for the hive, and every tiny bit of pollen has all the vites, mins, enzymes, amino acids, and carbohydrates needed to bring us great health. It's nutritionally complete and has been analyzed chemically and found to contain every nutrient we need. It's vegetarian and richer in protein than any other vegetable or animal source, containing five times more amino acids than meat, fish, eggs, milk, or cheese, plus of course it has so many other nutrients (vites, mins, enzymes, etc.) that the others don't have.

There's also a natural antibiotic that's been isolated and found to be very active in pollen, making it a germ killer in which bacteria can't exist. It destroys harmful intestinal flora and protects the body against all infections.

I take two tablespoons every morning before the Dynamite Energy Shake and have been doing so for a long time.

My Daily Do

This is what I take every day to feel terrific. It may seem like I do an awful lot (but the whole thing including *all* my exercises and meditation, plus taking the vites, takes less than an hour a day), but can anything be too much that makes me feel so great and so full of energy?

And my less than one hour a day of discipline gives me *twenty-three* hours of feeling fantastically "up," and eight of those twenty-three are spent sleeping like a baby—a *healthy* baby!

<u>On awakening</u> (before breathing and face exercises
and meditation)

one tablet   GH3

First thing on getting up and out of bed (an hour before breakfast)

three tablets $\left\{\begin{array}{l} \text{SOD, 3,000 units} \\ \text{each} \\ \text{Glutathione, 4,500} \\ \text{units each} \end{array}\right.$ $\left.\begin{array}{l} \text{Kal makes a combo} \\ \text{of both of these} \\ \text{in 1 tablet} \end{array}\right.$

two tablets vitamin C, 1,000 mg each
one tablespoon Silica Gel
nine drops Ginkgo biloba in glass of water

BREAKFAST

four tablespoons Dynamite Energy Shake in two
glasses apple juice
four tablets Dynamite Vites
two 1,000 mg tablets vitamin C
five 400 mg capsules vitamin E
two tablespoons Bee Pollen
one glass vial Zell Oxy
three 10 mg capsules CoQ10,
one ACF 223

one big red Delicious apple

MID-MORNING

two 1,000 mg tablets vitamin C

one pear or other fruit

LUNCH

my meal soup or salad or vegie burger

one or two large glasses carrot juice and garlic
four tablets Dynamite Vites
two 1,000 mg tablets vitamin C
three 10 mg capsules CoQ10,

MID-AFTERNOON

two 1,000 mg tablets vitamin C

one yellow Delicious apple

DINNER

my meal any delicious vegetarian dish

four tablets Dynamite Vites
two 1,000 mg tablets vitamin C

| three 10 mg capsules | CoQ10, |
| one | ACF 223 |

BEFORE BED

two 1,000 mg tablets	vitamin C
from two to six (or more if needed)	dolomite pills (chewed, followed by some water)
nine drops	Ginkgo biloba in glass of water
one tablespoon	Silica Gel

No Wheelchairs Here

I feel that after the years of abusing my body as a kid and a young adult, the least I can do now is give it every chance to be healthy, thriving, and bursting with energy so I can stay as energetic as I am now when that adorable Willard Scott puts me on *The Today Show* with all of his other one-hundred-year-old friends. . . . . .

Do miracles exist?
When Good leads you
to what you want,
it will <u>seem</u> like a miracle. . . . . .

6

How to Stay Young and Sexy Looking

This chapter is *not* just for women. Guys want to look great and stay young and sexy-looking too.

I don't think a person exists who, given a choice, wouldn't opt for great "juicy" skin, clear eyes, strong teeth and gums, a supple body, and lots of thick, healthy hair.

It's really not an ego thing. Our bodies *are* our temples of Good, and who doesn't want to express Good and look young and sexy while doing it right up to the end?

I know I don't want a wheelchair and a toothless smile. And I'm *positive* I don't want wrinkly skin and a bent-over body.

Many centuries ago, the average life span was mid-forties, then it expanded a bit to the mid-fifties. Now because of incredible technology and disease-controlling drugs, most of the killer diseases are in check, so we now can live to our nineties or beyond.

I had dinner a couple of years ago with George Burns (and three other people) and he was absolutely incredible, sharp as a tack and *very* funny. But had he known about these new discoveries that I'm telling you about, he would have *looked* younger and juicier. Mind you, he looks *terrific* for late nineties, but how exciting if he could be in his late nineties and look sixties.

You may think I'm pushing it, but I honestly don't think so. There are so many new products out that *work* and *do* make you feel better, think better, and look better. And I've tried them and I'm still using them.

Now each of us is an individual and has an individual body chemistry. My body is *extremely* sensitive, and if a nutrient's directions say "take two to four tablets daily," I'll take one the first day and see if it agrees with me, then maybe go to two or more or maybe stay with the one if I feel good.

You really have to monitor everything you do in life. A day (if you're under a lot of stress) can make a big difference. And certainly your body is a *lot* different now than it was at fifteen or twenty. Listen, your body could be *better* than then if you're really putting the right things in it.

And who's to say men shouldn't use moisturizers? What's wrong with keeping your skin supple? Your skin really *is* your body's largest organ. It's not feminine to take *care* of your self and your body, it's intelligent.

I try to read *everything* that will tell me ways to stay healthier, younger, and more energetic. I never fear aging. The reason I don't fear getting older is because most of the little signs of age had come to me when I was very young. At eighteen, right after I moved out and got my own apartment and just before I started college, I met a man who got me a job at a club dancing. Now I had never danced before in my life, but this man said he would teach me, and that he did.

He had an African kind of record with drums, he got me a leopard bikini, and soon I was wowing the patrons with my sexy little jungle dance. But it took hours and hours to teach me the routine, and because I wasn't a dancer and had had no training, it took unbelievable patience on his part and unbelievable work on my part.

The second day of my training, after hours of rehearsal, I got home, and when I looked in the mirror I saw my first white hair. Now mind you I was eighteen, so how awful could it be at eighteen to see a white hair? Had I been forty or fifty

I might have panicked, but at eighteen you're so young that *nothing* could make you feel old.

Soon after that I got more white hairs, so at age eighteen I started to color my hair.

Every week I went to Gene Shacove's great hair salon in Beverly Hills to have my hair done. It usually took about three hours from start to finish, what with the coloring first, then the shampoo/set, and then the long under-the-dryer bit. *And* it was expensive. I had to do it every week because my auburn hair grew so fast you could see the *horrible* white in the part.

Gene did my hair for several years, and then I couldn't afford the cost or the time spent anymore, so I watched him do it and he told me the exact color he used, and being a do-it-yourself kind of person, I figured out (with his help) how to do it right, and it was much better for me, costing a *lot* less money. It went from twenty dollars every week (back *then!*) to about two dollars. And just as important, it took a lot less time. At the salon you always had to wait because Gene was *always* behind schedule (I've never known a doctor or hairdresser who wasn't). At home I did it at night or on Sunday, so I never lost precious work time (or looking-for-work time).

I've been doing my hair myself ever since.

Henna

Several years ago I was out at CNBC-TV in New Jersey to do a wonderful TV show that Clint Holmes hosted, and Montel Williams, Keith Washington, and my self were the guests. While I was doing my makeup, the hairdresser, a guy, was fooling with my hair. I told him I used henna on the new growth but I hated it 'cause it was flame red. *All* henna was flame red. I told him someone should come out with a henna that's blonde or brown or strawberry. He amazed me when he told me there *was* a henna on the market that does those other colors. I was so thrilled to get this info, and of course I wrote it right down.

But before I tell you about that, let me tell you how I got into henna in the first place.

I already told you that I got my first white hair when I was eighteen and I started coloring my hair at that point. I really didn't think about it then, but obviously putting on peroxide (creamy or not) couldn't be too good for your hair. I dyed every week for many, many years, because I didn't want even a smidgen of white to show. I didn't realize it, but my hair never got longer than shoulder length. I really never thought about it, probably because I didn't think it important to be longer than beyond my shoulders.

Then about six years ago I noticed my hair was not as thick as it used to be, and it was breaking off *above* my shoulders. I have my last passport photo, and my hair looks awful. It's sort of stringy, and definitely not full, and about two inches above my shoulders, and I had never cut it—it just kept breaking off.

Then I watched a San Francisco show I did on tape, and my hair looked like you would imagine a "bad hair day" to look.

Something inside my brain clicked, and I "saw" the logic of the peroxide and dye hurting my hair. The chemicals go right into the shaft of the hair and change the color chemically, thereby weakening it. The thought of henna popped in, and I went out and got some. I knew that henna is a natural plant that grows outside, and the henna paste that you make with hot water actually *coats* your hair and becomes a protective barrier.

Ordinary henna will make your hair anywhere from bright flame red to bright brick red. I really wanted to stay blonde or reddish blonde, but I thought I had no choice. So I was a bright red redhead at the roots and my hair gradually was less red as it got to the end. Not too great, but better than dye and peroxide and stringy, broken-off hair.

I noticed within a few weeks that my hair wasn't falling out as much and was getting much thicker (because the henna *coats* the hair, it will appear thicker even before it grows in thicker). Slowly, it started to get longer because the ends stopped breaking off. And once all the weakened hair shafts grew out, my now strong hair is the longest it's *ever* been, even when I was a teener. It's about six inches below my shoulders, and I have to cut it often or it would be all the way down my back.

Now cut back to CNBC and the hairdresser telling me about a company, Avigal, which has lots of blonde and strawberry and brown and black shades of henna. I went right out the next day to the hair salon that he told me carries it, and the place was one and a half blocks from my house!

Strangely enough, that particular shop is owned by the people who *make* Avigal Henna. They sell it to shops around the country and also sell it to individuals who can order it for themselves (phone number in back of book). Because it's different from the red henna, I had the hairdresser do it the first time so I could see exactly how to do it (I am by nature a do-it-yourself kind of person, but I *always* either have someone show me how to do something the first time or I get my feet wet and *slowly* learn how to do something by my own experience). It was fairly easy to do this new henna, so the second time, two weeks later, I did it on a Sunday morning, and I've been doing it ever since.

It comes in twelve different shades from blonde to black. I use the "topaz" shade on my roots (it was originally put all over) once every two weeks (because my hair is not as dark as it used to be I don't have to do it every week), and my hair is now a strawberry-blonde color.

The name of the henna again is Avigal Henna. It doesn't lighten because you don't use peroxide (which damages the hair shafts), but it coats each hair shaft and makes it stronger and thicker. If you want brown (in all variations) or black, you can put it on over *any* color. It also comes in neutral that just coats the hair shafts and doesn't color them at all, so even if you do bleach, you could put this neutral henna all over it.

And if you want really strong blonde or strawberry blonde, and yours is dark, pray for white hair.

Retin-A and Fruit Acids

About three years ago Alan Burke, a dear friend of mine, came up from Florida with his wife and stayed with us in our house. He was a well-known TV/radio personality (originally from New York), and she was his sometime-producer. I knew Alan was in his sixties, but I didn't know how old Claire was. When she said sixty, I couldn't believe it. Her skin was so perfect, with no lines or wrinkles, so I complimented her, and she said it was all due to Retin-A.

Now I had heard of Retin-A, but not much. A girlfriend of mine who was a heavy smoker told me she loved it, but I hadn't seen her in a while, and her skin didn't impress me. But Claire impressed me. Her skin looked gorgeous.

So I called a dermatologist, set up an appointment, and got a prescription. At first my skin really peeled a lot every single day (I covered it with makeup), and it took many months before the peeling stopped. But my skin did look better. I was blessed with good skin, but it did start to look thicker. You can't go in the sun at all when you use it, but I don't do that anymore anyway.

Sela Ward, one of the stars of *Sisters* and in her thirties, told *Longevity* that she uses Retin-A to keep her skin "rosy." And that it does. It makes the tissue-thin top layer of skin slough off, and the "rosy" new skin is now on top.

I started with .05 strength and after about a year graduated to the stronger .1 strength. I used it for three years up until I started reading a lot about the fruit acids (alpha hydroxy acid and lactic acid) and decided to try them on my skin about a year ago. I then stopped the Retin-A and started the daily use of the fruit acids, and they really do make a difference. As good as the Retin-A was for my skin (and it absolutely made a difference), the fruit acids seem to be even better. There are lots of brands, and you should try several till you find the one that you like the best for your skin.

My favorite is La Prairie. I use all their products. But Estée Lauder has fruit acids, as does almost every other skin-care company. A girlfriend, Leslie, told me that Ponds has a great one that she uses and it's *very* inexpensive.

The reason fruit acids work is they gently peel off the top layer of skin and retexturize, oxygenize, fuel, and repair your skin. And who doesn't want that?

Frizzy Hair

My whole life I fussed with my hair. Certainly my whole adult life (from eighteen on) I spent *at least* an hour a day putting it up, waiting for it to set, and combing it out. At a very young age I bought a professional hair dryer (not a mickey mouse kind of home number). It was all chrome, very large, with a long chrome pole and four big chrome feet, and I bought it secondhand (formerly used in a beauty shop).

My hair was naturally curly, but in my case it was more naturally fuzzy than curly. So my whole daily hair routine was in straightening the fuzz and making curls. I used to put wave set on the strands, then roll them tight on rollers, then sit under this huge silver machine for thirty minutes (an hour when I washed it and it was all wet, not just damp) till it was dry and straight and curly-wavy. I did this for most of my life.

I'd ship my big dryer from coast to coast whenever I moved. I was literally a slave to my hair. I'd always have to plan an hour in my morning schedule for my hair (like getting up an hour earlier). Then hot rollers came out, and I switched to them only because I didn't have to sit still under the dryer for thirty minutes, I could walk around with them on my head as my hair baked with the wave set. When I tried it without the wave set, the fuzz stayed in and it didn't curl, and when I tried it with water, it took longer than forty-five minutes to dry. So every single day I baked my hair.

Then in the early eighties the "natural look" came out, and women had an "unset" look. I loved the all-curly look, but it didn't work for me. Every week when I washed my hair and blow-dried it in preparation for the wave-set routine, it got even fuzzier. I looked like a Ubangi. I envied all those women lucky enough to be able to just wash their hair and leave it alone.

So I continued with the wave set. But one night serendipity stepped in. In the middle of the night when I was walking to the bathroom, I must have fainted or lost consciousness somehow for just a moment, and I fell onto the back of a great big chair. Most chairs are soft and upholstered, but this one was very big and mostly wood. My head hit a big wood knob at the top, and the hit was right on my left eye.

I gained consciousness right away, and the blood was pouring down my face. I was really scared and woke my husband, who jumped up and was horrified by my bloody face. He threw on some clothes, I put on my big coat, and he took me to the Manhattan Eye, Ear, and Throat Hospital a few blocks from the house. They took me immediately, and the doctor stitched up my split upper lid and told me how lucky I was I didn't lose my eye. He put a big bandage on it and told me to keep all heat away from it.

The next day I wanted to wash all the blood out of my hair and I couldn't use the blow dryer, so I let it dry by itself, and the most amazing thing happened. Curls started forming and hanging down. I couldn't believe it! There was no fuzz, just long, curly hair. Every time I had blow-dried it, the heat had obviously taken the soft ringlets and fuzzed them all up.

But I had to wash it every day to *keep* it in ringlets. If I didn't, the day after I washed it and slept overnight in it, it got fuzzy again. So to keep *that* from happening, I gladly washed it every day. I hated doing it every day, but I was thrilled not to have to set it, and also, that it was nonfuzzy with very little work was terrific.

Then about two years ago I saw an ad in a magazine with a

"Before" and "After" shot of a dark-haired woman. In the shot on the left she had bushy, fuzzy hair, and on the right she had ringlets and curls. The product was called Frizz Ease, and I went *right* out (that very *minute!*) and bought a bottle. I washed my hair, put a rinse on (the best shampoo and cream rinse I've found so far is Pantene Progressive Treatment extra body shampoo and extra body Creme Conditioner). Then I put the Frizz Ease on, and when it dried, my hair looked GREAT!

But the *best* part is that every morning after I'm all dressed and made up, I put some warm water on my hands and then put it all over my hair and scrunch the damp hair up with my hands, and it keeps looking better every day. It's amazing stuff. I don't have to wash my hair every day anymore, I now only do it once a week, and sometimes every two weeks. What a thrill!

Hey, maybe next week or next year something even better will come along. The point is, keep your eyes and ears open to new things, and if you have *any* kind of problem, there's an answer out there waiting for you to find it.

H_2O_2

About two years ago I woke up one morning and my right earlobe hurt. It hurt a *lot*. I went to the bathroom mirror and looked, and the lobe was swollen about four times the normal size. I touched it and it *really* hurt. I looked around the bathroom for what to put on it and all I could find was hydrogen peroxide, so I got a cotton ball and sopped it with the H_2O_2 and touched the earlobe. The liquid bubbled and fizzed and foamed all over my lobe, and it felt a little better. About every ten minutes for an hour or so (until I left for work) I re-dabbed it. That night it was still swollen, although a little bit less, and I repeated my hydrogen-peroxide treatment several more times.

The next morning it was down by half and I put the H_2O_2 on again a few times and repeated it that night. The following morning my lobe was back to normal and I was so impressed by the simplicity of my treatment, which worked, that I decided that hydrogen peroxide must be *very* good for your skin for it to have healed my lobe that was swollen four times its size. Usually, the doctor gives you a prescription and you put some ointment on and it takes days to work. This simple, *cheap* (less than a dollar for a *big* bottle that lasts forever) liquid bought in any pharmacy worked in two days.

So that night after taking off my makeup and cleansing my face with a complexion brush and soap, I sopped a cotton ball with lots of H_2O_2 and gently rubbed it all over my face. I've been doing it ever since.

After it dries, I put on my fruit acids, moisturizer, and creams.

It's a great toner and I feel/intuit that it's a daily healing dose of nutritious oxygen to help keep my skin healthy!

Steam

Every morning when I get up (after the stretching, breathing, and face exercises and meditation), I go into the bathroom. I brush my teeth with peroxide and baking soda (coming later), and then I do my hot-compress bit.

It all started years ago when a facial steamer came on the market. The ads said it was great for your skin to make it sweat out the impurities and get the circulation going to your face. I of course bought one and used it for about a year. It was good, but there were two drawbacks. It took time to get the steamer steaming and to stand over it long enough to get your face nice and rosy. And the second drawback was to travel with it. It was bulky and took a lot of room in a suitcase.

I figured out that the really important part was to get all that nourishing blood to your face, so one day I got a new, thick washcloth, folded it in half, and held it under the hot water tap. I then squeezed out a lot of the extra hot water. Then, after testing it that it wasn't *too* hot (that would burn my skin), I placed the folded hot cloth over my forehead down to just over my eyes.

I counted to thirty, and with each count I wiggled my ears (I had read as a teener that you should imagine a string is attached to the top of both your ears pulling you up and that will keep your face muscles in shape, so I went a step further and figured that *wiggling* the ears would even be better to keep your face muscles in good shape, so I always looked for a time and place to secretly do this, and this was a *natural!*).

After a count of thirty ear wiggles, I immediately (you don't want to give the folded cloth a chance to cool off too much) put it over my eyes and cheeks and down over my mouth. This time I count forty-five ear wiggles (I want my cheeks to *really* get rosy!).

Then I quickly put it over my mouth, chin, and under my chin and count thirty ear wiggles. Then my neck gets thirty, and last I hold it on the top of my chest (just under my neck) for thirty.

Now I take the cooled-off folded washcloth (a thick one holds the heat much better than a thin one) and hold it again under the hot water. This time I leave in a little more of the hot water, I don't wring it as much as the first time because my face has gotten used to the hot steaminess, and as long as I don't burn my self (obviously you can't use too hot or boiling water, just hot tap water), my skin will benefit from the moist heat.

After the second round of forehead and eyes, eyes and cheeks, mouth, chin, and under the chin, neck, and last, top of the chest, I wash my face with a vegetable oil-based soap with aloe and lecithin that I get at the health store and I use a complexion brush. Many years ago when I first started acting, I met a film director, Winston Jones, with whom I worked, and he told me that the reason men usually had younger-looking skin than women of the same age was because they shaved, and shaving "thins" the skin, takes off the outer layer every day and allows the fresh new skin to come through. He told me that a complexion brush would do for a woman what shaving does for a man. So he went out and bought me one, and I've been using it ever since. It was inexpensive and it's great. I'm still using the original white plastic one he bought me over twenty-five years ago, and I bought a pink plastic one for my suitcase so I won't forget it when I travel.

After steaming and washing, I pat my face with warm water. Then I take a cotton ball, sop it with H_2O_2 (hydrogen peroxide), and gently wipe it all over my face and neck and upper chest. Then I put on the fruit acids all over my face (except my eye area), neck, and upper chest, followed by Skin Caviar, Creamy Skin Conditioner, Eye Caviar, Eye Cream, Day Cream and Neck Cream, all by La Prairie. They're very expensive, but I figure two things: First, I spend very little money on clothes—I buy almost everything from catalogs (what a break not to have to "shop") where nothing is terribly expensive, and second, my skin is very precious to me and I want to nourish it from *both* the inside with the very best and most potent foods and vites I can find, and the outside with the very best and most potent creams I can find.

A few years ago when I hit my forties, after having had two miscarriages and losing a baby (about which I've never been able to speak) and very much wanting a child, I heard about a doctor in the Caribbean—Nassau, to be precise—who specialized in live-cell therapy (including ovarian cells) from Switzerland. I'd read about it in *Cosmo* and I was intrigued (it all started at La Prairie in Switzerland). I called the doctor, Dr. Ivan Popov (originally from Hungary), and told him what I wanted, and he said the ovarian-cell therapy would probably help me to become pregnant. I left for a week in Nassau, had the cells, and Dr. Popov assured me it would help.

I had dozens of tests done in New York, but nothing happened. So I went down another year and tried again and still nothing happened.

Dr. Popov, a brilliant and wonderful man, died, and another brilliant and wonderful doctor took his place, Dr. Ted

Allen. He was born in Nassau of black parents, educated in Switzerland and Germany, and is married to a German woman. One of his brothers is a Harvard-trained psychiatrist, another is pastor of a church in Nassau, another brother is a college professor of economics, and another is a multimillion-aire self-made electronics expert. Dr. Allen's son is in medical school and his daughter is studying law, and another daughter is in art school, all in Munich. Talk about a family of achievers!

I tried several more times with the cells with Dr. Allen, but nothing happened. Nobody knows why.

In the meantime while browsing in Saks Fifth Avenue, I noticed La Prairie face creams, and I bought a jar of the Day Cream and one of the Night Cream. I'm not exaggerating, the *very first day* I used them I saw a *major* difference in my skin. I was so amazed that I went back and got the whole line and have been using it ever since, except now Bloomies, close to my house, also carries them, and Francis at La Prairie keeps me abreast of anything new.

There are other great skin products, Lancaster, Estée Lauder, Ultima, and probably many more, and they're all expensive. Again, I feel my skin is worth it, that the skin I wear is more important to me than the clothes I wear.

Now, after my face is all creamed, I take a warm-to-hot bath—warm in the summer, hot in the winter. About fifteen years ago while I was taking a bath one morning, an intuition hit me— if I believe so much in getting the blood to my face via hot compresses, what about other parts of my body that *never* get outside heat? When I take a bath, my feet and legs and rear end get lots of heat, and when I lie down after soaping, my back and arms get lots of heat, but my breasts and tummy *never* get heat. When I thought of this, I touched both breasts with my warm hands, and my breasts were *cold*, very cold. And so was my tummy. Bathtubs are not deep enough to let the water cover your entire body, so these two body parts (three?) never get outside heat. Right then and there I turned over and soaked my upside-down body. It felt terrific, and after several minutes I turned back over, and my breasts and tummy were all pink and very warm.

I've been doing this for over fifteen years, and every time I do it, I imagine all my nutrient-loaded blood rushing to my breasts, nourishing all the cells inside and keeping them really healthy.

I love doing simple things for my self that I *know* have to be good for me. It makes me feel that I really like my body and am doing everything in my power to keep it healthy and feeling good.

Now, after soaking both my front and my back in the tub, I start letting the water out and I stand up and put on the shower and let the warm-to-cool water rinse off all the soapy residue clinging to my warm and clean body. I must admit I didn't figure this one out my self and I can't understand how I went my whole life *without* figuring it out, but I did.

Barry Farber, who is a dear friend ever since my very first book came out (my vegetarian cookbook), had a New York radio show on WOR-AM (he's now on the Major Talk Radio Network all over the United States) and I did his show so many times that it really helped to make my vegie cookbook successful.

Barry and I were talking one day a few years ago about baths and showers, and he said that he loves a bath but always follows it with a shower. As soon as he said it, my mind clicked. How brilliant to wash off all that soapy water, which is drying to the skin. How ignorant I was to take baths all my life (I never was a shower person—as a kid I started with baths and stayed with 'em) and leave all that soapy residue on my skin. I knew that soap was drying to the skin—how come I never thought of washing it off with plain clear water? Well, I didn't, and thank Goodness Barry brought it up, because since that day I've become a bath/shower person, and again, I feel I'm doing good for my skin.

You just never know where brilliant ideas are going to come from, and if you keep receptive, you'll learn so many new things every day. It's one of the many things that makes life exciting . . . and Good.

Zsa Zsa

I met Zsa Zsa Gabor on a plane from Miami to Los Angeles in 1993. We had both just done the Cristina TV Show in Miami, each of us having taped a different day's show. Zsa Zsa had done the show on Wednesday and mine was on Thursday. She sat in the bulkhead seat in front of me, right next to her very handsome husband, Prince Frederick Von Anhalt. The seat next to me was vacant, and after takeoff she came back and sat next to me to get her dog from under the back of her husband's seat.

She is gorgeous! She *literally* looks in her thirties (I'm not exaggerating). I couldn't believe how young she looked—I know she must be at least in her early sixties—and I commented on how young she looks. She said she had made a choice of having a beautiful face or a slim body, and her face won out, so she started gaining weight till her face got as pretty and young-looking as it was when she was very young and as it is now. She said she has a large tush, but she doesn't care because her face looks so good. She does a very good job of concealing her voluptuous, zoftig body with loose-fitting clothes and scarves, and gorgeous she is!

Her sister Eva did *not* gain weight and opted to have her face done as so many women over fifty do, and as beautiful as Eva is and always has been, extra weight will make her look even more beautiful.

Face-lifts just keep pulling the skin tighter and tighter over your bone structure and can actually make you look older if you don't have a cushion of fat under the tighter skin.

Several years ago Peggy Lee was in New York appearing in a nightclub act. In every head shot she looked incredibly young and beautiful, and *she* must be in her seventies. Then I saw a full-length photo, and she was very heavy and wearing a muumuu.

Many years ago when I was writing my second book, *Everything You've Always Wanted To Know About ENERGY . . . But Were Too Weak To Ask* I was interviewing Hildegarde. Now I interviewed many fabulous celebrities for the book, from Bess Myerson (one of my favorite people) to Frank Gifford, but Hildegarde was extra-special to me. She had been a big star way before my time, but remained a singing performer well into the seventies. I saw her perform at the Persian Room at the Plaza Hotel in the early seventies, and I loved her. At that time she was in her late sixties, but surely didn't look it. She truly looked thirty-fivish.

Hildy (as lots of people called her) was the epitome of sophistication with her svelte figure and black strapless gown and her elbow-length white gloves. Her signature song was *"Darling, Je Vous Aime Beaucoup,"* which she co-wrote with her partner, manager, and lover, Anna Sosenko. They worked, traveled, and lived together for many years, and everyone in show biz knew they were gay, but everyone else thought Hildy was straight. Even though she never had a heterosexual relationship that the public knew about, she was so feminine and lovely that she looked all woman.

I asked a darling friend of mine, Gary Stevens (who knows *everyone*), to set up an interview once I started my book. I met Hildy at the Barclay (now the Intercontinental) Hotel on East Forty-eighth Street in New York. She was even lovelier up close, and I asked her lots of questions, even very personal ones, and she answered them all. But the part I remember the most was when we were discussing age and she said her doctor had told her that all people over forty should be ten pounds heavier than their normal weight because they look better. And she told me she took his advice and was about ten pounds heavier than maybe she should be.

Looking at her, I thought, "She looks terrific! And she must be seventy-something." It's one thing to look good on a nightclub floor with all the flattering lights on you, but she looked great up close.

Because I was so much younger than she, I didn't put any real stock in what her doctor had said, at least consciously. It was only later, years later, that I remembered what she and he had said.

And because I have an extremely analytical kind of mind, I figured out why he had said that (to be discussed later). I don't know if her doctor had figured it out or only noticed that older people with weight looked better than those who were thin.

Now let's fast-forward to about three years ago when I saw my self on one of the many TV shows I was doing with one of my books. I saw a tape of a live show I had done in San Diego, and I thought I looked awful. I looked too thin and gaunt-looking even though I had weighed 139 for years. I'm 5'8" and 139 had been my normal weight for all the years since I stopped smoking. When I smoked I weighed five pounds less, and it was very difficult for me to curb my ravenous appetite once I quit smoking. Smoking definitely anesthetizes the salivary glands, tongue, and stomach, because I was rarely hungry when I smoked (for about fifteen years), and I never had to worry about my weight.

But when I stopped, my appetite was humongous and it never left. So I was constantly thinking of food and how I was *not* going to eat it. When I finally invented my Dynamite Shake, that really helped calm my appetite, make me healthier, and keep my food, cigarette, and drug addictions at bay.

Anyway, back to seeing my thin self on TV. I thought I looked thin and awful, and it was the first time I ever saw my self that I thought that. So now I tried to gain a little weight. It was really bizarre because all my life I tried *not* to gain weight, so it reversed everything in my thinking about weight and fat for me to *try* to gain.

At first I gained about five pounds and I looked better, so I went up to ten pounds heavier and I looked even better. My tummy got bigger, as did my behind, but I didn't care. I looked fuller and better in my face, so I went up another five pounds, making it a fifteen-pound gain.

By then I also got a double chin, which *didn't* look good, so I contacted a plastic surgeon and had my double chin removed. Now I looked much better. My dress size went from a ten to a twelve, which wasn't thrilling, but it wasn't awful either.

My tummy was pretty much pottsy (and I will never wear a girdle—the thought of wearing a tight elastic "thing" is awful), so I went to another plastic surgeon and had some of the extra fat sucked off.

Both these procedures were very simple, done in-office, inexpensive, and painless.

My breasts had gotten huge, which didn't displease me *too* much! However, I was shocked when I went to do a health poster in 1993 for my Dynamite Energy Shake. In 1981 I had done a poster in a bikini made out of vitamin E capsules, and my necklace and ring were *also* vitamin E capsules, and it was a *tremendous* success. The caption read, *D'ya think I'm healthy?*, a take-off on Rod Stewart's album *D'ya think I'm sexy?*, and everyone *loved* it. At the bottom left was a credit reading "Jewelry and bikini by D. Alpha Tocopheral," which is the scientific name for vitamin E (and everyone wanted to know who was that new Turkish designer?). Almost every health store put me in the window, I had great newspaper coverage using the poster in photos, everybody was talking about it, and I decided to do it again twelve years later in 1993.

I made another bikini, this time out of vitamin A and beta-carotene. Well, when I put it on, I looked gross—my breasts were so huge that it was ludicrous. When I got the photos back, tears were rolling down my cheeks I was laughing so hard. All those years of envying women with huge boobs and now I had 'em and they looked awful hanging out of my bikini.

So an idea struck me to use a tee-shirt instead of a bikini, and we again took a bunch of pictures. This time they turned out great. On the front of the tee it says, I'M DYNAMITE * and at the bottom of the poster it says, * AND SO'S MY

SHAKE, and there's a kinda cute tattoo of a tiny can of Dynamite Energy Shake on my upper thigh.

So for all of you pushing fifty, or looking back on it (it's only a matter of time till all of us get either fore or aft!), listen up. Because around fifty-ish (it *can* be as young as forty-ish) the collagen under your skin that plumps your skin out and keeps it "juicy" looking slowly starts to disintegrate and leave, and your skin starts sagging because the collagen-cushion is gone, so you need fat to take its place (I go into this later in this chapter).

So put on weight, and save your pennies to have your double chin taken off (and you *will* get a double chin, I don't care *who* you are!) and to do a little liposuction on your tummy. You can also suck the fat off your butt and/or thighs. My butt and thighs are about two inches bigger than they were at 139 pounds, but it doesn't really bother me. I'm firm because I exercise, and even my fat little (?) behind is firm because of my walking uphill (coming later).

Take Oprah, who's been going up and down with her weight for years. She practically starved her self and got thin and looked great in jeans, but it wasn't natural for her to be that slim. Now of course she's running and exercising like mad and looks healthy and gorgeous.

And Helen Gurley Brown, who's a beautiful woman, would be even *more* beautiful and *more* sexy-looking if she gained some weight. She says she misses men ogling her, but men *never* (or hardly ever) ogle skinny women over thirty, but they *do* ogle voluptuous sexy-looking women of all ages. She thinks it's because she's over fifty, but if she'd gain a few pounds, she'd look even *more* stunning. Again, the double chin may have to be taken off and the tummy may need to be reduced, but with *her* exercise regimen, (she's *so* disciplined), she'd become even sexier-looking. Helen says in her terrific book *The Late Show* that the reason she's so thin is because she doesn't want a fat behind, or a fat *anything*.

But with today's technology, you don't have to have a fat

anything, you can have just about any look you want. And it doesn't cost a fortune. Instead of taking a vacation or buying lots of clothes, start gaining weight and saving for a good plastic surgeon, and every day will be like a vacation once you look younger and more luscious again.

Smoking *and Your Skin*

I was watching A&E's *Biography* on Brigitte Bardot and saw her life progress from adorable teenager to giant movie star. When she did *And God Created Woman* for Roger Vadim, she was very young and very gorgeous, and each of her succeeding films showed how beautiful she was.

At the age of thirty-nine she saw her self on film and made a decision that because she had aged so badly, she would never star in another film.

She was a chain-smoker from the beginning, and when you see photos of her in her forties and fifties, you see the awful deterioration of her skin. From gorgeous and juicy she goes to masses of wrinkles and deep lines all over her face caused by heavy smoking. It's pathetic because it's self-caused.

Now everybody knows that smoking is very harmful to your lungs and heart, but not everybody knows that it's even *worse* for your skin. Smoking and sun are two great skin agers, and now that people are so aware of sun damage, look how few people bake in their bikinis like they used to.

I mentioned earlier that my mother was a heavy smoker all her life and that I too had smoked from age eighteen to my mid-thirties.

When I was thirty-four, I heard my "inner voice" tell me to stop smoking—it said to me that when I got older, my skin would look awful, and that mental image was enough to scare me off cigarettes. My mother had wrinkled skin when she hit her forties, and she got more wrinkled every year, and all I needed whenever I thought of having a cigarette was the vision of her skin for me never to smoke again.

If people really knew that cigarettes are much *worse* for their skin than the sun, I truly believe they would give them up. I realize that the fear of heart and lung damage doesn't usually stop most people from smoking, but those organs are *inside* the body, and because they can't be seen, it's too easy to think "it'll never happen to me."

But if people truly realized the inevitability of the beginning of deep wrinkles and heavy lines all over their faces while they're still relatively young (forties and fifties), because of smoking, how *could* they continue puffing (unless their emotionalism was overwhelming them)?

Emotionalism is subjectivity. People smoke because they can't "see" how bad it is—to do that is to be objective about your self, to stand outside your self and "see" what you're doing, and to be unemotional. When you're subjective, you're all "inside your self," and emotional.

But if you're a smoker, and if your intellect *does* finally take over, there's a pretty good chance that imagining looking as grotesque as the older Bette Davis (who was *never* shown except puffing a weed), will do the trick. If you saw her on TV in the 1970s (when she was in her sixties) and of course when she got into her seventies you know how *horrible*—as in horror—she looked, and the fear of your skin and face looking as grotesque as hers, or John Carradine or William Holden (both heavy smokers who aged way beyond their years and looked awful) will get you to stop. Wouldn't it be great to hit your sixties or seventies (or eighties or nineties!) and still have younger-looking skin?

If your self-image is important to you, if you really want to stay younger-looking, then start the above kind of imagining (imaging in) to stop smoking (or to stop *any* bad habit). Émile Coué, the French psychologist and philosopher who lived from 1857 to 1926 said:

When the will and the imagination are antagonistic, it is always the imagination which wins, without exception.

Juiciness

Years ago my adorable friend Earl Wilson, the late syndicated columnist, told me he thought I was "juicy," and we had a big talk on juiciness. He said juicy was huggability (you felt you wanted to squeeze the person), a ripe look (a ripe juicy tomato as opposed to a hard green one), and roundness. I said it was a plumpness (not skin over bones but lots of flesh) and particularly a moistness that comes from flesh. You can't be juicy and not fleshy (a plum, not a prune).

Earl said he wanted to do a column on it and asked me to name some juicy people of the early eighties. I came up with Pia Zadora, Harry Belafonte, Raquel Welch, Zsa Zsa, Bette Midler, Ryan O'Neal, Lena Horne, Arnold Schwarzenegger, Dolly Parton, to name a few. You can see this has nothing to do with age—few of these people were kids when Earl did his column, and *none* of them were thin.

It's pretty difficult (if not impossible) to be juicy and thin.

Again, the reason why a person (man or woman) needs to gain weight nearing fifty is that the collagen starts slowly disappearing from beneath our skin, and it can start as early as our forties or into our fifties, and gets worse as we get older. Collagen is the gelatine-like substance right under our skin (composed of calcium, vitamin C, and protein, so be sure you get lots of all three every day) that keeps our skin firm. When it starts to leave, we need fat to take its place. With fat under our skin, it looks exactly the same as when the collagen was there. And the collagen is not just in our face, it's all over our body, so we need body fat on our legs and arms and all over (to keep from getting "bird legs," etc.). To keep from getting flabby, we must exercise, not a lot, just enough to keep our muscles toned (coming later this chapter).

I remember many years ago someone did an interview on the Queen Mother (she was probably in her fifties), Queen Elizabeth's mum, and she said she's glad she has wrinkles and lines on her face because they show all the worries and problems she's lived through and she's proud of each line and each wrinkle. And I thought to my self how *awful!* How much prouder she could have been if she'd had all those worries and problems and *not* have wrinkled her brow or scrunched up her face while worrying about those problems. Why not work on staying calm, cool, collected, and detached, making contact with Good inside your body and all around you, figuring out how to solve your problems, and not getting worry lines?

Winston Jones (aka "Jonesie"), the same film director who gave me my first complexion brush, also taught me not to wrinkle my brow. I was twenty, and he was working with me on a part for a film and I kept wrinkling my brow as we rehearsed, and he said, "Do you have any idea what those lines on your forehead will look like in a close-up ? Your face will be twenty feet high, so your forehead will be probably over six feet high, and those lines will jump out at you." So he got me so aware of what I was doing (most people don't have a clue they're wrinkling their brow, and of course I didn't either), and I started concentrating on keeping my brow still no matter what I said, either in the script we were working on or in real life. It took me a while, but I did it.

Another time when I was living in Brazil and Argentina for a couple of years making several films, I was deplaning in Buenos Aires after a trip from Rio, and a photographer took a shot of me walking from the plane. I was unaware he was there—my mind was a million miles away thinking of something else. Well, a couple of days later the producer showed me the picture, and I looked so glum and down and unhappy, and *awful*, that from that day to this I try to have a pleasant "up" expression on my face. Not a smile (you sure can't smile all the time) but a pleasant, happy look, like I'm not *un*-happy.

So many people are unhappy, and I'd like everybody to know I'm not.

Baking Soda & Peroxide

A few years ago, probably about ten, I read an article about a dentist who discovered how hydrogen peroxide (H_2O_2) mixed with baking soda was the very best toothpaste and treatment for not only your teeth but also your gums.

It said that the soda is an antacid, and that, with the H_2O_2's extra oxygen, kills bacteria under the gums and all around the teeth, keeping them both healthy.

In the article it explained that you poured a little baking soda, about a level teaspoon, into a small bowl or saucer, then poured just enough peroxide to make a paste, and you used this to brush your teeth and gums.

Well, I'm a simplifier, so I figured out why do all that to make a paste when I can dip my toothbrush into the bottle of peroxide and then dip the wet brush into my little plastic container of baking soda and then brush my teeth. And I've been doing exactly that ever since I read the article. When I'm finished, I put a little peroxide and a little water in my mouth and squish it around to get even more oxygen to my teeth and gums.

Before I started this, I had some gum problems, but every time I've been to the periodontist and/or dental hygienist since then, I've been told that my gums and teeth are in good shape, and when I told them what I've been doing with the H_2O_2 and soda, they were surprised, and not wanting to be responsible for my teeth falling out, said to continue whatever I'm doing.

Because I always like to give credit to whoever has a great idea, I searched and searched for that article and couldn't find it. I was quite certain it was the *Reader's Digest*, so I called and they said no, it wasn't in their magazine. They sent me an article about another dentist, but it wasn't the same. So whoever this brilliant innovative dentist is (and I think he's in the D.C. area), I apologize for forgetting your name and losing the article, and I thank you from the bottom of my heart and my pink and healthy gums.

Also about five years ago my periodontist told me to buy at the pharmacy a Perio-Aid 2, a plastic stick with a hole at each end in which to stick a small piece of toothpick. Then he told me to rub it between my teeth every day to get rid of plaque. So every morning and every night I do my baking soda, peroxide, and toothpick bit. It's worth the extra work every day to feel I'm doing everything I can to keep the teeth I was born with.

Exercise

I exercise every single day without exception. And that's why my extra twenty-five pounds don't make me look blubbery. When you keep your muscles toned, they act as a girdle on your tummy and upper arms and butt and thighs and legs.

I was in Australia in 1993 touring with my *HOW TO SATISFY A WOMAN EVERY TIME* book, and every Hilton hotel I was booked in (I went to six cities) had a health club for the guests. Now up until this trip I jogged every morning up Park Avenue to Sixty-eighth Street, across to Third Avenue and back to the house, about a mile. But when it rained or snowed (not too often), I didn't go.

Now the Australian health clubs all had treadmills (which I'd never tried before) and they were great. So every morning at 6:00 I'd go and do butterflies and lift weights and run like mad on the treadmill. I got back to New York on a Saturday late afternoon, and the next day, Sunday, I went down to Paragon on Broadway and Eighteenth Street and looked at treadmills. They had lots of them, but one caught my eye with a big *SALE* sign on it. It was a floor model and huge and the price was cut in half, which was exciting enough, but the salesclerk said it was *again* cut in half, making it 25 percent of the original price because they were having a special sale just that Sunday for floor models. Well, I grabbed it and it was delivered the next day.

From that day to this I haven't missed one day of using the treadmill. It's fabulous. But even *more* fabulous, about six months ago I read a magazine interview with Tina Turner and in it she said her trainer told her to use her treadmill uphill only. The click went on in my head and I thought, "You dummy, why didn't *you* think of that." Tina explained that it uses all the leg muscles better and it's sort of like a stair-climber. Boy, was she right. As of that day I do ten to fifteen minutes and go sometimes as high as 8 percent slant. Usually, I do ten minutes of 6 percent slant, and I can really feel the backs of my legs stretching. It's made a big difference. Doing the treadmill flat is good aerobically and makes me breathe hard and deep, but the hill climb really uses all my leg muscles. I can even feel the pull on my tush muscles, and my butt has definitely gotten much firmer and looks better than it did when I was eighteen because I'm using all the muscles there I never used before. The treadmill is really great.

Then about ten months ago I went to Detroit for some TV and radio shows and the hotel had a health club and some terrific machines (but no treadmill!). So I used all their arm and leg and tummy machines that weekend, and that Monday back I went to Paragon and got two fairly inexpensive machines, one with the butterfly bars, two kinds of push bars and one pull bar. The other is a bench with leg curls and a twenty-pound push-up bar. Now I do those every day. And just a month ago while watching part of the Westminster Kennel Club dog show on TV, I saw a commercial for a bicycle/rowing kind of machine (Health Rider), fairly inexpensive, so I got that. The treadmill and bike/rowing are in the bedroom, and the other two are in the basement.

Rebounder (Trampoline)

All exercise opposes gravity, and by doing that, strengthens whatever part of your body you're exercising. Push-ups, sit-ups, butterflies, weightlifting, *all* use the opposing force of gravity on a specific part of your body. And the aerobics, walking, running, jogging, depend on gravity to be effective.

The trampoline, or rebounder, opposes gravity with the *added* force of acceleration (when you jump up) and deceleration (when you bounce down and sink below where you started on the springy surface), and by using this, you strengthen *every* cell in your body (instead of only specific cells) every time you bounce, and all your internal organs are made up of all these cells, so you're building stronger vital organs and stronger muscle cells.

We have three times more lymph fluid than blood in our bodies, and lymph is water containing nutrients going *to* all the cells, and waste by-products, toxins, and extra-cellular poisons coming *from* all the cells on the way to be excreted. The lymph fluid is constantly moving around all the cells, and when the wastes are excreted and the fresh lymph is filled with oxygen, electrolytes, amino acids, fatty acids, carbohydrates, and hormones, every cell in our bodies is healthier.

Now the blood has the heart to pump it and circulate it throughout our bodies, but the lymph system works on a pressure hydraulic system, the pressure built up below the valve causes it to open, and the pressure above the valve keeps it closed. *The only thing that moves the lymph fluid is body movement.* Every time you bounce on the rebounder, the lymph valves are forced to open and close, and the lymph fluid does its job.

All the toxins and waste materials are sucked into the lymph tubes to be filtered by the spleen and the lymph nodes, and the *best* way (better than walking, running, or exercise) to stimulate the lymph system to circulate, clearing out cell garbage and sending in cell nutrients, is the rebounder. So every time you bounce, your lymph fluid is moving through your body, collecting garbage and bringing oxygen, etc.

Other forms of exercise strengthen the parts of your body that you move by opposing gravity, but when you use the rebounder, the added force of acceleration and deceleration strengthens every cell in your body by increasing the G (gravity) force in every cell, and that increases the strength and health of every muscle and every internal organ.

The body's strength results from the combined strength of

trillions of cells, and that depends on how well your circulatory system works. Rebounding gets your lymph *and* blood circulation moving, so how can your body *not* get stronger with very little effort?

If you start out slowly and gradually jump higher and stay on it longer, your body is going to amaze you with its improvements.

Cells become stronger to the point of rupture (it's called controlled stress), and that's why exercise should always be started slowly. You don't run a twenty-mile marathon without slowly building up to it, and at the end of a year's training you're ready for the big-time. As long as you push your body enough to slowly increase your exertion, the cells will continue building stronger cell-wall membranes to keep up with the ever-greater stimulation. So the more you bounce, the stronger your cells are getting.

And every time you bounce, your synovial fluid, which is part of the cartilage covering all your joints, is also moving through your body. Cartilage receives no blood supply, and the synovial fluid carries the waste out and puts the nutrients in whenever your body moves. Just like the lymph, the synovial depends *totally* on body movements to function. So the rebounder is perfect for circulating *both* body fluid systems.

I learned about the rebounder many years ago through two books, *The Miracles of Rebound Exercise* by Albert E. Carter (the "king" of rebounding!), and *Hidden Secrets of Super Perfect Health at Any Age* by William Fischer. As soon as I found out how fantastic rebounding is for every cell in my body and how it's the very best way of getting my lymph fluid moving to get rid of all the cell garbage and put in all the cell nutrients, I sent away for my first (and only) rebounder. I've had it for over ten years, and I use it every day at *least* ten minutes in the morning, and five minutes at night (and many times ten at night too), and it's great.

Whenever I travel, I can't take my rebounder with me, so

I use the hotel bed for my bouncing. I don't hurt the bed because I don't jump hard, I just bounce a little for five or ten minutes. Of course, the rebounder is better, but hey, sometimes you gotta improvise. . . .

And the best part about rebounding is that even elderly people can benefit enormously by using it very gently, even just by sitting in a chair and putting their feet on it and having someone else rebound. What it does is strengthen the legs so that fragile older people can eventually stand on it and gently use it to strengthen *all* their body organs.

Surprisingly, the shape of the eyeball changes under stress, and vision improves when the many millions of eye cells and the muscles controlling the eye are stimulated because of the controlled stress of using the rebounder.

My eyes have strengthened because the rebounder has done for them what it's done for the rest of my body cells, clearing out the cell garbage and bringing much-needed nutrients there by the increased stress of the acceleration and deceleration every time I use the rebounder.

My other exercise machines work my muscles, but my rebounder has strengthened not only all my muscle cells, but also all my internal organs. I keep mine in the bedroom, and it has screw-on legs, but lots of the newer ones have folding legs so you can lean them against the wall for added room space.

One of the best parts of rebounding is you don't have to jump high. You can jump as high as you want, of course, but even if you just bounce a little (maybe an inch—hardly at all), it still moves that lymph fluid (and synovial fluid) and does you more good (your vital organs) than strenuous muscle exercise.

Q-Tipping the Eyes

Since I became an adult, I've had at least fifteen eye infections of the lower lid. Several of them became so bad that I had to have an ophthalmologist actually cut out the infection from inside the lower lid. It seemed as if I was constantly getting these sty-like things, and they were painful and looked awful.

After the first ten years of my getting them, my ophthalmologist prescribed Neodecadron, which, if you put it in right away as soon as you think you're getting one, gets rid of it in a few days—which seemed like a real blessing to me. I didn't have any problem for several years with the drops, but once I was in Brazil and had run out of them and couldn't get them, so by the time I reached the U.S., the infection had already grown and I had to have another operation when I got back.

Finally, after more than twenty years of going through this, I met a New York eye specialist, and I told him about my constant infections. He said that all I have to do to make sure I never get another one is to take a clean, dry Q-tip every morning and every night and gently wipe it once along the rim of the bottom lid. Since I started this a few years, ago I haven't had *one* infection!

Thank you, Dr. L'Esperance, for this simple non-drug answer.

Yoga Breathing Exercises

Many years ago when I started my daily morning meditation (Chapter 9), I also started to do a simple yoga breathing exercise that takes only about five minutes to do, but it clears out all that stale "sleeping air" and fills my lungs with lots of fresh air and oxygen and makes me feel terrific (it also makes a lot of water in my eyes, which cleans 'em out).

The first thing I do as soon as I wake up and I'm still in bed is take the pillow away and lie perfectly flat, stretch all my muscles, legs, arms, torso, fingers and toes, then slowly exhale through my mouth all the stale air from my lungs, and when there's not a drop left, I hold my breath for five seconds, then very slowly inhale through my nose until my lungs are *completely* filled, then I hold it for a count of fifty and then very slowly exhale through my mouth. I repeat this four more times, and by the end of the fifth exhale I really feel terrific and *very* wide awake, and my head and my mind both become very clear and alert.

Face Exercises

When I started my yoga breathing every morning, I also started to do some simple face exercises. I had once read that you should open your mouth as wide as a baby loudly crying, so I start with that. I open it and then flex all my face muscles for about five seconds.

Then I squint and unsquint fifty times using just my eye muscles, then I push my nose up and down fifty times using my nose muscles. At the end of that when my nose is still up, I slowly pull my nose down as far as it will go and flare my nostrils out, then I raise my nose and do it again. I do that ten times.

Then I stick my lips out and move them in and out of a pucker about ten times. Then I open my mouth wide and stick out my tongue as far as I can and try to wiggle the tip, then move it from side to side ten times.

Then I stick my jaw out and flex the muscles in my neck for about ten seconds. At the end I again do the open wide mouth and flex all my face and neck muscles for about ten seconds.

The point is to use *all* the muscles, most of which probably never get used. It's the same as your body muscles. *All* muscles need to be used to keep them in shape so they in turn can hold your skin and flesh in place, and I feel my face is just as important as my body.

Firm Up!

When you're voluptuous (zoftig!), it's even *more* important to keep your muscles toned, 'cause now you've got a bigger body with more curves (more fat replacing the missing collagen) to keep pulled together.

I'll never forget a photo I saw of Leona Helmsley in a bathing suit with Harry (before their troubles) coming out of the ocean after swimming and I noted how firm her body looked even though she was big. She's another remarkably young-looking woman for her age. She must be in her seventies, and her face looks thirty years younger. I don't know if she started out thin, but she's got enough fat well distributed on her face and body to keep her young and juicy looking now. And she's very athletic, which is why she's not flabby.

And why I work out every single day.

Sex With Love Is
Heaven on Earth . . .

7

Sex and Love

I believe that sex belongs in a loving, committed, married relationship. I also believe that when a husband and wife love each other, the sexual pleasure they give each other is the cement that holds that marriage together. Without it the stresses of everyday life can strain it to the breaking point, but with it, their love and their marriage will thrive and last a lifetime.

Sex is the greatest *physical* pleasure that we can experience. Succulent and delicious food can make us salivate like mad, and gives us and our bodies a "high" when we chew it and when it slowly slides down our tongues and throats and into our stomachs.

But the pleasures of sex are even *more* tantalizing, and when sex is attached to love, the pleasures are boundless. When two people are in love and each gives the other the ultimate pleasure of an orgasm, that is the highest and deepest ecstasy on this plane physically, mentally, emotionally, and spiritually.

And it *is* a spiritual experience. It's the closest to "heaven" that we can ever come here on earth. How many of us have wondered why so many religious leaders are caught philandering? It seems that spirituality and sex are closely related. The deeper the well of spirituality, the stronger the love instinct (or vice versa), and sex is the deepest expression of love. From Jim Bakker to Aimee Semple McPherson to Jimmy Swaggart. Unfortunately, many turned out to be dishonest, but their sex drives were and are all strong.

Sex is not only an expression of love, it's also an expression of bio-chemical drive. The more estrogen and testosterone, the more the desire. And the more the desire, the more the capacity for love and giving. It is unnatural to stifle desire, to bury the feelings of pleasure. And yet so many do because of fear and of guilt. These are negative emotions and are not reasons to deprive us of the most important, the most healthful and relaxing, of all of life's pleasures.

In one way sex *is* like food: The more food you eat, the more you want, and when you abstain from food, the desire starts to leave, and with sex also, the less you do it, the less you want or need to do it. But when you have a robust and healthy sex life that is being expressed every day, the more you want it and need it every day.

An orgasm lowers our blood pressure, gets rid of tension, gets rid of depression, and releases endorphins in the body that give us a feeling of well-being. Because it's so much easier for the man to have an orgasm (his sex organs for the most part are on the outside of his body), a man generally has more orgasms and more endorphins than his woman.

But that's only up to now. Men are beginning to learn *how* to pleasure a woman *every time*. My marriage manual is teaching men all over the world *how* to make love so that they are not the only ones being satisfied; now their women are having orgasms in intercourse every time too.

And the most amazing thing is (and I've been telling people about it on radio and TV since I thought about it in 1982) that a man must have an orgasm to procreate a child, but a woman could have fifteen children (literally) and never have an orgasm. So obviously our sex organ, the clitoris, is *just* for pleasure; it's not needed for anything else. And I believe it was given to us as a "pleasure bond," to bond us with our husbands, our "soul mates," for a lifetime.

The ignorance used to be overwhelming, and not just the men's ignorance, but also the women's. I faked it in my marriage for eight years until it led to my divorce, and it was as much *my* ignorance as my husband's.

Because the book was *overwhelmingly* successful (sixty-two weeks on the New York Times Bestseller List in 1992–93 plus being the #1 best selling hardcover nonfiction book in the United States in 1992), I had literally thousands of people ask me when would I write the sequel, *"HOW TO SATISFY A MAN EVERY TIME . . . and have him beg for more!"* I usually said that all a woman has to do to satisfy a man is . . . show up! That was the only original joke I ever made up (and it was fun getting a laugh), but I decided to put into this chapter my thoughts and ideas on totally satisfying a *man* sexually . . . every time . . . and having him beg for more. . . .

HOW TO SATISFY A MAN EVERY TIME . . .
and have him beg for more!
(for women only)

Teasing really turns a woman on when her husband drives her wild with physical promises of orgasm that he deliberately keeps lovingly withholding till she's absolutely crazy with desire (and if you haven't had your mate try intercourse with my new technique, you haven't *lived!*).

And as exciting as that is for a female, it's just as exciting to a man to have his woman take charge of *his* body and drive him wild by sexually teasing him and then giving him the greatest orgasm he's ever had in his life.

When you do decide you're going to take charge of your husband's body, you should tell him either at breakfast, or call him early at work, that *tonight* is the night you're going to drive him crazy—you're going to take complete control of his body and tease him till he goes out of his mind, and *then* you're going to give him the greatest pleasure he's ever had. Let him think about it all day.

And when he comes home, either before dinner or after, you tell him you're now in charge, and you want to undress him. Lead him to the bedroom and then slowly take off his shirt, belt, slacks, undershirt, till he's in his underwear. Tell him to lie on the bed and then you'll take off his shorts.

When he's lying there with his shorts on, slowly start to take *your* clothes off. First your dress or blouse and skirt/pants, then your bra, and then your panties. Go over to him, and before you take his shorts off, take both of your hands with your fingers extended and lightly run them over his chest and arms.

Tell him he's not allowed to move or to touch you, that's part of the deal of *you* taking charge. So tease his chest and arms and then slowly take off his shorts. Now you can softly tease the inside of his thighs with the pads of your fingertips. Then tell him to bend his legs, and gently go with your fingertips behind his knees and tease him there.

At a certain point (and *you* are in control of whenever you want), gently touch his balls and tease them all over. Then go to his penis and gently run your fingers up and down it. Wet your fingertips and run them across the tip, and as he gets more aroused, go back down the shaft, then do the same thing with your tongue.

When he *really* gets hot, stop what you're doing with his sex organ and go back to teasing his chest and arms.

Do not let him touch you.

He must be passive, because you are totally in control. You can continue going from teasing his arms and legs and nipples back to his penis. Start over again as many times and as long as you want. It's *your* game and *you* are the coach calling every play. And he knows it.

Whenever you feel like the time has come for you to give him an orgasm, you very gently climb onto his body, straddling him, and *slowly* lower your self onto his penis, *very* slowly.

When it's about halfway in, raise up a little, very slowly go in and out halfway down a few times, then slowly go all the way down.

You are still in charge, still on top, and he will erupt very soon. Just keep slowly going up and down on his penis till he explodes into your body with the most intense orgasm he's ever had.

Or if you'd rather give him an oral orgasm, once you've got him really aroused, go back to his penis and start softly tongue-teasing it again, except this time you're going all the way to make him erupt into the greatest prolonged pleasure he's ever had.

Gently take the head in your mouth and let your tongue tenderly caress the head. Then take a little bit more, very gently, and let it go in and out of your mouth until he has an orgasm. And what an orgasm it will be. And what a sense of power and love you'll feel for the man you love.

Or let's say you decide to take charge of his body on the spur of the moment and your husband is already in bed and you reach under the covers and gently take his penis in your hand and softly caress it. It starts to get hard, and you continue fondling as it grows bigger and harder.

Now you pull the covers back and softly put your mouth over the tip and very gently suck it. Then you run your tongue gently up and down the shaft. He's out of his mind with pleasure and probably seconds away from orgasm when you take your mouth away and begin to softly kiss the inside of his thighs.

You can gently whisper, "I'm not ready yet, sweetheart, to give you an orgasm." This will really rock him, because you have totally taken over his body. You are in charge and he knows it. "I'll let you know when I'm ready," you whisper.

After gently kissing the inside of his thighs, you might want to go back to his sex organ and tease a little more. The more you tease, the stronger the orgasm when he finally has it.

If you want to continue teasing, you might go to his nipples and very gently rub your tongue around the sides and very softly kiss them. And you might want to continue fondling him while you kiss his nipples.

By now he's fully crazed with desire, and you might feel you're ready to give him an orgasm. It's *your* call, so do whatever *you* feel you want to do.

If you're ready, go back and start your tongue-tease again, gently, very gently going up and down the shaft. Then very gently climb onto his body and lower your self onto his penis and slowly, *very* slowly, go up and down as he gets more and more excited until he explodes with an incredibly intense orgasm into your body.

Or again, if you'd rather give him an orgasm orally, when he's very aroused and excited, take the head in your mouth and just let your tongue tenderly caress the head. Then take a little bit more, very gently, and let it go slowly in and out of your mouth. You're in control and he *loves* it!

He will have an orgasm at any moment that will be an *explosion* of love, and he'll be so turned on to the fact that *you* took control, that *you* made him wait till *you* wanted him to have an orgasm.

What a turn-on to a guy to be *sometimes* passive and masochistic, to *sometimes* surrender to his woman.

And once you've done that for *him*, please trust me, he will do *anything* for you (just to guarantee that you'll do what you did to him *again*). Just let him know that you'll do this as often as he wants if he'll do intercourse à la "the little red marriage manual."

What you want him to do is tease *you*, not with his hands and not with his tongue, but with his penis.

Until a woman has had an orgasm through intercourse alone, she has never experienced the *ultimate* pleasure. It's beyond words.

It's a fusing of the man and the woman together in a sexual climax that is so beautiful and so total that it bonds them closer together than they've ever been before.

The woman has *totally* surrendered emotionally to her man, and the man has felt a power over the woman he loves that is so strong that every time it happens, his love grows deeper, and so does hers.

You *cannot* have this kind of pleasure outside of marriage, and that's why I always call my *HOW TO SATISFY A WOMAN EVERY TIME* . . . book a "marriage manual."

You can have just plain old physical sexual pleasure, but you *cannot* have the quadruple whammy of the physical, mental, emotional, and spiritual melding that this kind of ecstasy brings to two people who not only love each other, but are *committed* to each other, and are married to each other.

Self-Pleasure

The ultimate turn-on is love. And when you and your beloved find each other, heaven-on-earth enters your life.

But some of us are not so lucky to have found a "soulmate" and we're still alone. Or our "soulmate" is out of the country or on a six-month assignment, or has passed away.

Self-pleasure is good. *Anything* that gives pleasure, and is healthy and hurts no one including our selves, is good.

So why is something so good reviled by so many? Because it's not understood and it's cloaked in ignorance and guilt. Most people accept a man's self-pleasure without any problems, so I'm really slanting this to women's pleasure.

Would *anyone* think wrongly of a really hungry person going into a well-stocked kitchen, looking at all the edibles, choosing a plate of steaming pasta primavera, and sitting down and slowly eating every last bite? Obviously not.

Then why would anyone want to deprive himself or herself or anyone else of another need that is just as important? If you don't eat food for a long enough period of time, your body will die. You need good healthy nourishment to thrive.

And if you don't have an orgasm for a long period of time, your body will get very tense, your blood pressure will go up, you will not feel really good, and you will definitely get depressed. And the instinctive physical way to get rid of depression is anger.

So when you see an habitually angry and tense person, know that that person hardly ever or never has an orgasm. Those substances called endorphins, which give you a sense of well-being when they're released in your body via an orgasm, will be withheld, and you will get more tense, more depressed, and more difficult to be around.

All those awful sexist stories about a cranky female needing an orgasm are true, but they are equally true for a cranky male. Except if a man went months or years without an orgasm, he'd be *worse* than cranky, he'd be violent!

Think about *that* with all the violence in the world.

If a woman is married and her sexually ignorant husband doesn't know how to intercourse correctly, and she, just as ignorant, doesn't know what to tell him to do to give her one, you've got a tense and unhappy wife. And if she's single and alone (and tense and unhappy), her own ignorance about self-pleasure is obvious.

And all older men and women who think that sex is now unimportant for them should know that part of the reason for their depression is that their bodies haven't lost their need for the now missing endorphins. They may think it has, their minds may be telling them that sex is only for the young, but *all* older people who are active and not depressed and/or tense and angry, are getting sexual pleasure, either with a spouse or alone. Of course they don't talk about it, but I've interviewed many seniors who do, and many who don't, and the happy, non-angry, non-tense ones do.

One woman's terminally ill husband made her promise that she would pleasure her self after he was gone. She told me he was extremely loving all their forty-two years of marriage—he *always* wanted her to have sexual pleasure, and he *always* made sure she did.

Sex is a part of nature. Our sex drive is a physical need just as our hunger drive is. We didn't *ask* for our sex organs, but they're part of the package. And to ignore them isn't just ignorant, it's stupid.

When a single woman learns about self-pleasure and sensualizes with it, her compulsive need to be with a man (whether he's good for her or not) leaves her, and she can wait for sex till she meets the right man and falls in love with him. This makes her more self-reliant and a happier person.

Any time you can rely on your self, you're going to be happier. Dependence on others can be a mirage—when you really need them the most, that's when they're usually not there.

But your self is *always* there. So nurture your body with really good nutritious foods, drink lots of water, get plenty of rest and sleep, and pleasure your self as often as you want so that you'll always feel Good.

Respect

A very important fact that many men are not aware of (and not many women are either) is that if a woman doesn't *respect* her husband, doesn't look up to him as a strong person (weak is what she *doesn't* want) who warrants respect, she won't have an orgasm through *his* efforts.

This is very important to know and understand, because if she feels all respect for him is gone, if she feels he's not capable of taking charge of her body (not her life, not her money, but her *body!*) sexually, she will either look around for a man who turns her on (and to be "turned on" a woman must have respect for that man), or she will close up physically and emotionally and be grateful she doesn't have to have sex anymore. She's at the point where she doesn't *want* an orgasm, but the truth is she won't *allow* her self to have an orgasm because an orgasm is *sexual surrender*, and she doesn't *want* to surrender to this weak man for whom she has little or no respect.

Inner strength is *very* sexy.

If you, a husband, are in a sexless relationship with your wife, you *must* change it for the sake of your marriage, your physical, mental, and emotional health, and last, but certainly not least, your wife's physical, mental and emotional health.

How do you command respect from a woman who no longer feels that you're worthy of it, who feels you're too weak to *take charge* of anything? You obviously can't force it, but you *can* slowly coax it from her.

Respect can start in the bedroom. If you don't make much money, you're not a titan of industry, you drive a beat-up old car, never mind. All you need is the *attitude* of "take charge," the letting her know that you *sexually* are stronger than she is.

If you learn how to drive her crazy in bed and *make* her have an orgasm every time you have intercourse, you will have love like you've never had before. Trust me, she will respect the fact that you are no longer tentative, that you are now in charge of her body (and as you hopefully already know, she's in charge of your body).

A totally sexually satisfied woman will do *anything* for her man, and you'll soon find out how *much* she'll do once you've given her this total pleasure.

How did she lose the respect for you in the first place? (I talk about a man respecting his wife later in the chapter.)

She probably romantically fantasized when you met and got married that you were a strong person who would take care of her in all areas. Remember, inner strength is sexy. Even if she was more successful than you at that time, she still wanted a man who would be able to take care of her if necessary (all women in love, subconsciously or consciously, want this).

Maybe you're basically a more passive type of person than she, and maybe you've had business reverses and you both fight now about finances—whatever it is, the respect she had for you (and whatever inner strength she thought you had) at the beginning is gone. It's now up to you, her husband, to learn how to play the game of sex.

But first, before anything, you *must* learn how to make love and how to intercourse correctly.

LOVE SHOULD *NEVER* BE A GAME. . . .

SEX SHOULD *ALWAYS* BE A GAME!

The games people play in *LOVE* can be very destructive— she flirts with another guy and her husband gets jealous. He makes goo-goo eyes with the hostess at the party and his woman gets crazy with insecurity.

Games like that are not fun, *ever.*

Love should bring security and warmth and a feeling of togetherness and the fun of compatibility, not the fear and jealousy that come from flirting games.

Sex on the other hand should be fun from the start. Two people who love each other can drive each other wild with desire by playing the "teasing game" because it's so important to great sex.

I keep coming back to teasing. I was the very first one who came out with it in 1982 with my marriage manual, and thank Good I did because it's the bottom-line answer to the greatest physical pleasure you can have.

All you need is love, imagination, and a sense of fun and play. Just imagine what would turn *you* on, and then do that to your mate. Everybody (man and woman) has a touch (in varying degrees) of masochism, so "torture" him or her lovingly with teasing. I cannot repeat this enough—it's very important you know *how* important it is for real deep sexual pleasure.

Start getting your mate excited, and then stop for a minute. Re-start and get him (her) even more excited, and stop again.

Now there isn't a doubt who's in charge, is there? And if your mate complains and says he (she) doesn't like that, believe me it's based on fear because the recipient of teasing has *totally* lost control. But basically this is what the giant turn-on in sex is all about: SEXUAL SURRENDER.

When you let your partner know you love him (her), but that *you* are definitely in charge at this moment, that is the biggest turn-on of all. Just make sure your mate finally *does* have an orgasm.

And if your mate persists in complaining (see "letter" below), do not listen and stop, just totally ignore it and continue till you make him (her) have an orgasm. It will be the most unforgettable sex experience he (she) ever had.

Letter From A Married Man

At the end of my *HOW TO SATISFY A WOMAN <u>EVERY TIME</u>* book there is the most extraordinary letter I've ever received (out of literally thousands I've gotten from couples since the book came out), a fourteen-page handwritten letter from a man whose wife had never had an orgasm in eighteen years of marriage.

He wrote me that he's madly in love with her, they have three kids and a very happy marriage, *except* sex had gotten very boring.

He says she'd always rushed sex just to get it over with, and it had become so dull for him that he was considering having an affair or even possibly a divorce because sex was *very* important to him and he couldn't stand the boredom of the bedroom anymore.

He wrote that they had tried marriage counselors, sex therapists, read many, many books on the subject, but nothing had worked. He thought it could be that she might have been sexually abused as a child and was now possibly "frigid."

One night he heard me on a radio talk show while he was driving his son to a Little League soccer game. He said I sounded so sincere in my promising every wife an orgasm through intercourse alone that early the next day he went out and bought the book and read it.

His wife refused to read it (it is a marriage manual and should be read by both husband and wife) because she said she'd failed so many times before, she didn't want to fail again.

That night when they went to bed, he started to make love, but she quickly got on top so she'd be in control and could get it over with fast. He said it took all his strength to roll her over and get on top in the controlling (missionary) position, which is what my technique needs.

He started gently teasing her nipples with his fingers, and she tried to stop him, saying it tickled. He said she'd always said that in the past and he'd always stopped before, but this time he paid no attention to her and continued.

She started to get angry and again told him to stop, but he didn't.

He continued to tease her nipples with his lips and tongue, and she got angrier and struggled to get him to stop.

Now he started teasing her clitoris with his penis, and she really got mad and demanded he stop, but he didn't. He says he sensed that he was on the right track just like I had said in the book.

She was starting to get aroused and she didn't *want* to (she obviously was very afraid of surrendering), so again she told him to stop. He said it was so exciting for him because he felt a loving power over the woman he loved that he'd never felt before.

He felt her getting more and more excited, which really frightened her and turned him on.

Then he started my technique.

Now she got even *more* excited, and the more he did it, the more excited she got. She finally *really* got angry now and *demanded* he stop.

Of course he didn't, and all of a sudden she had an orgasm.

He goes into graphic description of her ecstasy, and he says that night she fell asleep holding his hand, which he said had *never* happened in their eighteen years of marriage.

He says his life and his marriage were both changed incredibly for the better.

I spoke to him six months after I got the letter because I called him to see if he and his wife would appear on *Oprah* with me (he wanted to, but his wife was shy, so I got another couple who had written me a letter), and he told me that up to that night six months before, *he'd never been in charge*, and that's why his wife (who was afraid to let go, afraid to have an orgasm) had never had one before.

He said that the power he felt over his wife's body made sex for him better than it had *ever* been before, and six months later it was even *better* for both of them than it had been that night.

Sexual Power

Not only is it tremendously exciting for a man to feel sexual power over the woman he loves, it is even *more* exciting for his wife to feel his sexual power. A woman in love with her man really desperately wants this.

I can't tell you how many times women have called me on live call-in talk radio shows and screamed at me that every married woman should be in control of her own orgasm and should learn to masturbate so she's not dependent on her husband.

I have argued that the only reason women say this (and write books about it) is because these women have given up on their husbands *ever* learning how to give them orgasms, and how sad this is.

But once a husband learns how to do this, real sexual excitement will take over the marriage, and if he felt love from her before, he won't *believe* the love he's going to feel from her now.

My Two Surveys

My *HOW TO SATISFY A WOMAN <u>EVERY</u> <u>TIME</u>* book came about after I did a survey of 486 married women from all over the country in 1981 and found out that I was not the only woman "faking" it with my husband (remember, this was 1981 and nobody talked about faking then, it was still in the closet). Up till then I honestly thought I was the only one, and I also thought there was something wrong with me, because every time we made love, my *husband* had an orgasm, so there was obviously nothing wrong with *him*—it had to be me.

This ultimately led to my divorce. I didn't say to my self, "I'm not having orgasms, I want a divorce," what happened is I became cranky, crabby, bitchy, and yelled at my husband, who of course yelled back, and the fights escalated.

So many times in divorce court the husband and wife will tell the judge they fought over money. But the truth is if the wife is sexually satisfied every time her husband is, (and of course if the love is still there), a towtruck could be repossessing their car in full view of the couple (they obviously have money problems, right?), and the wife will *not* yell at her husband, she will feel loved and part of the marital "team" who is working *with* him to solve their problems.

Back to 1981, in that survey *every* woman said that she faked it at least *some* of the time, and the great majority said they faked it every time, just as I did.

After my survey, having found out there was nothing wrong with me, that faking is a universal problem, I came up with my foolproof technique for intercourse (done a *little* bit different than usual).

In 1994 I did a *second* survey of married women, this time 1,102 of them. In this survey, thirteen years later, not all of the women said they faked it; this time many said they don't even bother to fake it, they just lie there while he has an orgasm, and then they get their husbands to use oral sex or hands to give them one, which of course won't have to be done once he learns *how* to intercourse.

By the way, a husband should *not* ask his wife if she fakes it—of *course* she's going to say no. She fakes it because she doesn't want him to know she's not having an orgasm, and *that's* because she loves him, is sensitive to his feelings, instinctively knows how important being a good lover is to him (*all* we women instinctively know that) and also doesn't want him to think she's "frigid" (and of course there's no such thing as a frigid woman, only a woman whose husband hasn't learned how to make her "hot"!)!

There's enormous ignorance, and it's not just the husband's ignorance. If the wife knew what to tell him to do, she'd tell him. I was just as ignorant as my husband all those years I was faking it.

So ignorance is to blame for sexual unfulfillment, not lack of love.

But several of my questions in the survey, and the answers, I think you'll find *very* interesting.

I asked, "Would you rather be in control sexually or have your husband in charge?" and 88 percent said husband in charge. Many of the 12 percent who would rather be in control themselves had never had, or hardly ever had, an orgasm; in fact 11 percent of the 1,102 women surveyed had never had an orgasm.

And 46 percent of the women thought all men are selfish, but 79 percent thought only their *husbands* were selfish (interesting, no?), which would lead many to think of cheating, thinking, "Maybe there's a guy out there who won't be selfish like my husband, and who will care enough to give me an orgasm, because my husband sure doesn't care," (of course not realizing it's ignorance, *not* lack of caring).

And 56 percent of the married women replied that they believe some women are frigid. I find this sad because so-called frigidity is only the ignorance of both spouses.

These two surveys were enlightening and I believe accurate because they were 100 percent anonymous. Many surveys are one-on-one, and I believe most people will not be totally frank when talking to a person, but will be when alone, filling out a form.

And the one thing I absolutely am positive about is that

men are *not* selfish (even though many women in the survey said they were).

Any man who loves a woman enough to marry her, to want to spend the rest of his life with her, would do *anything* to give her an orgasm, he just doesn't know how. But once he learns my technique and his wife starts having an orgasm every time they make love, both of them will be amazed at how their love will grow and how much better their marriage is going to be.

Cheating

Many women are so afraid of losing control that they keep their husbands as little boys. But this makes them unable to have an orgasm, because again, an orgasm is sexual surrender, and you don't surrender to a child, you surrender to someone you look up to and admire, and love.

Just as many men are afraid of surrendering to their wives, so they have just a "physical release" and don't become a "soulmate." Because of this they rationalize that there's no good sex at home and they cheat.

And of course some men *like* to be treated as little boys because this relieves them of any responsibility of husbandly or any other kinds of duties.

Now the men who are afraid of surrendering to their wives and who go out and cheat with any number of other women are *never* going to experience the intense joy of an orgasm with deep love. An orgasm without love is physically pleasureful, of course, but with love it's overpowering, overwhelming, and the ultimate ecstasy.

And if your wife is "cold" and unresponsive, logic tells you that sex is obviously not pleasureful to her, because if it were, she'd be as "hot" as you are. So it's up to you to learn how to drive her crazy with desire.

Boredom with the same person and the same routine, day in and day out, can be a motivating influence to fool around.

204 *Good Is Alive and Well and Living in Each One of Us*

The imaginative excitement of "sinful sex" with a new, exhilarating body promises to change a humdrum life to one charged with electricity. But it's also charged with guilt, remorse, fear of discovery, and that ever-present possibility of some sex-related disease from herpes to AIDS.

Cheating on your wife is in reality cheating on your self. A clandestine affair might seem exciting (in your mind or in actuality when it happens), but it *cannot* compare with giving an orgasm to the woman you married, the woman whom you love and with whom you share everything in your life. And when you *do* learn how to give her this incredible Good-given pleasure, you might be amazed at how *she* will become a more exciting person to be around, and how that life-numbing boredom that led you to think about possibly cheating (or maybe actually doing it) will disappear once excitement-with-an-excited-spouse has entered your life.

And of course the *only* reason a woman would cheat on the man she loves and is married to and wants to spend the rest of her life with is she's sexually frustrated, she keeps "getting to the edge of the cliff" and never goes over it. This is about the most horrendous physical frustration that any human body can endure. Men can't even *imagine* getting to the point of *almost* having an orgasm and never having it, because they never experience that. It's truly beyond their comprehension. And some women have endured this for years!

Many people say a wife is really looking for affection, for a hug and "I love you," but trust me, if her husband takes the time and trouble to learn how to give her an orgasm every time they intercourse, *that's* the kind of affection that will keep her faithful and will let her know you cared enough to learn how to *show* her she's loved. And who says the hug and "I love you" won't be there with the orgasm? Why do so many women think it's either one or the other, not both?

Obviously, if the marriage is over, that's a different thing. I'm talking about if the love is still there but she's sexually frustrated.

Soul Mates

Let me give you a short scenario on why marriages break up and why the husband and the wife cheat. Everyone is looking for a "soulmate." I don't care who you are, a bachelor-type man or a career-oriented woman; underneath it all there is a longing to find your "better half" and become a perfectly together whole.

Now two people meet, fall in love, and get married, each confident that the other is the missing half, the long-sought-after soulmate.

The first few months are divine, and then once in a while the wife will get a little testy and he responds testily. If an orgasm gives endorphins, her body is screaming out for the missing endorphins resulting from the missing orgasms. And as more months go by, more spats.

How many men could go six months or a year without an orgasm or hardly ever having one? And how cranky, crabby, bitchy would *he* be if he *did* go six months or a year without one?

So she bitches about the top he left off the toothpaste tube, the bills, etc., and he screams back. But she's not bitching about bills or toothpaste tops, her body is very tense and nervous, making her mind and spirit tense and nervous just as his would be if *he* never got satisfaction.

As the spats continue and slowly worsen after several years, and the yelling gets louder, each starts to think, "This can't possibly be my soulmate. I made a mistake." And each starts to secretly re-look for a new and different soul-mate. And the marriage is figuratively over.

And again, when they go before the judge for the literal ending of the marriage, they both will cite financial problems as the cause, because most people do. They will say they fought about money.

But if the love they once shared had been nurtured by sexual satisfaction for *both* of them, not just the husband

(and this *always* strengthens the bond of love), no financial problems, no problems of *any* kind, could have split them up.

Sex is much more important than many people give it credit for. Love is the *most* important part of any relationship, especially marriage, but sex is the deepest *expression* of that love. And if the love is not being expressed sexually for either partner, the marriage is doomed, either to an eventual divorce, or a life full of bitching and fighting, and devoid of joy.

When a husband and wife love each other, sexual pleasure *is* the cement that holds that marriage together.

Beautiful, warm, loving sex between husband and wife is Good.

Rape

There is a widely held belief that women secretly want to be raped. Secretly, very secretly, this desire is supposed to exist within all women.

I will tell you where this myth arose and why.

As I continue to say, an orgasm is sexual surrender for both men and women.

How can you surrender to a possibly violent stranger, someone you don't know at all? Will he hurt me physically? Will he leave when he's finished, totally abandon me and hurt me emotionally? Is she cruel and could she cut off my sex organ? Will I love her and will she leave me? This works both ways.

First let's examine what men want in sex. Now we're talking about normal or fairly normal men, not real neurotics who are into sadomasochism (on either side), or psychotics or sociopaths.

A normal, fairly well-adjusted man wants a challenge. He wants a woman with inner strength who won't fall apart if he loses his job, a woman who'll help the partnership in all areas.

He *doesn't* want a clinging, helpless, weak woman (respect is not a one-way street—a man *must* respect a woman too—if he doesn't, the relationship is over).

Now he may not be aware of this. He may think he wants a woman who looks up to him, who thinks he's great, who adores him, and there's nothing wrong with that. Isn't that what love's about? But under the adoration, he wants inner strength, a woman who's not totally dependent on him. A little dependent emotionally because she needs his love (as he needs hers), but that's it.

Well, a woman wants the same thing. She wants a man who is strong, who loves her deeply, and who can take charge.

Some women unfortunately had a bad childhood experience (incest or other sexual abuse), or they were taught that sex is dirty or that men are selfish and only want their own sexual gratification.

Even these fearful and sometimes controlling women dream, fantasize, and long for sexual release. *All* women dream of sexual release. It starts in high school and sometimes even earlier, depending on the woman's physiology.

When the sexual stirrings begin for teenage boys, they also begin for teenage girls, but more subtly. He either masturbates or goes out and gets a girl. She fantasizes being in love and having the sexual release just happen.

She dreams that the man, whoever he is, will love her and *make* her have an orgasm (or surrender). This means she had no active part in it and relieves her of any possible guilt.

Because a man's sex organs for the most part are outside his body and a woman's for the most part inside, from puberty a boy/man has an orgasm easily. But a girl/woman doesn't, and that's when fantasy enters in.

A boy doesn't have to fantasize—he goes to his bedroom or bathroom, or he goes out and finds a girl who is looking for someone to take her out to the movies Saturday night, or to go to the football game with, and she gives her body in exchange for having a boyfriend. She doesn't have an orgasm—the pleasure she gets is knowing he wants her body, he *needs* her body, and that he will be her boyfriend in exchange for her body.

Because it *is* more difficult for a woman to have an orgasm and because of the overwhelming ignorance of how a man should intercourse done the usual way, she doesn't want to struggle for it. She doesn't want to try and try and keep getting excited and then constantly be disappointed. She doesn't want to keep getting to the edge and never go over it.

What she *does* want is for a man to *make* it happen, to *make* her have an orgasm. Many psychiatrists and analysts have mistaken this desire for loving force for a wish to be raped—to be violently taken by a stranger.

What she wants is force and control leading to an orgasm by someone who *loves* her, or *will* love her, not violence from a stranger. Rape does *not* give a woman an orgasm.

Because so many women have been in what turn out to be loveless (sexless) marriages, many of these women fantasize sex with a bold stranger, but it's never violent and painful, it's forceful and pleasureful.

What they *really* want is an orgasm, sexual surrender, with a man who loves them and whom they love. Or if it *is* a stranger, he will fall in love with her and she with him.

No woman wants rape and violence—every woman (who loves a man) wants him to be knowledgeable about how to give her an orgasm, forceful so that he *makes* it happen for her.

Sex And Love

I want to explain that what I have to say is *only* for a woman and a man who either now have or at one time had a deep love and need for each other. I consider my self a feminist (I've always supported my self, I believe in equal pay and all *other* equality, I bought my own home, etc.), but some feminists who have never been deeply in love with a man don't understand that sexual surrender is what happens to *both* the husband and the wife, and it's what makes a truly great and successful marriage.

And I also want to say that I believe so deeply in sex with

love and commitment that I want to warn you that casual sex can be dangerous. I don't mean the obvious disease-danger, but the emotional batterings that can scar you for life when you go from one body to another with no feeling emotionally, or a lot of feeling emotionally that is not reciprocated.

The great pleasure of sex was given to us originally to insure that we procreate, and way down deep, way beyond our conscious mind, that desire to further the species is still with us. Even though we use the pill and condoms and other birth-control methods, way back in the recesses of our beings is the need to create another human being with a caring partner. And because we *do* have feelings, to have endless affairs without love or caring isn't fair to you or your affair-partner.

Pay Attention Instead of Alimony

In my last book I had an original saying that came to me as I was writing about love and marriage:

Pay attention instead of alimony.

I now want to expand that to:

Pay attention instead of alimony, psychiatrist bills, teenage drug-addiction costs, doctor bills, etc., etc., etc. . . .

When you focus your loving attention on *anything*, it will thrive, be it your spouse, your kids, your parents, your employees, your boss, your pals, your animals, your plants—attention is like warming rays of sunshine.

And one of the things to pay attention to is sex. Don't make the mistake of thinking it's not important (as so many women told me when I toured the country with my marriage manual).

It's *always* important to a man (a normal, healthy man), and it *will* be important to every woman when her husband learns how to give her this beautiful, loving pleasure every time they make love.

And don't forget your self. If you don't pay attention to your self, you really *can't* pay attention to anyone else. If you don't eat right, you won't feel right, and how can you be loving and kind to *anyone* else if you're tense, anxious, depressed, or have pains in your stomach?

So paying attention starts with your self, spreads to your spouse, kids, parents, and friends and never ends.

If you truly care enough to pay attention, *real* attention, to listen and respond with care, the rewards are far greater than you might imagine—in fact, you might really be surprised. . . .

Tribute of Love

Everyone knows how deeply I believe in marriage and commitment and faithfulness and love, so I want to share with you a beautiful quote from our seventh U.S. president, Andrew Jackson, who was obviously deeply in love with his wife:

> Heaven will be no heaven to me if I do not meet my wife there.

Aphrodisiac

The greatest, strongest, most powerful aphrodisiac is LOVE!

Love Is Good

Finding love, *any* kind of love, is the beginning of finding Good. . . .

The LOGIC of astrology will help us find out
the things about our selves
that we need to know—
all the positives
(which we may or may not be aware of)
and all the negatives
(which we probably are not aware of).

8

The LOGIC of Astrology

We can't express Good (*or* love) until we like our selves, and we can't like our selves until we understand why we are what we are and why we do what we do. Astrology will help us understand our selves.

The thing I like the most about astrology is that it's *logical* (my fourth book is called *ASTRO-LOGICAL LOVE*). Most people think of astrology as occult, a telling-the-future kind of thing, but it's not. As I said earlier, if astrologers *could* predict the future, they'd all be multi-zillionaires—they'd do charts on the two fighters in a huge boxing match and accurately predict which one would win, they'd do charts on the stock market to predict which stock would go up, they'd go to a horse race and do charts on all the horses and find out which one would be first, which one second, etc. They don't do that because they *can't* do that. *No one* can predict the future. No astrologer can tell us what we'll be doing next week, next month, or next year.

But what astrology *can* tell us about is character analysis; it *can* inform us of personality traits. The value of astrology is to point out our positive and negative qualities so we can strengthen our good and try to eliminate our negatives.

We cannot express Good until we get rid of these negatives, and astrology was given to us as a tool to help us help our selves.

A few years ago there was a survey done under the supervision of a psychology professor, Dr. Patricia Greenfield, by an astrologer who identified 87 percent of the character traits of a group of grade-school kids, using only astrology for information. Alice Lane was the astrologer, and she did astrological charts on ten second- and third-grade students whom she had never seen or met, using only the birth dates and time of birth supplied by their teacher, Alice Lauran.

Then Lane, the astrologer, and Lauran, the teacher, each answered twenty-seven questions about the character traits of each child. When the two separate lists of answers were compared, the astrologer had answered 235 out of 270 questions correctly, which is an 87 percent accuracy rate. She had unerringly described the intelligence, creativity, aggressiveness, and went so far as to say which ones had a tendency to gain weight.

Dr. Greenfield, the psychology professor under whose supervision the survey was done, said that as a result of the survey, her opinions about astrology had totally changed. She said that she hadn't thought that the results would be as positive and as accurate as they turned out to be, and that her skepticism was now giving way to belief.

The science of astrology is based on the fact that the sun and the moon and the earth, and all the other stars and planets, are interrelated and part of a giant cosmic plan or design.

Sunspots and solar flares (huge magnetic storms on the sun) strongly affect the earth's weather, and positive and negative ions in the atmosphere have been proven to affect the way we think and feel, and ultimately behave. The brain is an electrochemical system, and electrical charges, geomagnetism, and electromagnetism affect humans, animals, and plants (we've all heard of luna-tics whose symptoms worsen with a full moon, and we've seen photos of animals howling at the full moon).

The specific conditions and varied positions of the stars and planets influence the earth and everything and everybody on it by emitting these magnetic forces and cosmic rays (radiation), which alters DNA and RNA, the nucleic acids in all living things. All the planets' gravitational and electromagnetic fields of influence in our solar system interact with our sun, and we are the recipients of this interaction and these rays and forces.

Just as we can't see radio waves and sound waves, we can't see cosmic rays. But when we turn on the radio, we experience the sound traveling on those radio waves. We can't see the sun's ultraviolet rays, but when we're outdoors in our swimsuits, we experience a suntan. We can't see infrared rays, but we can see the outlines of our body's bones and organs in a finished X-ray film. Cosmic rays are as real as radio waves and sound waves and ultraviolet rays and infrared rays. We can't see any of them, but we know they exist by their effects.

We may not know *how* radio waves work, we just know that they do, and we confidently switch on our sets knowing the sound will start.

The same with astrology. You may not understand how cosmic rays and magnetic forces work, but after you do a self-chart and see how accurately it pinpoints *you*, or you do a chart of your family and are amazed at how your spouse was so correctly categorized in personality and character traits, you'll begin to believe in astrology as a tool for self-discovery and other-discovery too.

You'll become aware of facets of your self that you never knew existed. Some of these will be positive and some will be negative. It's up to you to accentuate the positive and eliminate the negative (and don't mess with Mr. In-Between, as Johnny Mercer said).

The more I know about astrology, the more I can see how accurate it is. And I believe as you do charts on your self, your love, your family, friends, etc., you'll develop an even stronger belief in astrology than you might already have.

The reason I call this chapter "The LOGIC of Astrology" is because astrology *is* logical. The more you delve into it and learn about it, the more you'll see the logic in it. Certain signs have certain traits that they give to those born under them. Librans *are* indecisive and *do* weigh things because they are able to see both sides of an issue. Aries people *are* egocentric and must lead in what they do. Sagittarians *are* outspoken and very frank and blunt about everything.

So let's take the mystique out of astrology, really delve into it and really learn about it.

Later on I will explain that our chart is *not* just the Sun sign (and each of us is aware of our Sun sign, the month and day we were born) but includes our Moon and Mercury and Venus, etc. (there are eleven total), and it's the *combinations* of all our planets that tell the whole story of what our characters and personalities are. The Sun sign is just a part.

And of course astrology can do more than just analyze your own qualities, it can do a character analysis on everyone you know and even those you don't know. You can do a chart (it takes about five minutes with my *ASTRO-LOGICAL LOVE* book to do a very simple chart) on a prospective employer and find out what his or her basic nature is. A person could be either generous or stingy, easygoing or a martinet, even-tempered or a blusterer. I never hire anyone without doing a chart first, and whenever I've gone against the chart and my better judgment and overlooked negative traits because I was dazzled by a personality, I've been sorry.

You can do a chart on your family and find out why you always felt close to your sister and not your brother (or vice versa), why you always loved your father's company and not your mother's (or vice versa), or why you loved both their company or why you couldn't bear either one of them and moved out when you were eighteen.

If you're going to get married, wouldn't it be great to see if your beloved will be faithful? Of course, before that you'll want to see how faithful *you* will be.

You can do a chart of Adolf Hitler and see where his cruelty came from. And his warlike attitude.

Or do one on Franklin Delano Roosevelt and find out why he was so likeable (and why he *always* prefaced his speeches with "My friends"), and such a humanitarian, and also you will see why he cheated on Eleanor for many years with his mistress.

Or one on O.J. Simpson and find out the drives behind his actions, why he's so emotional, moody, and such a compulsive womanizer, and why he shows signs of violence.

And how about discovering why Ronald Reagan has always been so faithful to Nancy. The first time I did Nancy Reagan's chart, I was stunned to find her Venus in Gemini. I literally couldn't believe it, because Venus in Gemini makes a person compulsively unfaithful, and if anyone appeared to be faithful to her husband it was Nancy. Every book I read said that Nancy was born in 1923, and of course I believed what I read.

I was so sure that there had to be a mistake that I called a friend of mine in Tampa, a newspaperwoman named Bethia Caffery, and I told her that Nancy *couldn't* have her Venus in Gemini. So Bethia, with all her journalistic skills and tactics, got in touch with a school where Nancy went as a young girl in Chicago, and sure enough, the records said she was born in 1921. I immediately looked up July 6, 1921, and *voilà!*, Venus in Taurus, a placement that almost guarantees faithfulness. The two Venus placements that are the most faithful are Taurus and Pisces, and Ronnie's Venus is in Pisces.

Now remember, I am very logical, I'm not into occult. I don't believe for a second that someone can tell me a future event in my life, but I *know* how accurate astrology is in showing me someone's basic nature, including my own.

I see in my own chart *why* I'm a very logical person, and that same Sun placement of Libra makes me so indecisive that it's pathetic. I love the story about Barbara Walters, a Libran, who, when asked about her indecisiveness, responded that she had been seriously considering seeing an analyst about *why* she's so indecisive and finding out what she can do about it, but when she looked in the phone book and saw hundreds of names, and then friends recommended dozens more, she knew she could never make the decision as to *which* analyst to go to.

And it seems in my case I *always* have two or more things to make a decision about, and of course I go back and forth a hundred times. But because I'm super-aware of this negative trait, I'm constantly working on it, and I really *am* getting better (it wouldn't be possible to get worse) by *forcing* a decision. A great quote from *Middle of the Night* by Paddy Chayefsky: "When a decision is called for, the most *important* decision to make is the decision itself. Whether it's right or wrong, only time will tell."

I also know why I'm such a perfectionist and a nitpicker. I drive my self crazy in my constant search for perfecting things, and of course when I compose a letter, it's at *least* five drafts and sometimes more, which drives my assistant nuts, but my letters are always *exactly* what I want to say. This is my Virgo Mercury.

We all have basic natures, and it's amazing that most of us don't have a clue what we're *really* like. When you do your own chart, you'll be surprised to see all the facets that the planets give to your personality and character and basic nature.

You'll find out *why* you've never been able to keep a secret, or *why* you're a very talkative person. You'll be happy to discover you have a mean streak because now you can work on sublimating that little bit of meanness that, had you not become aware of it, would have continued to make the people around you unhappy.

You'll find out what makes you vindictive, and that aware-ness will allow you to change it. I had *always* been vindictive and I honestly thought everyone was, but then I found out about the Scorpio in my chart (which also gives some great positives). I realized what a negative vindictiveness was in my life, and I became aware of what it was doing to me (forget the recipient of my vindictiveness). So I worked on it and now can say honestly that I am *never* vindictive anymore. Not that I don't think about it—it will always be a part of my nature. Whenever anyone does something to me that's not nice (that dirty rat), my nature is to figure out how to "get even." But I *immediately* push it out and get on to something else. I *never* act on it anymore, because I can now clearly see that it is *I* who will get hurt, not the other person. Vindictiveness is a self-killer.

You see, you can't change your basic nature. That's what you are. But you *can* change the way you act or don't act upon your basic drives arising from your nature. But of course you have to *find out* what your nature and drives are. You have to become *aware* of the negs so you can begin to *not respond* when the negative part of your nature starts to push you to do something (or not to do something).

The one very important thing to remember is that your Sun sign is only a part of your chart.

All the other ten planets affect you as much if not more than your Sun sign, and it's important that you find those ten so you will really understand your character and personality, why you are what you are and why you do what you do.

Let me give you a simple positive/negative look at all the signs:

Astrological Sign	Positive Traits	Negative Traits
ARIES	Bold, a leader, avant garde, aggressive, innovative, daring, a pioneer, forthright	Egocentric, impatient, warlike, easily angered, temper tantrums, impetuous

Astrological Sign	Positive Traits	Negative Traits
TAURUS	Sensual, earthy, prudent, patient, practical, home-loving, self-reliant, great memory	Obstinate, a mean streak, argumentive, plodding, bovine, dogmatic, gluttonous
GEMINI	Charming, quick-thinking, clever, fun-loving, witty, entertaining, versatile, alert	Restless, dual-natured, fickle, unreliable, elusive, scattered, critical, glib
CANCER	Supersensitive, talkative, home-loving, nurturing, great sense of humor, sentimental, gentle	Moody, brooding, fearful, possessive, talky, grasping, overly emotional, touchy
LEO	Sunny disposition, romantic, stylish, generous, dynamic, dramatic, philanthropic, self-confident	Arrogant, closed-minded, tyrannical, vain, proud, immodest, snobbish, imperious
VIRGO	Precise, witty, organized, quick-thinking, perfectionist, analytical, lucid, discriminating	Critical, nit-picky, repressed, cautious, rigid, reserved, methodical, prudish
LIBRA	Logical, fair, diplomatic, cooperative, adaptive, sociable, just, charming, gracious	Indecisive, self-indulgent, narcissistic, procrastinating, love-obsessed, self-doubting

Astrological Sign	Positive Traits	Negative Traits
SCORPIO	Loyal, intense, courageous, passionate, indomitable, magnetic, dynamic, self-confident, mysterious, fearless	Vindictive, sadistic, demanding, ruthless, secretive, suspicious, selfish, warlike, jealous, domineering, self-destructive
SAGITTARIUS	Philosophical, cheerful, adventurous, optimistic, enthusiastic, solicitous, travel-loving	Blunt, outspoken, impulsive, tactless, insensitive, rash, reckless, careless, hypocritical
CAPRICORN	Determined, responsible, ambitious, persevering, realistic, disciplined, dependable, organized	Calculating, materialistic, social-climbing, conformist, headstrong, rigid, demanding, authoritarian
AQUARIUS	Humanitarian, inventive, idealistic, original, humorous, silly, inquisitive, friendly, a visionist, gregarious	Eccentric, willful, thoughtless, opinionated, stubborn, quirky, fantasizer
PISCES	Intuitive, sympathetic, sensitive, devoted, receptive, psychic, understanding, perceptive, spiritual, unselfish, idealistic	Passive, self-indulgent, drug-prone, depressive, indirect, escapist, fearful, masochistic, submissive

The most confusing part of astrology to most people I think is that most of us are aware of only our Sun signs and think that's the whole story. *Everyone* knows his or her Sun sign because, again, all it takes is the month and the day (to get deeper you need the year), and that is only one-eleventh of your chart.

For instance, you may be a Gemini and you saw the "unreliable" negative trait and you think, "This is ridiculous. I'm the most reliable person in the world." But what you don't know is that you probably have your Mercury in Taurus (a *very* reliable, prudent sign). Or maybe your Moon or Mars could be in Virgo, another super-reliable planet, and either of these could overwhelm your unreliable Gemini.

Or you may be Pisces and you think, "Passive, hah! I'm the most aggressive person I've ever met," but you don't know that Aries is your Venus or Mercury (or both!), and the Aries boldness may totally overcome any Pisces passivity.

Let me just explain the rudiments of the different placements:

1. SUN: your basic essence, your conscious self-expression, the bottom line of you
2. MOON: your character, your subconscious, your instincts, inner desires, and emotions
3. MERCURY: the way you think, communicate, and express yourself mentally
4. VENUS: your love sign, your attraction sign, influences your love life
5. MARS: your sex drive, your forces of energy, assertiveness
6. JUPITER: your super-conscious, your expansion and opportunity sign
7. SATURN: your ability to analyze and determine
8. URANUS: your ability to be original, inventiveness
9. NEPTUNE: your intuition, inspiration
10. PLUTO: your regeneration, transformation
11. ASCENDANT: your personality, sense of identity, self-image, as the world perceives you

Your Ascendant is your rising sign, the planet on the horizon at the moment of your birth.

So there are eleven different influences and each one is important. However, the first six, up to Jupiter, plus of course your ascendant if you know the exact time of your birth, have the most influence on you. The other planets are at even farther distances, and although they *do* have influence, you're not as affected by them as the first six and your ascendant.

One of the most logical proofs of the accuracy of determining personality traits and characteristics is to look at families with several children. The children have the same mother and father, hence the same genes, and they have had the same environment. So why are some of them so *totally* different and why are some in various stages of alikeness?

In my own family, my brother and I are totally different. I'm a Libran with double Cancer, Capricorn, Scorpio, Virgo, and Aquarius rising. My brother, John, an English lit. professor at the University of California, is a double Sagittarian with Leo, Scorpio, and double Virgo. Now I'm very logical, indecisive, eccentric, super-sensitive, a perfectionist, love silly humor, and I'm sentimental and emotional. My bro is not at all sentimental, eccentric, or indecisive; he's cheerful, organized, blunt, a tad arrogant, and has a witty, dry sense of humor (he's *very* funny). We are not at all alike. The only thing we share are memories.

Try a chart on your own family. But before you do it, write down the outstanding positive and negative traits of each one. Make a list of your mom and dad, sisters and brothers, sons and daughters, and your spouse and/or friend and friends.

Now do a simple chart (it only takes about five minutes and is very easy with my *ASTRO-LOGICAL LOVE* book) and compare with your list. I guarantee you your list will match the charts that you do.

Let's look at some famous people:

O.J. Simpson is a triple Cancer (Sun, Mercury, and Venus), making him *extremely* emotional, moody, and possessive. His

Moon is in Pisces, the *other* very emotional/sensitive sign (boy is *he* emotional!). The three water signs are Cancer, Pisces, and Scorpio (water is the emotional element). His Jupiter is in Scorpio (ruled by Mars, the god of war), giving him great passion and loyalty, but also great jealousy, vindictiveness, and a warlike attitude. His Mars is in Gemini, and when either Venus or Mars is in Gemini, it's almost impossible to be faithful.

Jackie Kennedy Onassis was a double Leo (Sun and Mercury), which gave her great strength and her life great drama. Leo unfortunately also gives great arrogance, particularly when in Mercury, but her soft-spoken demeanor certainly did not show this side of her. She surprisingly had her Venus in Gemini, which, again, almost assures unfaithfulness. The only times I've *ever* seen anyone with Venus or Mars in Gemini be faithful (and out of all the charts I've seen, I've seen this only three times) is when the person is extremely religious. The three people, two married men and one married woman, told me how strong the pull is to cheat on their spouses, but because all three are strict Catholics, they didn't give in to their urges. I would believe this to be true of Jackie. Her first husband, JFK, had the *same* Venus in Gemini, and the world knows how he didn't fight *his* nature—he was compulsively unfaithful. Catholicism means different things to different people, as do *all* religions.

Adolf Hitler was a triple Taurus (Sun, Venus, and Mars), and this made him extremely faithful in any of his romantic relationships and gave him not only his patient and prudent side, but also his obstinance and dogmatism with a definite mean and cruel streak (*all* Taureans have this mean streak, and he was a *triple* Taurus). His Aries Mercury made him think and act boldly, be easily angered, warlike, egocentric, and want to be Number One. He was a double Capricorn (Moon and Jupiter), making him determined, persevering, disciplined, and organized. Capricorn Moon *never* gives up—ever!

Marilyn Monroe was a double Gemini (Sun and Mercury),

and her Moon and Jupiter were in Aquarius. This gave her quadruple air, which made it difficult to keep her feet on the ground and gave her a fey quality (some people called it "flaky"). The Aquarius made her friendly, eccentric, and a real fantasizer living in her own fantasy world, and the Gemini gave her a dual personality and made her unreliable (was she *ever* on time to a movie set?), fun-loving, and wanting to be taken seriously as an "intellect" and a good actress. Her Venus in Aries gave her a sexual boldness (and just a little bossiness), and her Pisces Mars gave her intuitive ability, sensitivity, and a bent toward drugs.

Franklin Delano Roosevelt was a triple Aquarius (Sun, .Mercury, and Venus), making him a warm and friendly guy. Aquarius is the "friendship sign," and all his radio speeches began "My friends" (listen to Sun-sign Aquarians say "my friend" a lot in conversation). It's also a sign of eccentricities and humanitarianism, and he had a lot of both. His Cancer Moon gave him sensitivity and emotion, and his constituents really felt his nurturing nature, which is a strong part of Cancer. His Gemini Mars brought his unfaithful nature, and his ten-year-long affair with his mistress brought great unhappiness to his wife, Eleanor.

Martin Luther King, Jr., had a Capricorn Sun, giving him determination, discipline, and organizational skill; an Aquarius Mercury gave him some eccentricity and the ability to communicate great humanitarian desires; double Pisces Moon and Venus gave him sensitivity, a spiritual bent, and faithfulness, which made a conflict with his Gemini Mars, which impels toward unfaithfulness. Whenever Taurus or Pisces (the two most faithful Venus or Mars signs) is in either planet with the other in Gemini (the most unfaithful), the unresolved conflict will go on for a lifetime: "Do I or don't I cheat?"—and this always causes unhappiness (as does all conflict) until it's resolved.

King Henry VIII was Cancer Sun with Leo Mercury. The Cancer gave him his emotional, nurturing side, and the Leo

Mercury gave him his incredible arrogance. His Moon was in Aries, giving him boldness, leadership , temper-tantrums, and making him easily angered. He had a double Gemini, Venus and Jupiter, and the Gemini Venus impelled him to be often bored sexually and to need new romantic partners (he was *sooo* unfaithful), and his arrogance led him to divorce and behead wives, rebel against Rome, and start his *own* church, the Church of England.

There are certain placements that are easily defined and easily spotted. One of these is the *Leo* arrogance, not necessarily in the Sun sign, which is sunniness, generosity, dynamism (although the arrogance is *sometimes* expressed there), but in the Mercury and Moon, where the arrogance becomes overwhelming and makes those people mentally rigid and unaccepting of any ideas besides their own (they are *always* right!), which really limits their growth. But remember, *becoming aware of this arrogance makes it easier to control it*.

Leo Mercury gives a mental rigidity and arrogance:

Napoleon Bonaparte, Rasputin, Leona Helmsley, Fidel Castro, Henry Ford, Mae West, William Kunstler, Jacqueline Susann, President Bill Clinton, Mary Baker Eddy, Ivan the Terrible, Julius Caesar, George Wallace, Peter Sellers, Mata Hari, Huey Long

Leo Moon gives a certainty of always being right (aka, arrogance):

Winston Churchill, Burt Reynolds, Peter Sellers, Nero, Barbra Streisand, Oscar Wilde, Mao Tse-tung, George Wallace, Bryant Gumble, Prince Phillip, Zubin Mehta, Carly Simon, Chiang Kai-shek, Catherine the Great, Jesse James, Aimee Semple McPherson

Cancer Moons give a warmth and a vulnerability:

Babe Ruth, Theodore Roosevelt, Ralph Waldo Emerson, Henry David Thoreau, Phyllis Diller, Janis Joplin,

Jimie Hendrix, Humphrey Bogart, Eleanor Roosevelt, Franklin Delano Roosevelt, Calvin Coolidge, Ethel Barrymore, Alexander the Great, Ethel Merman

Capricorn Moons never give up until they get what they're after, and this usually comes not early in life but a little later:

Abraham Lincoln, Johnny Carson, David Letterman, Thomas Edison, George Washington, Mia Farrow, Lucille Ball, Dick Cavett, George Washington Carver, Charles Darwin, Clara Barton, Adolf Hitler, Adolf Eichman, Joseph Goebbels, Claude Debussy, General George Patton, Georges Bizet, Napoleon Bonaparte

There are several double, triple, and quadruple *Scorpios* (sometimes called "Scrappios"—they *can* be warlike) that are interesting, Scorpio being a very strong sign of loyalty, passion, invincibility, courage (the soaring eagle), *and/or* vindictiveness, sadism, and ruthlessness (the stinging scorpion):

Charles Manson, quadruple Scorpio; Joseph Goebbels, triple Scorpio; Marie Curie, triple Scorpio; Martin Luther, triple Scorpio

Cancers are so emotional, and when people have Cancer several times in their charts (I, for one), they really have to become aware of their overly emotional natures and work on controlling them:

Ernest Hemingway, Princess Margaret, the Duke of Windsor, Joanne Woodward, Nelson Rockefeller, Lord Byron, Alexander the Great, Henry David Thoreau, Judy Garland, O.J. Simpson, Gina Lollobrigida

Gemini Venus and/or Mars have a tremendous pull to be unfaithful (but remember, this *can* be overcome):

Reggie Jackson, Cher, Franklin Delano Roosevelt, O.J. Simpson, Jackie Kennedy Onassis, John F. Kennedy, Bob Hope, William Shakespeare, Rembrandt, King

Henry VIII, Martin Luther King, Jr., Tyrone Power,
William Randolph Hearst, F. Scott Fitzgerald, Mary
Baker Eddy, Bob Dylan, Amelia Earhart, John Barry-
more, Rudolph Valentino, Julius Caesar, Johannes
Brahms, Louis Armstrong

Taurus, although sensual, earthy, and self-reliant, can also
be obstinate, argumentive, dogmatic, and quite cruel, and
finding out about it can really help in getting rid of the cruelty:

Bing Crosby was a triple Taurus; Gary Cooper, triple
Taurus; Henry Fonda, triple Taurus; Adolf Hitler, triple
Taurus; Karl Marx, triple Taurus; Lenin, triple Taurus

Aquarians are eccentric, and that's part of their charm:

Zsa Zsa Gabor, Eva Gabor, Tallulah Bankhead, Ernie
Kovacs, Mia Farrow, John Barrymore, W.C. Fields,
Carol Channing, Red Buttons, Dick Smothers, Jack
Benny, Ernst Lubitch, Vanessa Redgrave, Norman
Mailer, Gertrude Stein, Jimmy Durante, Humphrey
Bogart, Oprah Winfrey

Pisces are very receptive, sensitive, and intuitive (and
very romantic):

Elizabeth Barrett Browning, quadruple Pisces; Casa-
nova, quadruple Pisces; Elizabeth Taylor, triple Pisces;
Rimsky-Korsakov, quadruple Pisces; Maurice Ravel,
triple Pisces; Michelangelo, triple Pisces; Henry Wads-
worth Longfellow, triple Pisces

Many people have triple and quadruple of the same sign in
their charts:

Capricorn: Elvis Presley, triple Capricorn; Louis
Pasteur, quadruple Capricorn; Henry Miller, triple
Capricorn; Joan of Arc, triple Capricorn

Sagittarius:
Ludwig von Beethoven, triple Sagittarius; Mark Twain,
triple Sagittarius

Aries:

Emile Zola, quadruple Aries; Raphael, triple Aries; Gregory Peck, triple Aries; Tennessee Williams, triple Aries; Gloria Swanson, triple Aries

Libra:

Giuseppe Verdi, triple Libra

Gemini:

Dean Martin, quadruple Gemini

Aquarius:

Wolfgang Amadeus Mozart, quadruple Aquarius; Adlai Stevenson, triple Aquarius

Virgo:

Lyndon Johnson, quadruple Virgo; Leo Tolstoy, triple Virgo; Joseph P. Kennedy, quadruple Virgo

An interesting fact is that many times a person will be attracted to a partner whose Moon is the same as his or her Sun sign:

Frank Sinatra's Moon is Pisces—Barbara Sinatra's Sun is Pisces

Paul Newman's Moon is Pisces—Joanne Woodward's Sun is Pisces

Rose Kennedy's Moon was Virgo—Joe Kennedy's Sun was Virgo

Elizabeth Taylor's Moon is Scorpio—Richard Burton's Sun was Scorpio

John Lennon's Moon was Aquarius—Yoko Ono's Sun is Aquarius

My father's Moon was Aries—my mother's Sun was Aries

It's so important to do your chart and to find out *your* Moon, Mercury, Venus, Mars, Jupiter, etc., and find out *why* you're like you are and how you can change whatever you want to make yourself better and happier.

Then you'll do other people's charts and find out what *they're* really like.

Until you find out, you're really working in the dark. And when you *do* find out, you're going to be way ahead in your search for self-discovery.

Science/Astrology

Most of the great minds of ancient and modern history started out being astrologers—from Hippocrates to Ptolemy and from Copernicus to Newton.

Dr. Franz Hartmann, M.D., wrote in the *Saturday Review*:

> It is extremely difficult for people living in a space age technocracy to realize that the majority of the world's greatest scientists and philosophers of the past were in fact astrologers. Only a few scientists today are studying the influence of the stars and planets on human character . . .

Psychology/Astrology

Carl Jung studied astrology and used it in his later studies of personality. He said that if he were to start over again, he would use astrology even *more* as a tool with psychology. Dr. Jung found that people born under the same zodiacal sign have many personality traits in common. He said that human personalities "coincide in the most remarkable way with traditional astrological expectations."

I have a very close female friend who went to a shrink for three years and then didn't see him for a year or so. Then she went back, and when one day I met her and her doctor right after she re-started, he said to me (in front of my friend) that he couldn't believe she learned so little in the time they had spent together. Then he said to her, "I'm embarrassed that you worked with me for over three years and you haven't changed at all; you've totally rejected any of my suggestions and you're in the same place you were three years ago."

I know my friend very well and I know she's an Aquarian with triple Cancer (Moon, Ascendant, and Jupiter). She's a fantasizer and very emotional. When people fantasize, they don't *have* to change, because in their fantasy they're *already* perfect.

She decided to stop seeing the shrink and work with me in a very unconstructed kind of way.

I spoke to her every day, usually on the phone, and kept reinforcing her slowly growing awareness of being a fantasizer. *All* Aquarians are fantasizers, and that helps them creatively become great composers, writers, actors, and any other profession that takes a lot of imagination. But the downside is they sometimes lose hold of reality. A dear male friend of mine is a *double* Aquarian (Sun and Mercury), and in his mind he's a great musical conductor. He doesn't really have to go out and work at it and get an agent and knock himself out looking for jobs, because when he sits home watching TV he can fantasize about all the great symphonies he's *going* to conduct.

My girlfriend could have gone to the psychologist for years, and he would have been even more perplexed that she wasn't changing and growing. Aquarians can be *very* willful, and of course her shrink didn't know this. But my constant reminder to her that reality is where it's at slowly sank in, and the more she realized that all the things I was saying about her nature were true, the more closely she paid attention.

Also, being a triple Cancer, she's *extremely* emotional, and I keep reminding her that her intellect is shriveling because she uses it so seldom, and she's beginning to at least *try* to detach her self from her strong and so far uncontrolled emotions, and she is improving. It's the first time I've known her that I can definitely see changes, and it's exciting. And it's all happening via the insights of astrology.

If you *truly* want to change, find out about your self. Do a simple, easy, five-minute self-chart with my book *ASTRO-LOGICAL LOVE*. When you do, you will instinctively know that what you're learning is the truth. And you might find conflict there, like one planet making you faithful and the other pulling you to be unfaithful.

Or one warlike planet and one receptive, loving one. Lots of us have conflict in our charts and in our lives, and it's certainly better to know about it and try to work it out so that we understand our selves, rather than blindly going through life being confused and confusing those around us, and never understanding *why* we're so confused as we're being pulled in two different directions.

We cannot express Good until we get rid of the negatives in our personalities, our characters, and our lives.

Astrology was given to us as a tool to help us help our selves. It's there, it's free, and it's probably the biggest help you'll *ever* have to know your self.

Go**o**d is alive and well
and living in each one of us.

9

Go̬d

All my life I thought of God as a person. A spirit-person, but a person. A very wise, kind, good, all-knowing, and all-powerful person. And a He—God has *always* been a male, Father God or God the Father (as in the Catholic Apostle's Creed: "I believe in God the Father almighty, creator of heaven and earth" . . .)

Everyone thinks of God as person. Even those who think they don't, if they search deep enough in the subconscious, will find a feeling about a super-being who in reality has all the human qualities of a person—love, anger, compassion, etc.

The great German philosopher Nietzsche said, "The German imagines even God singing songs!"

The only ones who appear not to think of God as a person are those who don't believe in God altogether. Atheists say there is no God; however, the God they don't believe in is a person-God. They reject the concept of God and the emotionality of the belief in God.

And that belief *is* emotional, is full of feeling. I went twelve years to Catholic school, and I got heavy doses of religious training. And I'm glad I did. It led me to where I am now.

Everything we experience leads us to where we are now. All those hours of catechism stirred up my questioning mind.

"Who is God? God is Love." What could that possibly mean to a five-year-old, a ten-year-old, or a fifteen-year-old? I was a very inquisitive child and I asked a lot of questions. The answers always were, "That is one of the mysteries that we must accept on faith," so I did. Sort of.

But I always was uneasy because no priest or nun ever answered my questions logically. I accepted the mysteries because I was a Catholic and truly believed that Catholicism was the one true church because that was what I was taught. I personally felt sorry for people in other religions because they didn't know that the Catholic Church was actually founded by Jesus when he said to his apostle Peter, "Thou art Peter and upon this rock I will build my church," and of course the name Peter means rock (or so I was told), and Saint Peter was the first pope. My whole life up till I was nineteen I believed Catholicism was the one true church.

When I hit nineteen, I had what I call a "reverse conversion." Just as Saul had been struck by lightning, knocked off his ass (donkey), and suddenly saw that he should change his life for God, and he did, the opposite happened to me.

On a particular Sunday I arose and started getting dressed for Mass as I had done thousands of times before. Up till then I had not only gone to Mass and Communion every Sunday of my life, I had also arisen at 5:30 A.M. every one of the forty days in Lent for many years, made and packed breakfast for my self to take, and gone to 7:00 A.M. Mass. So I was obviously extremely religious up to this point.

But on this particular Sunday when I was nineteen, I got totally dressed and was checking my self out in the bathroom mirror when something clicked in my head. Something—to this day I don't know what, but it must have been my inner voice—got me to take all my clothes off and go back to bed, and I have never been to Mass since then.

At this point I decided to study other religions. Now before this I had converted a few people to Catholicism, six that I know of, so my belief was a deep one. But as I studied the Lutherans and Episcopalians and Christian Scientists and Unitarians, I began to see, at least surfacely, that people actually believed as strongly in their religions as I had in mine.

One of the major problems with all organized religions is that people tend to think *their* religion is the best. Isn't that what's been going on for years and centuries and eons with Protestants and Catholics in Northern Ireland, the Serbs and Muslims in Bosnia, the Jews and Arabs *anywhere*, and all the so-called "holy wars" in history?

If your mom and dad were both Baptists, you probably are one too, and don't we usually think our football team is better, our politics are better, our thinking is better than someone else's? So of course we think our religion is better. If we didn't, we'd join whichever one we *did* think was better.

What my leaving the church boils down to, I believe, is that I was unconsciously rejecting the blind faith and searching out the intellectual answers, if they existed.

I read omnivorously every book I could find on different religions, and my mind was gobbling it all up. As a Catholic I had memorized all the dogma but in reality had understood little. What I *had* felt and loved was the beauty of the pageantry, with the mystery of the Mass in Latin, the incredible incense, and being part of something I believed was good. I am one of the most disciplined persons I've ever met, and I made my self be a fantastic Catholic because I was taught that that was what I should do to go to heaven. And I wanted all good things, including at the very end, heaven.

All my years from then to now I've been searching, through my own thoughts and the thoughts of others, for the true sense of God.

And a few years ago I started to get it. I actually started to see exactly what it's all about. And the more I understood it, the more sure I was of its truth.

I have to have logic in my life. Things have to make sense. And when my catechism asked, "Who is God?," right there it was wrong. "Who" is a person, and I wanted to know *what* is God?

It started to come to me that God is Love (my grammar-school catechism asked and answered: "Who is God? God is Love"), the act of loving.

And in my first book, my dedication is:

"To Love, which is God . . ."

My second book: "To Love, which is God, which is Love . . ."

My third book: To Love, which is God, which is Love, which is God . . ." etc.

I started to see and believe that the *act* of loving was what God was.

But later on I finally *really* got it. I started thinking about Goodness, and I remembered that another answer in the catechism was God is Good. What *is* Good? Good is a universal power. You can't see it, but it's everywhere. Good is all-powerful and all-knowing.

Good is everywhere. It's in the air surrounding you. You breathe it, your pores absorb it, it's everywhere.

Good is all around us and inside us. You don't have to cajole it, you can't plead with it, it can't get angry with you, nor can it be pleased by what you do. Only *you* can do all that. Those are human things.

Good is there, all over, just like electricity is. Electricity always was, yet only recently have we learned how to harness it and use it for our own good. Eons ago people marveled at lightning and thunder. It frightened them because it was uncontrolled. But when we learned how to plug into the wall to make our TV go on, our lights flash on, or our CD player play beautiful music, it didn't frighten us anymore—it gave us great pleasure and a feeling of our power over the elements.

Good is unemotional. God is emotional. God gets angry. Good doesn't. God is pleased and happy when you do the right things, Good isn't. *You* are pleased and happy when you do the right things.

Good just is. Good just exists, sort of waiting for us to realize its presence. Goodness is the expression of Good, and when Good's presence is realized and felt and expressed, a joy and feeling of love unlike any other you've ever felt comes over you.

It's unconditional joy. You can't anger Good and you can't please it. You can anger and please your self and other people, but not Good.

Good is all the Good things you've ever wanted, peace of mind, love, happiness, and it's all there waiting for all of us to feel and realize and tap into.

If we worship Good, that in itself tells us what our thoughts and actions *must be*. And when we worship the Good within us, how could we possibly think or do wrong or feel fearful when we're adoring our own Goodness? And when we worship the Good inside others, even though they may be obnoxious, negative, and destructive, we see the *potential* for Goodness, even if they don't, even if they have totally blocked all of their Good from being expressed.

Every time I see the word "God," I substitute "Good." The word "Good" gives me a feeling of power, that the force of Good is *my* force of Good, that I am actively thinking, feeling, and doing everything to further Good and Goodness in my life and in this world.

But I'm probably the first person who even talked about the God/Good connection, and I'm sure I'm the first who ever substituted the word Good for God. God *is* Good. Good *is* God.

The Golden Rule is supposedly the foundation upon which every religion is based, but how many people who go to church "religiously" every week (and sometimes every day) will "do unto others as they would have others do unto them"?

That's the problem. Preachers preach and members listen, but how many base their lives on what the preacher, rabbi, or priest is saying? I can remember going to Mass and Communion every day in Lent and every Sunday every year till I was nineteen, concentrating on the Mass and sermon, praying to God, and enjoying the camaraderie of seeing my friends and talking and having a good time but not really *actively* trying to be a better person.

Why try to be a *better* person if you don't think you're a good person to begin with? If the priest or any of the nuns had made me feel good about my self, rather than pounding into me my weakness and unworthiness without Jesus, I could have saved over thirty years of shame and shrinks.

In the Catholic Church at that time (it may have changed by now), every Saturday afternoon I would go to confession and in the dark little cubicle tell the priest all the things I'd done wrong the previous seven days. I distinctly remember not knowing what sins I may have committed (or *if* I committed any) and wanting to go to Confession like all the other kids and making up anything that might be a venial sin (probably the other kids were doing the same thing), and always saying more or less the same things: "I lied once and got mad at my mother twice" or "I yelled at my brother and used God's name in vain," and the priest would give me absolution and my penance. "Say five Hail Marys and two Our Fathers," and then I would recite the Act of Contrition: "Oh my God I am heartily sorry for having offended thee, and I detest all my sins because I dread the loss of heaven and the pains of hell . . ."

And yet I grew up into an okay adult. But how much *better* I could have been had I been taught about the Good within me instead of the bad, and the awful guilt that went with it. Hell was always looming over me, and that was *eternal* fire, pain, and suffering. Hell was for *mortal* sins like murder, thievery, divorce, etc. Purgatory was also a threat, but at least it wasn't *forever*, it was just until certain venial sins were cleansed from me when I then could enter the kingdom of heaven (kingdom = king = God).

So many churches preach fear, and many people believe

it's deliberately done to keep parishioners from leaving, that the fear that they'll go to hell if they stop going to church keeps them in tow. I don't believe it's deliberate, I believe that the priest's or minister's mother and dad taught him, and their mothers and dads taught them, and their parents and teachers taught them, and you can go back centuries and trace the teachings of fear.

The thing that's the *most* wrong is that everyone is taught that in and of our selves we're nothing, that it's God and/or Jesus within us that are our strength and our salvation, that we're so nothing that without God/Jesus/Allah/Jehovah, etc., we are *doomed!*

We are taught *not* to believe in our selves!

I subscribe to a religious monthly newsletter called *The Plain Truth* and it has some very beautiful and interesting articles in it that I enjoy. But the November 1994 issue has a story "*I want to accept Jesus, but . . .*" and it says:

> ". . . If Jesus had not been resurrected, then we would have no salvation; we would have no hope; we would have no future. But he is risen . . ."

> ". . . Through Jesus, our sins are forgiven. Through Jesus, we have access to God and the Holy Spirit. Only by the name of Jesus are we given salvation . . ."

> ". . . As the Bible tells us, Christians are counted as righteous because of what Christ did for us. Not because of what we do. . ."

I couldn't believe the last line when I read it . . . "*Not because of what we do . . .*" What *we* do is totally irrelevant, it's only what Jesus Christ did that counts. No wonder so many people are having problems accepting personal responsibility. If what we do doesn't count, then you don't *have* to be a good person, you don't *have* to do the right thing, all you *have* to do is believe in Jesus. Talk about giving people an out regarding responsibility for our actions!

Then ". . . A commitment to Christ requires faith" . . . what about faith in the Goodness within our selves, belief in our own abilities? Now *that's* something that could *really* change a person—if one could *really* believe in one's self, mountains could be moved.

". . . Through Jesus we have access to God . . ." How sad that people are being taught that we can't get to God on our own, that we have so little power, so little strength, and so little *anything* without Jesus. According to this we can't "have access to God" without Jesus.

There has been a tremendous interest in angels in the last few years, and Robert M. Perry, Ph.D., a retired professor of religion, believes that angels are believed in because of an intense human need. He's quoted in *Longevity*: "I suspect it started with the idea of a God too perfect to contact. You had to have a means of access, and the perfect man or woman, an angel, becomes that means. So what's the truth in angel stories? Just the truth of human want, which is a very big truth indeed."

We can't reach God without an intermediary!

And this is not just Christianity, it's *all* religions. There seems to be no religion that preaches just goodness, kindness, and honesty; they all have temples, mosques, retreats, churches, reading rooms, etc., which you must go to to worship God, Jesus, Jehovah, Allah, etc. And if you don't go there, God will be upset (not to mention the preacher!).

Is God better than Jehovah, is Allah better than Buddha? The most wonderful thing about worshiping Good is that you can't say, "My Good is better than your Good." Good is absolute and is exactly the same for you as it is for me. Good just is.

I know a man who is extremely religious, believes that Jesus is his savior, and is also a very good man. He's honest, forthright, kind, and lives a highly principled life with his wife and five adult children. I know there must be many religious people who go to church daily or weekly, who believe in Jesus as their God and their savior, who are truly good.

Religions can be very Good. The fact that many Catholics are strong against unfaithfulness in marriage and for celibacy before marriage, that many Protestants believe that honesty is always the best policy, that many Jews believe that the family unit is the ultimate joy to be protected and cherished and they do exactly that, that many Buddhists believe that inner cleanliness of body is as important as cleanliness of spirit, and of course that many Mormons believe and practice the same outside and inside purity (no smoking, no alcohol, no drugs of any kind), shows us that there are religious people who are truly good.

The problem is that *many* people who go to church aren't. Many of these people are not honest, are full of fear, and are easily angered. And many of these people pray fervently to their God, and then figure out who they're going to lie to, cheat, put down, and take advantage of when they finish praying. They obviously believe in a God who will let them do anything they want as long as they continue to pray to Him.

Ralph Waldo Emerson said, "What you do speaks so loud that I cannot hear what you say."

Some religious people believe that God wants them to kill those who believe in religions different from theirs. Others believe that God looks the other way when they doctor the books of their business and cheat their partners or Uncle Sam. They think that as long as they go to church and pray, God approves their lying under oath in a courtroom.

There is a veil of mystery around God, but every thinking person, churchgoing or not, can see and understand that the *bottom line* to *all* religions should be Goodness and expressing Good. If believing in Jesus and/or God helps you be a Good person, then that's Good. But if believing in Jesus and/or God makes you shirk your responsibility and think you don't have to be or act Good as long as you go to church, you must know that you're kidding yourself.

Your conscience—your inner voice—will tell you if an act is Good or not, and if you follow that inner voice, it makes no difference whatever else you do or don't do.

From God to Go͎d

The most beautiful interior of any edifice I have ever seen is Temple Emanu-el in New York City. It's breathtakingly beautiful on the inside, and it's the largest Jewish temple in the world. For several months my husband and I used to go Friday nights for the 5:15 P.M. services, and that's where I started substituting Good for God while reading the prayer book:

Praised be the glory of Go͎d in all the world.

Our Go͎d and Go͎d of our fathers, may thy kingdom come speedily, that worship of thy name and obedience to thy law may unite all men in brotherhood and peace.

Of all things the most necessary to him who would serve Go͎d is trust in Go͎d.

But the Jewish religion, like most other religions, preaches that God should be not only loved, but feared:

. . . let the glories of a just, righteous and God-fearing people increase from age to age . . .

One of the things I love about Good is you don't have to fear it. All you have to do is love it, and you can even go so far as to adore it, in your self, in others, in animals and all of nature around us. And to adore Good, you have to *be* Good. And to be Good, you have to *do* Good. You don't have to concentrate on being Good, just *do* Good and you will *be* Good. To love Goodness means you love all the things that *are* Good, like truth, honesty, justice, courage, and principles.

The pain of being unloved is not the absence of love, but in seeing our selves as unlovable.

How sad that we are not taught about how Good and

wonder-full and loving we are, but rather how unworthy and bad and innately sinful we are. No wonder I had so many relationships with the wrong men—I needed to constantly verify that I *was* lovable. "Look how many men have loved me! I really must be a lovable person."

I started as a teen and didn't stop till I finally purged my mind of all my unworthiness that had been pounded into me by my mother and my teachers. They were all either well-meaning but ignorant, or emotionally unstable, and these kinds of role models, examples, and guides are what push millions of kids into drugs and/or crime.

If you see your self as unworthy and bad, how many good things are you going to do? And drugs are an escape—when you're high, you can fantasize what a great person you *really* are. The only problem is you can't stay high forever, and when you sober up, reality hits you hard that you're *still* unworthy and bad.

Mark Twain said, "Keep away from people who try to belittle your ambitions. Small people always do that, but the really great make you feel that you, too, can become great."

Most of us want and feel we need God to take care of us, to watch over us and keep us from danger. Sort of a strong father who loves us, protects us, gives us what we need when we need it, and is always there to forgive us when we're bad. Like a terrific parent *should* be (in our imaginations), for most of us who didn't have one. Or what we would imagine an ideal father to be. Someone we look up to, respect, love, and maybe even idolize.

When we have this omnipotent father, God, we can do anything we want and He will forgive us if we say we're sorry, then we'll do it again and He'll forgive us again, ad infinitum.

What we *don't* want is to take responsibility for our selves, our actions, and our lives.

The *only* answer is Good. When we see and understand that Good *had* to create us because Good just *is* and can't express itself—that's why we were created by Good—it *needs us* to express itself. When we *do* express Good, we *become* Good, we *are* Good.

Abraham Lincoln said, "When I do good, I feel good. When I do bad, I feel bad. And that's my religion."

Someone once said that "Goodness is its own reward," and it is. *Nothing* can make us as happy and as fulfilled as doing Good. But when we love and adore Good and it becomes something that we want to express *all* the time, there are lots of *other* rewards:

1. Peace of mind—being a Good person means we will have no qualms of conscience, we'll be relaxed and at peace with our selves and the world at all times. Euripides, that wise Greek, said, "There is one thing alone that stands the brunt of life throughout its length: A quiet conscience."

2. No fear—When Good is our Source and fills every crevice of our being, there is no room for anything *but* Good. Fear can't get a toehold because there's no place to hang on—every single space is filled with Goodness and truth.

3. No envy—we'll know that the Good within us will show us what we have to do to get what we want and will lead us there. And we'll know that whatever anyone else has we can *also* have if we use the Power of Good.

4. No jealousy—Good will lead us to understand that Good is *unlimited* in its scope. Up till now we've always thought there's only so much potentially available money or success in the world, that these are limited, so if someone else makes money or makes a success, we've always felt there's so much *less* left now for us. But the *truth* is that the Power of Good is *unlimited*, and whatever we can imagine (image-in) we want, with Good's Power behind us, we can and will get it. We will be genuinely happy when a friend succeeds because we will know that our friend's success only proves that

Good is working, and will work *equally* for us. There is *no* limit to Good.

5. No anger—fear is behind *every* negative emotion, and without fear, anger could never exist. Without anger, hostility and violence are gone. When we allow Good to take over our minds and our actions, all fear leaves. Good and fear *cannot* coexist.

6. No self-pity—"Why me, God?" will disappear from our minds. We will begin to realize that *we* are in charge of using our Good, *we* are the directors of Good inside us and around us. When a tragedy strikes, we will understand that this is for our growth and was directed by us (totally super-consciously) to happen. When John F. Kennedy was killed, his brother Bobby was inconsolable, and on a TV special it was said that Bobby "was reconciling his belief in God." When we believe in God, we want to know why our "Father" would do something so terrible as take a loved one, would allow children to die or be killed, would allow airplanes to crash, killing hundreds, would allow earthquakes, floods and wars, killing tens of thousands. When we believe in Good and adore Good and Goodness, we are beyond human understanding and see that even tragedy has a purpose in Good, and we begin to accept *everything* as either Good or the absence of Good.

Something I find extraordinarily interesting is the meaning of the word "sin." Sin comes from the Latin "sine" or "without," but of course sin has come to mean something inherently bad. But the *truth* of the matter is that sin only means "without Good" or "without God"—it has no moral good/bad connotation to it, but religions have made it mean bad in and of itself.

When you're without Good, all you have to do is become aware of Good, and then become Good by *doing* Good, to bring it back into your life, and any and all so-called sin leaves.

And "original sin," which some religions say we were born with (and I believed in for many years), is a heinous concept. I was taught that every baby ever born is and was tainted with the "original sin" of Adam and Eve and only baptism in that religion could expunge that "badness," and if the baptism doesn't happen and the baby dies, it spends eternity in Limbo. It never goes to heaven. Sounds like a pretty un-loving belief to me.

A few weeks ago I was lying in bed at the end of the day, tired and just a little down. I wanted and needed comfort. I was relaxing, and thinking and feeling regressively of Father God, and I felt safer and comforted. I felt for the moment that someone was taking care of me.

I wanted and needed to feel loved, which is of course passive. Children need to feel loved. All of a sudden I thought, "Why do I, an adult, need someone to take care of me? *I want and need to love, not be loved* (if I am *loving*, I will be loved by others in this life). So instead of wanting or needing Good to love me (impossible—Good is not a person), I want to love Good. I want to actively adore my Good, which created me to express itself, and that makes me feel not only loving, but also in charge of my own life.

"With Good I feel stronger and more able to take care of my *self*—Good empowers me to take care of me. If I think and act Good, that power of Good is *my* power. I no longer need *another* being to help me or take care of me, *I* will take care of me. I feel much *stronger* believing in Good. The weaker, more passive me needed to believe in a Father God who takes care of weak, passive me."

We all at one time or another (and probably most of us still) have believed that God is usually very loving but can get angry and punish us if we are bad, and will reward us if we are good. Now intellectually that is ridiculous. God is *not* a person, never was, and never will be.

But it's *simpler* to think of God as a person. It takes no real thought to imbue God with human feelings. "God loves me when I'm good and gets angry with me when I'm bad. And if I beg God for something, and I'm *really* good, God will give it to me." Of course, when we *don't* get what we want, we rationalize and think maybe we weren't good *enough* at that moment to get what we wanted.

It's just like it was when we were kids. We could cajole Mom and sometimes get what we wanted, and other times if she was in a bad mood, she would whack us if we asked for anything.

Everything was emotional then. We laughed, we cried, we yelled, we got angry, we were afraid. We were little more than our feelings.

The only place we used our brains was in school. We learned to read, write, add, subtract, and find Nigeria and Albania on the map.

But we never went beyond this. We accepted whatever we were taught about God. I learned my catechism from the nuns and priests. Some learned from ministers, rabbis, yogis, mothers and fathers.

We were fed religious info the same as were fed all other info—our little sponge-minds sopping up God as a sometimes loving and sometimes angry person who was our Creator.

We were also taught fear. "If you do that, I'm going to get the policeman to put you in jail." "Don't go in the water, you might drown," "If you're bad, God is going to punish you forever in hell." And this was the beginning of our negative emotions. This was when we left the Garden of Eden.

Conscious fear entered my life when my mother used to sing an olde English ditty to me. "Today is the day they give babies away with a half a pound of tea." She may or may not have meant to frighten me, but the panic I felt when I thought that she was going to give me away was so intense that it stayed with me subconsciously all these years, and only several years ago did the feelings of fear come back to me as I vividly started to remember this despicable song.

We exited Paradise when fear entered our lives. Fear is at

the bottom of *every* negative emotion, from jealousy to anger, from envy to panic. Fear is at the bottom of *every* negative action, from lying to cheating, from arrogance to cruelty. And many years ago, in 1976, to be exact, I realized that I had gone as far as I could alone in trying to banish fear from my life, that I now needed some kind of spiritual help to root out the terrible debilitating force of fear that was a part of my every thought and action. And that was when I decided to meditate.

Every single morning since 1976 I have done my daily meditation. I do it in bed right after I've done my breathing exercises, my stretching, and my face exercises. I have never missed a day. Once in a great while if I have a plane to catch or an early TV or radio interview and I'm a little on the late side, I will do it in a cab on my way to the TV station or the airport, or I'll do it at the airport as I await my flight, or I'll even do it on the plane. But I almost always do it when I awaken. I *never* forego it. It makes me feel so good and gets me in a good mood for the day.

It connects me with the Good inside me, and that Goodness makes me feel, think, and be the very best I can be, and that really makes me feel good.

Back in '76 when I started, I made up my own original meditation, and through the years it has changed a lot. It's very important that you make up your own *original* meditation. If you take a standard meditation that lots of other people do, it might help you to an extent, but if you make up your *own* meditation that's just for you, the more personal it is, the better it's going to be to help you.

Through the years I've asked for many good things, and as I've received them, I drop them out of my meditation.

Back in 1976 I believed strongly in God even though I didn't have a clear idea of what God was. I knew it wasn't a person, but in order to meditate I acted like God *was* a person. I would say, "God adores me and wants me to have everything I want." Now only a *person* could want me to have something.

I continued to think of God as someone who loved and

adored me and took care of me, sort of like my father did when he was alive. It was an emotional reaction to my meditation, but it seemed to work for me. It helped me to overcome some fears and to feel not so much alone. I felt there was *someone* taking care of me.

Then about 1985 I felt I needed something more to capture the feeling of being loved and protected, so I changed the "God" to father and mother nicknames. I actually started speaking *to* God, not *about* God. I was saying "Father (or sometimes Dad, Daddy, or even Mummy), adores me and wants me to have everything I want." The funny thing is I never had a "Mummy" or a mother who really expressed love to me, so this was kinda fun.

I felt much better emotionally about that. It gave me a feeling of closeness with God, that I could actually speak to this loving being and not just be objective—I was really *personally* involved with God.

But after a while my inner self grew to the point where my mind took a jump and I started to see and think and feel how weak and helpless I felt when I needed God, and prayed to Him. Then I began to see and think and feel the indivisibility of God and Good. As soon as these thoughts entered my consciousness, I grabbed them. I held on to them, and I kept thinking about them for days.

It really started sinking in that Good and Goodness, and the state of Good, are the source of everything. The more I thought about this, the more I felt the truth of it, the more I felt strong being a part of Good. It was the very beginning of the realization that Good and fear cannot coexist. If I am full of Good, there will be no fear. If I am full of Good, there *can* be no fear.

Good is the ultimate. It's not a person, it's not a spirit, it's not a thing, it just *is*. It's actually a Force and a Power.

And each one of us is born with it, and it stays with us till we depart this plane. But we don't always know we have it.

We are personalized Good. *We* are the directors of Good.

That's why we have brains and a free will. We can choose to express Good or we can choose not to.

What appears to be evil is but the absence of Good.

So when we choose *not* to express Good, all kinds of terrible things happen. Read the Bible about pestilence and war and plagues. Except the Bible calls "Him" God.

And many people really believe that bad people are those who make all the money and are successful, and good people are the schnooks in the world slaving away at stupid jobs they hate while they envy the successes.

But the truth of the matter is, if you recognize that Good is almighty, that Good is your one and only Source, and you truly *become* Good and express *only* Good (no lying, no cheating, no jealousy), you will tap into the Power of Good and you will not feel weak and helpless as you do with God. That's why we beg God to help us, because we're weak and God is strong. But believing in Goodness will make *you* feel strong, because Good is strong and empowers you to take care of *your self*.

To know what Good is and what you're adoring, just imagine the inside part of you that's beautiful, that's truly kind and gentle, that part that is loving and has a child-like innocence that wants to love and trust everyone. Just imagine the part of you that doesn't want to lie, doesn't want to cheat or steal. That's the Goodness, the Good in you, that's the *real* you. Take away the fear, and you will be amazed that all the anger and jealousy and vindictiveness will disappear, and what's there is what's always been there—Good and Goodness just waiting to be recognized and adored.

Let me show you my meditation. This I created for my self, and again, even though you could use mine or any other meditation, it's very important that you think up and do your *own original* meditation, that you make it personal with what's important to you.

Or start out with mine or any other one, and keep whatever

makes you respond positively, and gradually change the rest to words that mean a lot to you.

I always begin:

"Good is my source.
Good is my *only* Source.
Good is my Source of everything."

My source is the very bottom line of me, what I'm all about, my essence. And if Good *is* my source, then there's no room for any fear or any of the other negatives.

And I think about Good and Goodness and how I want to try to do only good—nothing dishonest, nothing mean, only Good. I am *totally* relaxed, no fears, no negatives, only love and relaxation.

Then I start with my own personal affirmations: "I am forever young" (and I visualize my self full of energy and electricity) "and healthy" (I visualize my body feeling great) "and up" (I unconsciously smile because I *feel* "up"). "Good is my Source."

Then I say, "Every cell in my body is young and clean" (I think about how I keep my body clean inside by taking all the antioxidants several times a day and that keeps my cells clean) "and filled with Good and love and energy" (I visualize all the cells in my body filled with the relaxed feeling of love and the excitement of energy) "and getting younger and younger and younger" (and I think about getting cleaner inside and always getting healthier). "Good is my Source."

Then I say, "I am forever relaxed and confident and feeling my love and my Good" (I think about my Goodness that wants to be expressed, and about the love within me that also wants to be expressed) "and self-reliant and decisive and energetic and organized and filled with Good." And I visualize the Power of Good filling up my body.

I used to use the word "fearless" after "organized," but I started to become aware that the word made me *fearful*; it conjured up visions of old fears, so I dropped that word and replaced it with "filled with Good," which *really* works for me.

"And having fun . . . life is an adventure." I love this last part because I don't want to do *anything* that isn't fun, and I visualize all the adventures awaiting me—love, travel, great success, and all the other exciting and fun things I expect to find in my future.

Now I say, "I adore my Good, and the Power of my Good with my thinking-without-emotion, will lead me to everything I want."

And then I list all the things I want (which I'll get to in a minute).

You know why the Power of Good works? Because you have to *express* Good. If you really love Good, you must *do* Good, and that automatically makes you *be* Good.

The *only* reason people lie and cheat and steal is because they are afraid that if they *don't* steal (ideas, money, belongings), they won't have good things. Think about the times you may have done any of these negative things, and you'll realize that fear was the motivation. You were afraid if you didn't steal, you would be powerless.

And trust me, Good is the most powerful force in the world. There is nothing as powerful as a good person, a good idea, a good anything. So *real* power comes with Good.

Good is fearless. And once you truly understand Good and tap into it, you will truly begin to change your life and get all the things you want:

"I adore my Good, and the power of my Good with my thinking-without-emotion will lead me to everything I want:

Love, energy, health, babies, children, a happy marriage, friends, excitement, travel, fame, fortune, multimillionairedom, success, feeling my Good and the power of my Good within me, feeling love for my Good and for Goodness everywhere, and fun—life is an adventure . . . Good is my Source."

Over a period of time I've mentioned many very specific things I've wanted (and you must put in every single thing you want), like getting a new mortgage, getting more respect for the one you love, making a specific business deal, getting money for something you may be working on, and of course I've dropped all the things I've received, like lawsuits I've won or settled, finishing my comedy film *PK*, finishing my new film GOOD (so I only want to release it successfully now), meeting a wonderful man and falling in love, and lots of other things that I meditated on. Sometimes I meditated for years and sometimes for months before they happened, but they always happen.

Because Good is my Source . . .

Vegetarians

I am a vegetarian and have been one since 1968. I stopped eating all meat and fish because I don't believe in killing. I also don't wear any leather or animal skins (I have the most beautiful polyurethane shoes, boots, purses, and belts you've ever seen. I bought three pairs of cowboy boots, one red, one black, and one white, and when I wear any of them, *everyone* always comments on how gorgeous they are. I always ask people how much they think I paid [of course they think they're alligator], and they say anywhere from $250 to $750, and they faint when I tell them $29.95.)

I have several gorgeous fake furs (I have recurring visions of an anti-fur person throwing paint all over my beautiful fakes!).

I don't believe in killing people and I don't believe in killing animals.

Up till now I sort of soft-pedalled my personal morals. You do your thing and I'll do mine. That's sort of what I said in my first five books. I told people I was a vegetarian, but I didn't push it.

But the longer I've lived, the more introspective I've become, and the more I feel like urging people to do the right thing. I've always tried to do the right thing and I personally would be happy and welcome it if someone pointed out to me my ignorance about some issue and/or my näiveté if I am doing something wrong. So I'm going to do unto you as I would have you do unto me.

Now I'm not saying you're deliberately doing the wrong thing if you're eating meat and/or fish. I ate meat my whole life till 1968 and I didn't have a clue that it wasn't right to do it. My conscience didn't bother me, because that's where I was mentally, emotionally, and spiritually up to that time.

But if someone I respected had talked and explained to me when I was a very young adult about vegetarianism, I would have stopped eating meat years earlier. Or if someone I loved and respected had advised me as a child, I would have done it then.

Then I went to Argentina, the beef capital of the world, and I lived there on and off for a few years. I was staying at the Palace Hotel on Avenida Florida, and one night for no apparent reason something clicked in my mind and I decided never to eat meat or fish again.

I had tried several years before that to stop because the idea and thought of killing animals seemed such a cruel and barbaric act to me, and was slowly getting more and more strong in my consciousness, but every time I'd go out to dinner (which was often then in my dating years), I'd look at a menu and see nothing vegetarian, and lacking the insight then to order a plate of all the terrific side dishes (which can be really delicious) that come with the meat and fish entrees, I'd always end up ordering a meat or fish dinner.

Then came my conversion in Argentina and I haven't eaten any animal since then.

Now if one had to eat animal protein to be healthy, we'd have no choice, but the truth is that vegetable protein is as good if not *better* for us to make us strong and vital and bursting with health.

Lots of people think being a vegetarian makes you weak,

but believe me, that's not true. One of the many health newsletters I subscribe to I cancelled because this ignorant doctor did two pages on how vegetarianism will weaken you, and he actually made fun of vegetarians and likened us to fragile little old ladies in tennis shoes (I would bet you I'm much healthier than he is). When I read that, I couldn't believe it. Now I know many doctors are closed-minded and resistant to new ideas (even long-term *proven* ideas), but this guy was *so* ignorant and fact-resistant about vegetarianism that he must have been about other new discoveries too. If he hadn't written anything, I never would have known, but he was so *proud* of his great knowledge about vegetarianism being totally bad for you that he was actually *arrogant* about it. Anyway, enough of ignorance.

I love the fact that the toughest and strongest animal in the world, the elephant, is a vegetarian. Also hippos and rhinoceroses, two very powerful animals, eat only vegetation. And one of the fastest animals in the world, a thoroughbred racehorse, never eats animal protein, only vegies. So you can see how ludicrous it is to think that vegetarians are weak.

And physiologically not one part of our anatomy is equipped to eat meat. Carnivores' teeth are long, sharp, and pointed, and their jaws *only* move up and down for biting and tearing flesh. We humans have flat molars for grinding side to side when we eat fruits, vegetables, seeds, and nuts.

In Harvey and Marilyn Diamond's best-seller, *Fit For Life*, Harvey says:

> I wonder how many vegetarians there would be if, when people wanted a piece of steak, they had to go out, beat a defenseless steer to death, cut it open, and wade through the blood and guts to slice out the particular parts of beef they desired.

I feel I must discuss something that will probably make you sick as it does me. The more sensitive you are to the pain and suffering of others, the more it will sicken you.

The abattoirs, or slaughterhouses, are to me the saddest places on the face of this earth. Whenever I see one, I literally get ill (a big TV station in Louisville, Kentucky, is adjacent to one, and I hate going there because I have to pass it to get to the TV show). Animals are sentient beings. Of course they can't communicate with us with language, but they have varying degrees of intelligence. And they *are* intelligent.

Anyone who's ever had an animal as a pet, from a dog or a cat to a horse or a bird, will know that what I'm saying is true. Animals have strong feelings. They know fear, they do get angry when provoked, and they certainly feel love. I've had many, many animals in my life, and I can honestly say that I've loved them as much as I've loved people, and when each one died, I felt I lost a close friend.

My French poodle, Maurice Chevalier II, was super-intelligent and I loved him dearly. We were together nineteen years and had an extremely close bond. Two instances of his intellect (if I may call it that): One day I drove my car with Maurice to go to the Unemployment Insurance Office in Hollywood. It's when I first started acting on TV and between jobs all actors went to U.I. (we called it that because Universal International was known as U.I., and when you told someone where you were going, it sounded like you had a major interview at one of the biggest studios in Hollywood).

I had a Ford convertible, and the top was up but the back window was zipped out. I parked across from U.I. on Santa Monica Boulevard in the street in front of a tiny little outside mall of about ten stores, seven going across and three going down this space of about 150 feet, looking like a 7, three across and five down. I went across the street to the U.I. office and left Maurice in the car. I had taught him *never* to go in the street. I used to walk him without a leash, and he never went past the curb. Once in a while to test him I'd throw a ball into the street, and he'd run to the curb and stop. He wouldn't go any farther.

I was in U.I. for about twenty minutes, came out, got in

the car, and drove off. I got to my apartment about ten minutes later and panicked when I looked for Maurice and saw he wasn't there. I must have been so preoccupied and thought he was asleep on the backseat floor. Well, I drove so fast back to U.I., I made it literally in less than five minutes.

I quickly parked the car and started looking for him in the minimall. I called him, but he didn't come. I started to go into each store, and each owner or manager told me yes, he'd been around several times looking for me, but he then went out each time. At the fourth store a woman told me she'd been watching him for a half hour as he went from store to store.

I kept yelling his name out, and finally he came bounding out of the next store toward me. I can't tell you how happy I was. This woman said she'd watched him go to the sidewalk curb several times, and he'd stop and come back to the stores looking for me. If he'd *ever* stepped into the street onto Santa Monica Boulevard, it would have been all over. This little sweetpea figured out I was somewhere around and he wanted to find me. And if you think *I* was happy to find him, you should have seen him when he found me.

The second instance was a *real* intelligent move on Maurice's part. I was now living in New York (boy was that hard to now get him to do his biz in the street—I'd pick him up and put him in the street near the curb and he'd jump back up, scared to death of doing wrong. He didn't def at all for days, till finally he understood it was okay now to go in the street).

Anyway, I had an apartment on Central Park South, an L-shaped studio. A ten-foot-long closet wall created an entry hall. One day Maurice was sitting at the front door and I put a large suitcase horizontally across the entry hall, one end against the wall and the other end of the suitcase against the sliding doors of the ten-foot coat closet, blocking Maurice's way to walk into the living room. I wanted to see how high he'd jump to come to me. I wondered if he'd try to jump over the suitcase, which was about two feet high, or if he'd decide it was too high to try and just give up and stay sitting there. I was on the other side of the suitcase and called him to come into the living room.

I watched him as he contemplated the height of the suitcase. Then he did an amazing thing. He turned to the closed closet, nudged the one sliding door open with his nose and his paw, walked into the closet and nudged the sliding door open from the inside, and walked out to me in the living room, bypassing the suitcase, which was blocking the entry hall.

That was a real thinking process. I don't know if a five-year-old kid would have figured that one out, but Maurice did.

If you think about killing animals, and I'd like you to think about it for a moment, you'll begin to see how barbaric it is. We take beings with lesser intelligence than we have, and we brutally murder them. I once by mistake started reading about *how* they are killed, and I was so upset I couldn't get it out of my mind for days. I won't tell you about it because it's too gruesome and it bothers me too much, but it's the most inhumane, brutal, and cruel act that any human can imagine.

And do you think these animals don't *know* what's going to happen to them? Do you think they cannot hear the screams of the other animals being murdered? And what happens when a body is panicked or terrorized? The glandular excretions into the body are poison. I only say this in case the pain of the animal doesn't reach you; I know the thought of all the hormones you get might really bother you.

This book is about Good. And I'd like you to think about how good could it be to kill an animal?

Those of you who read the Bible know that one of the Ten Commandments is, "Thou shalt not kill." It does *not* state "Thou shalt not kill people" or "Thou shalt not kill humans."

The Bible says, "Thou shalt not kill."

And here are some wonderful quotes from some far-seeing people. . . .

Leonardo da Vinci, 1452–1519
"I have from an early age abjured the use of meat, and

the time will come when men such as I will look upon the murder of animals as they now look upon the murder of men."

Isaac Bashevis Singer, a well-known Jewish writer, walked into a kosher dairy restaurant in New York that he'd been going to for years, and the by-now-familiar waiter who'd been attending him all this time said, "May I ask you a question, Mr. Singer?" and when he nodded, the waiter said, "Do you *not* eat chicken because of your health?" and Isaac Bashevis Singer said, "No, it's for the chicken's health."

Henry David Thoreau, 1817–1862
"I have no doubt that it is a part of the destiny of the human race, in its gradual improvement, to leave off eating animals, as surely as the savage tribes have left off eating each other when they came in contact with the more civilized."

George Bernard Shaw, 1856–1950
"But death is better than cannibalism. My will contains directions for my funeral, which will be followed not by mourning coaches, but by herds of oxen, sheep, swine, flocks of poultry . . . all wearing white scarves in honor of the man who perished rather than eat his fellow-creatures."

Adam Smith, 1723–1790
"It may indeed be doubted whether butcher's meat is anywhere a necessary of life. Grain and other vegetables . . . can, without any butcher's meat, afford the most plentiful, the most wholesome, the most nourishing, and the most invigorating diet. Decency nowhere requires that any man should eat butcher's meat . . ."

Albert Schweitzer, 1875–1965
"When so much mistreatment of animals continues,

when the cries of thirsty beasts from our railway cars die out unheard, when so much brutality prevails in our slaughterhouses, when animals meet a painful death in our kitchens from unskilled hands, when animals suffer incredibly from merciless men and are turned over to the cruel play of children, we all bear the guilt for it."

Ovid, 43 B.C.
"Earth is generous with her provision, and her sustenance. It is very kind; she offers, for your tables, food that requires no bloodshed and no slaughter."

Hindu Law Codes
"He who permits [the slaughter of an animal], he who cuts it up, he who kills it, he who buys or sells [meat], he who cooks it, he who serves it up, and he who eats it [must be considered as] the slayers [of the animal]."

Buddhist Sacred Text
"He who walks in compassion, therefore, ought not to eat meat."

Gandhi, 1869–1948
"I have always been in favour of a pure vegetarian diet."

Leo Tolstoy gave a dinner party, and when one of his friends, a Russian woman, entered the dining room, she was shocked to find a live chicken tied to her chair. Tolstoy, a total vegetarian, told her that because she was the only meat-eater there, he would greatly appreciate it if she would kill the chicken.

The word "vegetable" comes from the Latin word *vegetus* which means "lively," and when you become a vegetarian you *will* be more energetic. Amazingly enough, five percent of the U.S. (over 10 million people and growing daily) are vegetarians in 1994.

Several years ago I gave a birthday party for my friend Virginia Graham. Her birthday is July Fourth, so we had a barbecue in the backyard and served bogus burgers (called Sunshine Burgers). They are absolutely delicious, and I defy anyone to tell they're not real when they're cooked on a barbecue, and put on a sesame-seed roll with mustard, catsup, onion, pickle, etc. Of course I told no one. When all the burgers were eaten and Ginny, her daughter, TV talk show host Lynn Graham, and all her friends were still raving about how great they were, I *then* told them they weren't real meat. No one (including Ginny or Lynn) would believe me.

Every Thanksgiving and Christmas the "turkey" and "duck" with brown gravy would fool anyone, especially with fresh cranberry sauce, baked yams, brussel sprouts, and pumpkin-mince pudding.

And at parties, sesame "chicken" and "beef" with orange sauce are so delicious that people can't believe they're not the real thing. And the "chicken salad" in a sandwich (or in a salad) would fool anyone. You may not be ready to stop eating meat and fish yet, but think about all the yummy vegetarian meals you can easily make and eat.

Also, it's important for all you pet owners to know that now you can get vegetarian pet food that's amino-acid balanced, making it as good as meat or fish for your dog or cat. Some pet stores carry it and also some pet catalogs. Hairy, Maggie, Chauncey, and Nathan are all thriving on it.

My significant other became a vegetarian when we met. This was before I came out so strongly against killing, so he did it all on his own. He'd been reading about how bad meat is for you with the fat and hormones, etc., and of course he loved animals too. He'd tried for years, but no one else he was around would go along with him, so he didn't stick with it because he didn't know about great vegie recipes (he says, "How many baked squashes can you eat?").

He's now becoming a gourmet vegetarian cook, and his dishes are so delicious that you'll wonder once you try some of the great recipes why you never tried this before. I mean *really* delicious! His sauteéd portobello mushrooms are awesome!

And vegetables are a lot *cheaper* than meat too. You'll save money, you'll save your health, you'll gain enormous sensitivity, and your conscience will tell you every day what a Good person you are. . . .

Evil

One of the major problems with dealing with evil is that we tend to make excuses for the evildoer. I know I used to do this. I'd *always* say that anybody who did evil must be insane because a rational person *couldn't* commit a terrible crime. By my saying that, I was saying that evildoers were really not responsible for the evil done, that they weren't mentally capable of knowing that what they were doing was evil. And even lesser wrongdoings I would excuse because I always felt there was something beyond the person's control that made him or her do it.

I have since realized the fallacy of my thinking. Wrongdoing is not to be excused. We must pay for our negative acts because we *chose* to do them.

Everyone *does* have a choice, and I finally realized (with the help of some insight) that *all* wrongdoers know that what they're doing is wrong because they all try to hide the crime and/or run and hide themselves after the crime. This is a very important part, because it's obvious that the people know what's been done is wrong or they wouldn't have to lie and/or hide.

Didn't Susan Smith make up a story about the black carjacker who kidnapped her two small children? Didn't the Menendez brothers have a story concocted and an alibi at the ready? Didn't the killer of the abortion doctor in Florida in 1994 flee and hide? Doesn't *everyone* who does wrong hide? It's pretty obvious that evildoers *know* they're evil, else why the cover-ups? They know it's evil or they wouldn't try to hide.

There was a great cover story by Ron Rosenbaum in *The New York Times Magazine* in June, 1995, titled "Evil's Back,

(Staring Into the Heart of the Heart of Darkness)." He writes about Susan Smith's state of mind the night she killed her two young children and the degree of actual responsibility that she should take for her act. "Was it an "evil deed," or the product of dysfunction disorder, past abuse, mental disease? Since no one "in her right mind" could have committed the evil deed, she must have "lost her mind"; she wasn't really responsible . . . she was beginning to look less like the perpetrator than the victim."

But her pastor of the United Methodist Church in Buffalo, S.C., (where, before she confessed, she prayed that the black carjacker would return her children safely), Rev. Mark Long "insists on Susan Smith's moral autonomy that night. He believes she had a choice between good and evil. Had a choice and knew what she was doing when she made it."

Next Mr. Rosenbaum writes of the two ten-year-old Liverpool boys who beat a two-year-old child to death and left his body on some railroad tracks to make it look like he'd been run over by a train. "It was this last, all-too-clever, chilling touch that led the judge to denounce the young killers not as misguided, abused, troubled children . . . but as unequivocally wicked, evil."

Because evil is so heinous to us, we try to make excuses for those who do it: he was abused as a kid, she was sexually assaulted at the age of ten, he lived in poverty and never had an education, she came from an alcoholic home. There are thousands upon thousands of adults who were abused as kids, sexually assaulted, poverty stricken, had no education, and/or came from alcoholic homes but who have never done evil. It's those who are convinced that they will *get away with it,* are convinced that they will *never be caught,* who decide to be violent, or commit *any* kind of misdeed.

There are no excuses for evil—*no excuses*—and I am convinced that if every person were sure that he or she wouldn't get away with it, the evil wouldn't be done. So obviously there is a choice, obviously the person chooses evil, and obviously that person believes he or she will not ever be found out or caught.

And then we have evildoers who supposedly believe they are doing good by doing evil. I say supposedly because I don't believe it. Adolf Hitler was in a position of great power and did whatever he wanted, and because of his power, he knew he could get away with doing evil. He knew that if he blamed the Jews for the German economic woes, and promised the Germans jobs and economic prosperity once the Jews were gone, the majority would not rebel against him.

There are many people who do evil in the name of Good, but I will never believe that they really are convinced that they are right. Just as Hitler became more powerful the more he persecuted the Jews, those who do wrong and pretend it's in the name of Good do it to make themselves richer, more successful, more powerful, or more popular. It may appear they're working from another angle, but the truth is their wrongdoing will benefit them in some way. And the only reason anyone is successful in doing wrong is because they are allowed to get away with it.

So to be a Good person you must let others know that you want no part of dishonesty, injustice, or cruelty. It's up to each one of us to "become our brother's keeper" (and our sister's). We are responsible for our selves, but we're also responsible for those around us. We can't stop someone from doing wrong, but we *can* let that person know that we want no part of it, that our ethics and sense of right and wrong will not allow us to be a part of anything dishonest, unjust, or cruel.

Edmund Burke said: "The only thing necessary for the triumph of evil is for good men to do nothing."

Be a Do-Gooder

For any of you wondering how to change your life and become a Good person, it's really very easy.

You don't have to wonder how you can get your mind to

think Good thoughts and then wonder how to try to be a Good person.

All that is needed is to *do* Good.

When you *do* Good, you will automatically *be* Good.

And when you *do* Good, you will *automatically* be happy. Guaranteed!

Goodness is the only *permanent* happiness.

Many years ago, I started putting nickels, dimes, or quarters in parking meters that had expired, and it gave me a lot of joy thinking that maybe I saved the car's owner from a parking ticket.

And what's *really* fun is going into a big, open self-serve eating place (like at an airport), finishing your food, hiding a dollar bill under a plate, walking out, and then watching from a distance as the bus boy cleaning the table finds the money. Talk about giving joy!!!

Being anonymous makes it fun—but letting people know you're giving them something is fun too. *Any* giving of your self or your possessions makes *you* feel Good, makes the *recipient* feel Good, makes you a do-gooder, and makes life a lot more meaningful.

Good Helps Them Who Help Themselves

If you look back on any and all good things that happened in your life, you'll see that you had very little to do with their happening. Maybe you prepared for them by doing preliminary work, but you didn't "make" them happen. All the circumstances were right (and anything *could* have gone wrong but nothing did), and the Good thing happened.

Or maybe something Good out of the blue happened without *any* doing of yours, like when I was hanging on to my house by a hair and my mother left me $50,000.

My point is that all your worrying doesn't help one bit. The *only* thing that can help bring about something Good is your mind, and it can't be used *for* you, *you're* the only one who can use it.

From now on just *know* that Good is there and tap into it. Do your homework first, do everything you can to pave the way for Good to lead you to what you want. Worry and tension will only *stop* Good from happening. Relax and think about the power of Good, use your Good-given mind to give you solutions, and trust that Good things will happen. I promise you they will.

Reward the Good and Punish the Bad

The most important thing we must all do to make our world a better place is recognize Good and reward it. Praise it. Write notes to those who deserve it, from Good senators to Good moms and dads, to Good bus drivers to Good cops. Tell any Good person you know how much you appreciate his or her Goodness.

The other important thing we must do is punish the bad. We must let every one know we will not tolerate bad behavior. No lying, no cheating, no insulting, no stealing. When someone—anyone—does something bad, we must become involved. We must let that person know he or she is wrong. If it's something serious, we must let the authorities know. If we see someone stealing, we must report it, not ignore it.

If we don't get involved, the moral spiral downward will get progressively worse. It's accelerating rapidly now because we're allowing evil to be excused, we're allowing wrongdoers to plead "insanity," and then when they regain their "sanity," get released and go out and steal, rape, and murder again. We're allowing wrongdoers to make excuses. As Guess Jeans says: "No excuses!"

We're not holding people responsible for their actions. Each one of us is responsible for choosing every action we make.

We must reward the Good action.

We must punish the bad action.

We must get involved. . . .

The Hereafter or the Now . . .

Most religions preach happiness in the *hereafter* if we are good in the *now*.

When you believe in Good, and think and express, and *do* Good, you will have perfect happiness *now*.

And just as important, you will have success now. Not just spiritual success (which will help you feel as one with the universe), or mental and emotional success and happiness (which will help you feel Good about your self), but actual success in the physical plane, like earning money (which will help get rid of a lot of anxiety), and owning property (which helps your self-esteem), and being successful in whatever field you want, be it business, professional, entrepreneurial, or show biz.

Once you grasp the fact that God is not a person with human qualities of love and anger and pity, a person you can make deals with, but is Good, pure and vital Good, a Force stronger than any known power, and when that Force is used by any of us who understand the idea of right and *doing* right, and by all who use our brains without any negative emotion, you cannot *stop* Good from leading you to what you want.

We were created by Good to express Good because Good cannot express itself without us.

I believe Good always was and always will be. It is a Power, all-knowing and all-loving, but because it is a Power and not a being, it cannot express itself without us, its creation. And that's *why* we were created, to express Good through our bodies, our minds, our feelings, our creativity, our art, our music, but mostly through our Goodness.

We were given free will, because on this plane every positive has a negative. Every tree casts a shadow, light has darkness, perfect health has sickness, and Good has without-Good (aka bad). But if you can see that the tree is the reality, and the shadow is an image of the tree; light is reality and darkness is the absence of light; perfect health is reality and sickness is the absence of health; you will then understand how Good is the only reality, and evil is the absence of Good.

So with the intellect Good has given us, we can see the difference between right and wrong and we are able to make a choice. The animals don't have this gift—they just work on instinct—but we, Good's perfect creation, can climb the highest peaks of creativity and accomplishments, or we can also fall to the lowest depths of cruelty and depravity.

We have composed hauntingly beautiful music, painted breathtakingly beautiful art, written poignantly beautiful stories, and *we* did it with and through the Power of Good.

We have also tortured, maimed, and killed millions of innocents, and *we* did that when we pushed Good out of our lives.

It is *our* choice. Good is here and there and everywhere and it's up to us to love it, to adore it, and to use it. We have Good and we have without-Good. We have seen what Good is capable of doing and we also have seen what the absence of Good is capable of doing.

Can we go another decade, another year, another day, without changing our priority? Each one of us is a creation of Good, and if each one of us pushes out the phony baloney of our life, if each one of us pushes out the fear that overtakes us because we feel alone and tense, full of anger, jealousy, and self-pity that is dragging us down to drugs, violence, and unhappiness, the world will begin to change because our Goodness will start to spread and never end, like the sound waves of beautiful music.

And don't think that one person can't make a difference. Just by setting an example we can quietly influence those around us, and if we multiply that by thousands, and then tens of thousands, right can and will slowly begin to light the darkness of wrong.

What a potential for a world with no more religious fanatics, a world united by everyone's belief in Good.

The first step is each one of us listening to our inner voice, our conscience, which will *always* tell us the right thing to do. Then *we* make the choice. . . .

Good *is* alive and well and living in each one of us. . . .

Afterword

Just imagine for a moment that I want to start a new religion. I want to call it Good, and I want everyone who believes in Good to contact me so we can organize our new religion.

I of course will be the founder and head of the Good Church. We will have to start small with our first church here in New York, but with your donations we will very quickly build many new churches in all the major cities in the United States, then the world.

Our services will be every Sunday to worship Good. Please plan on bringing your family and all your friends so we can all worship Good together.

Ludicrous? Yes. Absurd? Yes. Possible? No.

Good doesn't *need* a founder, a leader, or a head. We don't need someone to tell us what's Good and what isn't. Our consciences do that.

Good doesn't *need* a church. We don't need a special place in which to worship Good.

Good existed since time began and Good will exist long after forever. It doesn't need me or you or anybody else to organize anything except our selves.

There are no special prayers, no hymns to sing, no bowing, kneeling, or collections.

We don't have to give money to Good, because there's nothing to support—no pastor, no building, no taxes, no nothing.

All we need in order to worship Good, to express Good, and to be Good is our selves . . . and our consciences. . . .

Suggested Books to Read

In 1976 I wrote my second book, *Everything You've Always Wanted to Know About ENERGY . . . But Were Too Weak To Ask*, and at the back I put in *Suggested Reading* and listed thirteen books that I thought everyone would enjoy and benefit from reading.

In 1980 I wrote my third book, *Isle of View (Say it out loud)*, and this time I listed nineteen books that I thought were terrific.

I am now ready to suggest to you my third list (with some repeats that are too great *not* to repeat), but before I do, I'd like to quote Mark Twain:

> A man who does not read good books has no
> advantage over the man who can't read them.

1. The Essays of Ralph Waldo Emerson
    "Self-Reliance"
    "Compensation"
    "Spiritual Laws"
    "Love"
    "Friendship"
    "Prudence"
    "Heroism"
    "The Over-Soul"
    "Circles"
    "Intellect"
    "Art"
    "The Poet"
    "Experience"
    "Character"
    "Manners"

Ralph Waldo Emerson was an American essayist, philosopher, and poet. He has the most brilliant mind of anyone either now living or dead that I've ever encountered. When I was nineteen, someone gave me *The Complete Works of Emerson*, and the insights I have received from this monumental writer (after rereading it every year) have helped me in every phase of my life.

2. *Power Through Constructive Thinking*, by Emmett Fox

If you read only the section in this book called "The Seven-Day Mental Diet," it may change your whole life. But let me warn you that it's tougher than any other kind of diet you've ever tried before!

3. *The 7 Habits of Highly Effective People*, by Stephen R. Covey

An incredibly enlightening book about the most basic lessons we should have learned but probably didn't, written in a "can't-put-this-book-down" style.

4. *Your Body's Many Cries for Water*, by Dr. F. Batmanghelidj

You must read this book for your own health and for the health of all those you love.

5. *Don't Know Much About History*, by Kenneth C. Davis

Because I always found history so boring (boring teachers, boring textbooks), I fell in love with this book. It's brilliantly written, and you will have fun reading about all the great and exciting moments of U.S. history that used to put you to sleep.

6. *Don't Know Much About Geography,*
   by Kenneth C. Davis

   Ditto the above, but this is about all the exciting *places* in the world. I only hope Kenneth C. Davis now writes a book about the history of the *world* (from the "Big Bang" to now) that I so desperately want to read.

7. *Neurosis And Human Growth*, by Karen Horney, M.D.

   Dr. Horney believes that under favorable conditions our energies go toward realizing our own potential. Under the influence of inner stress we become alienated from our real selves and in this book she stresses self-realization.

8. *Self-Analysis*, by Karen Horney, M.D.

   This is one of the best books about psychoanalysis and how to analyze your self, written by one of the most well-known psychiatrists in the world.

9. *How To Live Longer and Feel Better*, by Linus Pauling

   A fascinating book about nutrition, vitamins, and vitamin C in particular, by the Nobel Prize-winner.

10. *The Healing Factor: Vitamin C Against Disease,*
    by Irwin Stone

    Irwin Stone aroused Linus Pauling's interest in vitamin C and shares a dedication in Pauling's own book. Here, once and for all, you'll learn just about everything there is to know about this all-around curative vitamin.

11. *Psycho-Cybernetics*, by Dr. Maxwell Maltz, M.D.

    This is about "self-image psychology," and Max was a dear friend. It's one of my favorite books and I've read it probably ten times.

12. *The Delany Sisters' Book of Everyday Wisdom*

A wonderful book written by two black sisters who never married, Sadie (who became a schoolteacher) and Bessie (who became a dentist) Delany, who wrote this book at ages 105 and 103. It's loaded with common sense about how to lead a Good life through discipline, fun, good nutrition, love, and being a Good person.

13. *Vitamin E: For a Healthy Heart and a Longer Life*, by Herbert Bailey

My friend Herb shows us scientific data proving remarkable cures from using this life-enhancing vitamin.

14. *Word Power Made Easy*, by Norman Lewis

I am constantly trying to increase my vocabulary, because the more words I know, the easier it is for me to think (thinking does take words), and the better I can express my self. Building your vocabulary will enrich not only your thinking, but also your life.

Reading is one of my favorite pastimes, and many years ago, when I was in my earliest twenties, I asked my bro, who had become a professor of English Literature at the University of California, to send me a list of his opinion of the greatest books that everyone should read. He sent me the following, mostly novels that deal directly with human nature, they are all great, and I read each one:

1. *Madame Bovary*, by Gustave Flaubert
2. *The Red and The Black*, by Stendahl
3. *Vanity Fair*, by William Makepeace Thackeray
4. *The Good Soldier*, by Ford Madox Ford
5. *Huckleberry Finn*, by Mark Twain
6. *Anna Karenina*, by Leo Tolstoy
7. *Pride and Prejudice*, by Jane Austin

8. *Catcher in the Rye*, by J.D. Salinger
9. *Chrestomathy*, by H.L. Mencken
10. *Lie Down in Darkness*, by William Styron
11. *Adam Bede*, by George Eliot
12. *Lady Chatterley's Lover*, by D.H. Lawrence
13. *Waverley*, by Sir Walter Scott

Product List

1. Avigal Henna

   Avigal Henna of America
   P.O. Box 1064
   Long Island City, NY 11101
   1-800-722-1011

2. Frizz Ease

   Most pharmacies

3. Retin-A (face cream)

   Dermatologist prescription
   all pharmacies

4. Fruit Acids (face cream)

   All department stores
   many brands

5. La Prairie Face Products

   Most department stores

6. Rebounder (trampoline)

   Most sporting equipment
   stores
   or
   Rebound Fitness Society
   P.O. Box 703
   Canfield, OH 44406
   216-533-5673

7. H_2O_2

   All Pharmacies

8. Colon Cleanser
   Psyllium and Lava
   (Bentonite)

   American Botanical Pharmacy
   P.O. Box 3027
   Santa Monica, CA 90408
   310-453-1987

9. Bee Pollen

   CC Pollen
   3627 E. Indian School Rd.
   Suite 209
   Phoenix, AZ 85018
   1-800-875-0096

10. CoQ10	Most Health Stores	
11. Lecithin	Most Health Stores	
12. Dolomite	Most Health Stores	
13. SOD	Most Health Stores	⎫ KAL
		⎬ makes
14. Glutathione	Most Health Stores	⎭ combo
15. Silica Gel	Most Health Stores	

16. GH3

Pharmacies in Nevada, USA
Romania, Switzerland,
Germany, etc.

17. ACF 223

Gero Vita International
1027 S. Rainbow Blvd. #299
Las Vegas, NV 89128
1-800-972-7100

18. Ginkgo Biloba

Most Health Stores

19. Zell Oxy

Many Health Stores
or
Bio-Nutritional Products
P.O. Box 9
Harrington Park, NJ 07640
1-800-343-0787

20. (vegetarian animal food)

Nature's Recipe

Many Pet Stores

Wow-Bow Distributors

NY State 516-254-6064
o/s NY State 800-326-0230

21. Naura Hayden's Dynamite
Energy Shake

Many Health Stores

22. Naura Hayden's Dynamite
Vites

or

23. Naura Hayden's
Dolomints

1-800-255-1660

Health Newsletters (that I subscribe to)

Last Chance Health Report by Sam Biser
University of Natural Healing, Inc.
355 W. Rio Road, Ste. 201
Charlottesville, VA 22901
804-973-0262

Health & Healing by Dr. Julian Whitaker, M.D.
7811 Montrose Road
Potomac, MD 20854
301-424-3700

Health & Longevity by Dr. Robert D. Willix, M.D.
105 W. Monument St.
P.O. Box 17477
Baltimore, MD 21298
407-368-2747

Turn Back the Clock by Dr. Keith E. Johnson, M.D.
12020 Sunrise Valley Drive
Reston, VA 22091
703-476-2252

Naura's Other Books:*

*HOW TO SATISFY A WOMAN <u>EVERY</u> <u>TIME</u> . . . and have her
beg for more!*
  - A marriage manual and a marriage saver!
  - This is the first and *only* book that shows a man *exactly* how
  - *#1 Bestseller* 1992 Hardcover Nonfiction—*Publishers
    Weekly*
  - 62 weeks *The New York Times* bestseller 1992–1993
  - "It really works!"—*The Los Angeles Times*

*Everything You've Always Wanted to Know About ENERGY . . .
But Were Too Weak To Ask*
  - All about physical, mental, and emotional energy
  - Over 2-million-copy bestseller
  - On every bestseller list in the country
  - "Naura's energy is contagious. This book can make us all su-
    perstars."   —Dr. Robert Atkins

Isle of View (Say it out loud)
  - This book full of love energy will change your life!
  - " This upbeat book follows its predecessor onto the best-
    seller lists."   —*Publishers Weekly*

ASTRO-LOGICAL LOVE
  - A *logical* look at astrology!
  - Do the simple charts in just minutes and find out about
    personality and character traits of your self, your love, your
    ex-love, your future love, your children, friends, enemies,
    employer, employees, etc.
  - "Do a chart and find out about everyone you know."
                                                            —*People*

*on sale at all bookstores

or to order direct and use any major credit card call:

1-800-255-1660 M–F, 9:30–5:30 e.s.t.

The Hip, High-Prote, Low-Cal, Easy-Does-It Cookbook
- A vegetarian cookbook with over 200 delicious meatless recipes
- "Heartily recommended . . . the buy of the year"—King Features

*on sale at all bookstores

or to order direct and use any major credit card call:

1-800-255-1660 M–F, 9:30–5:30 e.s.t.

AMERICAN PRO SE ASSOCIATION
("Pro Se" is a legal term that means
representing one's self in a legal
action without an attorney.)

I had already finished my book and the manuscript was being typeset, when I sent a stockbroker friend of mine a birthday card and he called to thank me and catch up on what's going on, and to fill me in on what's news with him.

I was happily surprised to find out he just started the American Pro Se Association, which is not-for-profit and provides free legal information to the general public.

Anyone can become a member *except* lawyers and judges, and dues are very low (twenty dollars a year) because the four officers are unpaid (they all have paying jobs in other fields).

I joined immediately when I found out they provide:

1. Sample letters and other forms for dealing with credit bureaus and similar situations
2. Some standardized court forms
3. Publication lists and sources of appropriate legal books
4. Simple directions for drafting out a case for review by an attorney to save expensive billable hours
5. Advisory alert as to both bankruptcy and divorce
6. Access to attorneys who will review and edit double-spaced typed papers for $60 per hour and/or to handle certain matters for $90 per hour
7. Complete access to all forms and materials—members are able to access and download legal forms and other information on a twenty-four hour automated basis for creating their drafts for review by an attorney
8. Access to reference materials and library with free use of copier in conjunction with those materials
9. Free use of PCs, fax/modems and the programs, files, forms and other legal materials on those PCs—including nights and weekends when courthouse libraries are usually closed
10. Free copy of any special materials or compilations created for or by the American Pro Se Association if it appears it may have relevance to a member's particular problem

284

11. Membership list with telephone numbers and areas of first-hand experience that may be useful
12. Various forms and files on a diskette to save time typing and creating from scratch—just modify to suit

plus hundreds of other valuable services and pieces of information to enlighten us legally and to cut down our legal expenses.

"Pro Se," as I mentioned earlier, is a legal term that means handling a case by your self without an attorney, and with this group you could of course do that, or you could prepare your own papers (and cut your legal costs greatly) to use with an attorney.

I'm so happy someone finally did this, and how wonderful it's my friend Carl Frederick.

Of course I got the typesetter to send the manuscript back to me so I could add these pages, because I feel it's very important for all of us to know that this information is available so we can begin to try to solve our own problems.

How to contact: American Pro Se Association
1441 Prospect Avenue
Plainfield, NJ 07060

908-753-4516 (phone)
908-753-2599 (fax)

For all you Good people out there
who make me feel better about my self,
who make my life happier,
and just by being Good, bring joy to me
and to every one around you,
thank you. . . .

And for all you out there who don't,
who try to spread fear and self-doubt,
who think that lying and put-downs will bring you
what you want,
you who have not yet discovered your Good within,
I pray you recognize it soon.

For Good will bring you
the true joy you've never had,
and your Goodness will ripple and won't end
until it reaches
The Peaceable Kingdom
that Good wants all its creatures to live in,
filled with joy and happiness and peace. . . .

This is Good. . . .

Naura Hayden

Naura loves to write.

She loves to write books (six), screenplays (one), and musical comedies (one).

Naura loves to act, starring in TV shows (over twenty), and
movies (two).

She also loves to sing, in movies (two), on records (two),
and in musical comedies (one).

She wrote, produced, edited, and starred in a movie, *P.K.*,
where she plays the title role, with a cast that includes Sammy
Davis Jr., and Dick Shawn (both in their last film roles), Jackie
Mason, Sheila Mac Rae, Larry Storch, Virginia Graham, Anne
Meara, Professor Irwin Corey, Joey Heatherton, Louise Lasser
and Kaye Ballard.

She wrote, produced, and starred in an Off-Broadway
musical, *Be Kind to People Week*, where she played the lead,
Hope Healy, and she wrote the music and lyrics to all 14 of
the songs.

She produced, directed, and edited a second movie, *Good*,
in which she doesn't appear.

Naura loves animals, and has a poodle named Hairy, three
cats named Maggie "the Cat", Chauncey, and Nathan, two
turtles named Ozwald and Myrtle, and a one-winged pigeon
she rescued named Walter.

She testified before the U.S. Congressional Committee on
Nutrition, citing the effect poor nutrition has on all Americans,
and she is an honorary fellow of the International Academy of
Preventive Medicine.

Naura invented the DYNAMITE ENERGY SHAKE sold
in many health stores, and all the profits go into The John

Ellsworth Hayden Foundation, named after her late father, which gives free DYNAMITE ENERGY SHAKES to state-run prisons, mental health institutes, youth centers, and senior citizen nursing homes.

Naura had her own radio show, *Naura's Good News*, on WMCA in New York City, was a regular on *Good Morning, New York* and co-hosted *AM-New York*, both on ABC-TV.

The 5'8", 1?6 lb. Ms. Hayden lives in a yellow townhouse on Manhattan's East Side, jogs uphill on her treadmill every single day, and gulps DYNAMITE VITES and DYNAMITE ENERGY SHAKE which give her the energy every day to do all that running uphill.

She's impressive and impressionable, animated and ambitious, beautiful, and bursting with energy.